THE KARL MARX LIBRARY

EDITED AND TRANSLATED BY

SAUL K. PADOVER

Distinguished Service Professor of Political Science,
Graduate Faculty, New School for Social Research

ALREADY PUBLISHED

On Revolution

On America and the Civil War

On the First International

On Freedom of the Press and Censorship

Also by Saul K. Padover

THE REVOLUTIONARY EMPEROR: JOSEPH II
SECRET DIPLOMACY AND ESPIONAGE
(*with James Westfall Thompson*)
THE LIFE AND DEATH OF LOUIS XVI
JEFFERSON (a biography)
EXPERIMENT IN GERMANY
LA VIE POLITIQUE DES ÉTATS-UNIS
FRENCH INSTITUTIONS: VALUES AND POLITICS
THE GENIUS OF AMERICA
UNDERSTANDING FOREIGN POLICY
THE MEANING OF DEMOCRACY
THOMAS JEFFERSON AND THE FOUNDATIONS OF AMERICAN FREEDOM

∴

Edited by Saul K. Padover

SOURCES OF DEMOCRACY: VOICES OF FREEDOM, HOPE AND JUSTICE
THOMAS JEFFERSON ON DEMOCRACY
THE COMPLETE JEFFERSON
THOMAS JEFFERSON AND THE NATIONAL CAPITAL
A JEFFERSON PROFILE
THE WRITINGS OF THOMAS JEFFERSON
THE COMPLETE MADISON (also titled: THE FORGING OF AMERICAN FEDERALISM)
THE WASHINGTON PAPERS
THE MIND OF ALEXANDER HAMILTON
WILSON'S IDEALS
THE LIVING UNITED STATES CONSTITUTION
CONFESSIONS AND SELF-PORTRAITS
THE WORLD OF THE FOUNDING FATHERS
NEHRU ON WORLD HISTORY
TO SECURE THESE BLESSINGS

On Religion

THE KARL MARX LIBRARY
VOLUME V

On Religion

KARL MARX

ARRANGED AND EDITED, WITH AN
INTRODUCTION AND NEW TRANSLATIONS
by Saul K. Padover

McGraw-Hill Book Company

NEW YORK   ST. LOUIS   SAN FRANCISCO
DÜSSELDORF   LONDON   MEXICO   PANAMA
SYDNEY   TORONTO

123456789BPBP7897654

Library of Congress Cataloging in Publication Data (Revised)

Marx, Karl, 1818–1883.
The Karl Marx library.

Includes bibliographies.
CONTENTS: v. 1. On revolution.—v. 2. On America and
the Civil War—v. 3. On the First International. [etc.]
1. Socialism—Collected works. I. Title.
HX276.M2773 1972 335.43'08 78-172260
ISBN 0-07-048095-9
0-07-048096-6 (pbk.)

Contents

[v]

Judaism and Jews

Personal Letters

Contents vii

Introduction:
Marx's Religious Views

KARL MARX's views on religion, including his criticism of Christianity and antipathy for Judaism, are best understood in total context. His ideas were affected, first, by his special family background and, secondly, by the theological thought that prevailed in Germany in his early years. The family experience lent sharpness to his religious criticism and caused a particular idiosyncratic bias—hostility to Jews. In general, however, Marx's religious position was in line with that of contemporary German theological radicals, notably Ludwig Feuerbach and Bruno Bauer, the latter of whom was his teacher and friend at the University of Berlin. To their ideas Marx added a materialist-philosophical slant of his own.

It should be pointed out, however, that the subject of religion was one that did not occupy Marx for very long. He concerned himself with it primarily in his early years, when he was interested in philosophy, which then included theology, or vice versa, as the Christian theologians would have it. His main philosophical-theological writings are contained in his doctoral dissertation, *Difference Between the Democritean and Epicurean Philosophy of Nature*, for which he received his Ph.D. degree from Jena University in 1841, and in *On the Jewish Question*, which he published in 1844. The doctoral thesis, while dealing with classic Greek philosophy, also examined theological questions, such as the gods, the heavens, etc. *On the Jewish Question* was a philosophical-political essay ranging through a particular theology: Judaism, the religion of the Jews. Thereafter Marx lingered but intermittently on questions of theology, and then only as religion affected politics and economics.

The influences that shaped and colored Marx's early development, including his religious views, are of intrinsic personal and historical interest.

He was a descendant of rabbis on both sides of his family. The genealogy shows rabbis and rabbinical scholars going back at least to the fifteenth century. Many of these ancestors, of whom Marx, incidentally, was not proud, were men of great eminence and erudition. One of them, Isaac Katzenellenbogen, chief rabbi of Venice-Padua, Italy, published a learned edition of the great medieval Jewish philosopher Maimonides in 1550. Marx's maternal grandfather, Rabbi Joshua Heschel Lvov, was the author of a Hebrew book, *She'elot Uteshuvot P'nay Levana (Responsa: The Face of the Moon)*, published in Altona in 1765, which contained strongly democratic views. Records available since the seventeenth century show that virtually all the rabbis of Trier (French: Trèves), where Karl Marx was born, were his paternal kin. During Karl's childhood and boyhood, his father's brother Samuel was rabbi in Trier, as was *his* father before him.

Karl Marx's father, Heschel, was born in French Sarrelouis and raised in Trier, a German town captured by the French in 1794, about a quarter of a century before Karl's birth (1818). French revolutionary ideas came to Trier with the conquering army. Among other things, the French Revolution, for the first time in European history, granted Jews civil rights. In this new liberating atmosphere, Heschel Marx acquired a legal education and became a practicing lawyer in Trier. But after the French were defeated at Waterloo, and Trier was ceded to Prussia (1815), the government in Berlin issued an administrative decree barring non-Christians from a number of professions, including the law. A Jew could practice law only if he became converted to Christianity, a step which the pious Protestant Prussian Government strongly encouraged. Karl Marx was later to castigate the Hohenzollern monarchy for its arrogance and its "Christian" morality.

Karl Marx's father was confronted with a cruel choice. On November 22, 1814, seven months before the French Empire came tumbling down at Waterloo, Heschel Marx had married a Jewish Dutchwoman, Henriette Presburg, at Nijmegen (Nimêgue), in French-ruled Holland. Heschel Marx, who was thirty-eight years old when Trier suddenly became Prussian, now had to choose between renouncing his ancestral religion and giving up his career as a lawyer, a profession which he loved and which was the only way he knew to support his family. The Marxes' first child, Sophie (Karl was the second), was born in 1816.

To be sure, Heschel Marx was no longer a practicing Jew. Shaped by the ideas of the French eighteenth-century Enlightenment, he was an admirer of Voltaire and Rousseau and no believer in organized religion. Nevertheless, he had pride in his ancestry and his people. To be coerced to adopt an alien religion was an assault on his dignity as a man and as a citizen. It meant severing his ties to the Jewish community. Conversion to Christianity also involved hurting the feelings of his mother, the widow of a rabbi, and a break with his family, including his rabbinical brother Samuel in Trier.

After vain appeals to Berlin for a special dispensation, supported by leading Christian lawyers, Heschel Marx made the painful step of conversion to a religion in which he did not believe and which, under the circumstances, he could hardly respect. He was baptized a Lutheran sometime in 1817, and adopted the Christian name of Heinrich. It was not the proudest moment of his life. This took place about a year before Karl was born.

It is an indication of how little the Marx family believed in Christianity that Henriette Marx, Karl's mother, did not join her husband in the conversion. She remained Jewish during Karl's childhood and young boyhood, becoming converted only in 1825, a year after all her eight children, including six-year-old Karl, had been baptized (August 26, 1824). Here, too, moral compulsion came into play: by administrative decree, the Prussian Government barred non-Christian children from public schools.

Young Marx attended the Evangelical *Volksschule* (elementary school), directed by Johann Abraham Küpper, the pastor who had prepared him (and later, his mother) for baptism. This early schooling, it is worth noting, also involved a minority status, for the Protestants were a small group in a city that was well over 90 percent Catholic. In fact, Trier was steeped in Catholicism, abounding with churches and other ecclesiastical institutions. Within a few minutes' walk from Karl's home were the Archiepiscopal Palace; the immense Cathedral, begun in the fourth century and rebuilt in the early Middle Ages, which contained the Holy Coat, presumably the seamless coat of Jesus; and the brick Basilica, the construction of which dated back to the Roman Emperor Constantine I. In this ancient city the impression of Catholicism and ecclesiasticism was overpowering, as the German poet Goethe noted after a visit there:

> The town itself has a striking characteristic: It claims to possess more ecclesiastical buildings than any other of comparable size, and this reputation can hardly be denied it; for within the town walls, it is burdened—yea, oppressed—with churches, chapels, cloisters, convents, and colleges; and outside the walls, it is blockaded—yea, besieged—by abbeys, foundations, and Carthusians.

In this city, Protestants were such a minority that they did not have a church building of their own. Hence Marx's elementary school was hardly in the mainstream. Here he imbibed Protestant, rather than

Catholic, dogmas. In the Gymnasium (secondary school), which Marx attended from the age of twelve to seventeen (1830 to 1835), religion was a compulsory subject two hours weekly. His teacher of Protestantism was again Pastor Küpper, who was pleased with his pupil's "knowledge of the Christian faith and morals." The Gymnasium graduation diploma stated that young Marx also knew "a little of the history of the Christian church."

But Christianity was not one of Marx's favorite subjects. As a student he was much more interested in poetry than in religion. It is to be noted that he had a gift for languages, and mastered French, Greek, and Latin, but ignored Hebrew, which the Gymnasium offered as an elective subject.

More important was the immediate home environment. It was a household where religion provided, not certainty, but the reverse. With a Jewish mother (who probably did not attend synagogue) and a Christian father (who did not go to church), Marx as a young boy could obviously never be sure whether he was a Jew or a Christian. There is no record that Karl was circumcised, but he may have been, since according to Jewish law a child follows the religion of its mother.

It is not kown what, if any, religion or religious rites Karl was exposed to at home. Did his mother observe the time-hallowed blessing of the candles on Friday night? Were there any prayers said in the Marx home; if so what kind? Was there any observance of the Sabbath Day by the mother? Was it likely that Karl's mother, a woman of strong character, suddenly gave up all the cherished ancient Jewish rituals because of her husband's baptism?

As for Karl's father, it can safely be assumed that he did not preach or teach Christianity to his children. He was simply not capable of such hypocrisy. He was, after all, a product of the Enlightenment, skeptical of all organized religions. He seems to have had no interest in theological questions. His library, for example, while replete with historical and legal works,[1] did not contain a single volume on religion, either Jewish or Christian. But given his background and personal experience, it would be strange indeed if Heinrich Marx, an affectionate and sensitive man, did not talk to his children, especially his bright oldest son, Karl, about the long history of persecutions and humiliations of the Jews in Europe. Indeed, as late as the 1820s, when Karl was a little boy, there were pogroms in the Rhineland, although

---

1. Heinrich Marx's library contained such works as a ten-volume *Konversations Lexikon* (Encyclopedia); a six-volume *Dictionnaire Historique* (*Historical Dictionary*); a five-volume Pufendorf, *Einleitung zur Historie der vornehmsten Reiche und Staaten* (*Introduction to the History of the Foremost Empires and States*); and five volumes of the writings of Hugo Grotius.

not in Trier. But no Jewish family anywhere could escape the fearful reverberations of such occurrences.

The religious uncertainties and general insecurities of the Marx household were bound to have a splintering effect on the children. At best, they could not help being outsiders. Karl Marx was sensitized to this, as can be seen from his profound comments on the "alienated" man in one of his earliest writings, *Economic and Philosophic Manuscripts of 1844.* He himself became an alienated man in the classic sense, uprooted from his origins and estranged from the religion that had held his people together for two hundred generations. Such alienated men—or *déracinés,* as the French call them—if they are intellectuals, as Marx was, ultimately turn critics of the dominant ideas and rebels against the existing institutions, as the mature Marx did.

The process of alienation was completed at school. This was an institution connected with a church, the founder of which, Martin Luther, had preached (in 1543) the persecution and extermination of "this damned rejected race," after the Jews aroused "God's rage" by refusing to be converted to Christianity. Advocacy of anti-Semitism was not, of course, in the curriculum of Marx's school, which was probably a gentle and humane institution, but the spirit of the religion as a whole was inimical to Jews, although not to the converted ones. As an understandable defense mechanism, young Marx, deprived of a spiritual base of support in Judaism, imbibed the ancient hostility to his people and accepted all the ugly stereotypes of the brutally caricatured Jew then widely prevalent in Europe, and not only among Lutherans. He learned to despise and hate the people from whom he originated. This was an expression of what the Germans call *Selbsthass* (self-hate), a trait which Karl Marx displayed throughout his whole life. The extent and virulence of his anti-Semitism—which, it should be stressed, was expressed mostly in private, and only on a few occasions in his published writings[2]—can be seen in the letters published in this volume.

At school, Marx came to know the Bible, which in his mature years he occasionally cited, not with sanctimony but with a touch of irony. He also learned the usual Christian pieties and dogmas. These he obediently echoed in his graduation essay-test on religion (written, be it remembered, when he was a boy of seventeen), "The Union of the Faithful with Christ, according to St. John 15:1–14, presented in its Reason and Essence, in its Absolute Necessity and its Effects." In the light of Marx's later philosophy, this youthful effort has a special flavor. In retrospect, it can be read with irony, which Marx, who had a

---

2. See, for example, the selections from *Herr Vogt,* a polemic that had nothing to do with Jews, who were dragged in extraneously by Marx for obloquy.

devastating sense of humor, would have been the first to appreciate.

Young Marx began with a statement of the traditional Christological chauvinism, as taught by his pious teachers. History, he wrote, had "engraved with an iron stylus" on its pages the truth that in the pre-Christian era even those nations that had attained the highest levels of culture had no conception of God, suffered from superstition, and had no real morality. Non-Christian peoples, being moral savages, suffered from an inner conviction of their unworthiness.

"Thus," Marx wrote, "the history of nations teaches us the necessity of the Union with Christ."

Christ himself had expressed the need for such a Union in his beautiful parable of the vine and the branch, when he said he was the vine and his followers the branch. The branch cannot bear fruit, and the followers cannot do anything without him, the vine. But this applied only to those who accepted Christ; as for the others, they were —ominously—left to the judgment of the Lord.

Marx concluded:

> Thus the Union with Christ imparts a joyousness which the Epicurean in his frivolous philosophy and the deep thinker in his most arcane science have vainly tried to snatch at, but which the soul can attain only through its unrestrained and childlike Union with Christ and God, which alone makes life more beautiful and exalted.

But it is possible that Marx did not really believe what he wrote. Küpper, his religious teacher for nearly a dozen years, was not altogether satisfied with his pupil's essay. The pastor commented that, while the paper deserved praise for the "fertility of its ideas" and "vigorous presentation," Marx's concept of the Union with Christ was formulated "one-sidedly" and its necessity was proved "only meagerly." Küpper apparently sensed Marx's reserved attitude toward the Savior.

At any rate, the inoculation with Christian dogma had no lasting effect. Marx shed it while studying philosophy at the university, and by the time he took his doctorate, at the age of twenty-three, he was already clearly an atheist. In his dissertation Marx lauded Epicurus as the "greatest enlightener" for having freed ancient man from the bondage of the gods. He quoted with approval the remarkable eulogy of Epicurus by the first-century, B.C., Roman philosopher Lucretius:

> When, before the eyes of men, disgraceful life on earth
> was bowed down by the burden of oppressive religion,
> which extended its head from the high regions of heaven,
> and with gruesome grotesqueness frightfully threatened mankind,
> a Greek first ventured to raise his mortal eye
> against the monster and boldly resisted it.

Neither the fable of God, nor lightning nor thunder of heaven,
scared him with its threat . . .
Thus, as in reprisal, religion lies at our feet,
  completely defeated,
but as for us, triumph raises us up to heaven.[3]

In the appendix and notes of his dissertation, Marx explored the philosophical aspects of religion and examined the question of the existence of God and his relation to man. There was a strong undercurrent of skepticism in the annotations, particularly in his critical comments on such Christian German philosophers as Hegel, Kant, and Schelling.

In Hegel and Schelling, Marx wrote, the "proofs" of the existence of God were either contradictory or tautological. Hegel, he noted, rejected the theological proofs of God's existence only in order to justify them. "What kinds of clients are these," Marx asked, "whom the lawyer cannot save from being condemned without killing them himself?" Hegel had written: "Because the accidental is *not*, God or the Absolute is." But the theological proof states it in reverse: "Because the accidental has true Being, God is." For, in Hegel's view, God is the guarantee of the accidental world. Marx commented: "Obviously the reverse can also be said."

As for the ontological proof, Marx wrote that it meant only that "what I really conceive is a real conception for me," and nothing else. God is what the mind thinks he is: "in this sense all the gods, heathen as well as Christian, possess a real existence. Did not the old Moloch rule? Was not the Delphic Apollo a real power in the life of the Greeks?" Kant, in his *Critique of Pure Reason*, had criticized the ontological, cosmological, and physico-theological proofs of the existence of God as "speculative reason." Marx's comment was that this Kantian position "means nothing." For imagination could be as powerful as so-called reality. If someone, Marx wrote, genuinely believes that he possesses a hundred Taler, then this imagined money has the same value as if it were real money. The possessor of the imagined Taler would incur debts in his imagination, and these would have the same effect as the

---

3. Lucretius, *De Rerum Natura* (*On the Nature of Things*):
   Humana ante oculos foede quum vita jaceret,
   In terreis oppressa gravi sub relligione,
   Quae caput a coeli regionibus ostendebat,
   Horribili super aspectu mortalibus instans:
   Primum Grajus homo mortaleis tollere contra
   Est oculos ausus, primusque obsistere contra;
   Quem nec fama Deum nec fulmina nec minitanti
   Murmure compressit coelum . . .
   Quare relligio pedibus subjecta vicissim
   Obteritur, nos exaequat victoria coelo.

debts humanity owes to its gods. Real Taler have about the same kind
of existence as gods which exist in the imagination:

> Introduce paper money into a country where its usage is not
> known and everybody will laugh at your subjective imagination.
> Bring your gods to a land where other gods prevail and it will be
> proved to you that you suffer from imaginings and abstractions.
> Rightly so. He who brought the old Greeks a different god would
> have had to find proof of his existence. Because for the Greeks he
> did not exist.

Existence, like nonexistence, can be proved only in the "country of
reason." Such proofs, Marx noted, were nothing but the proofs of
the existence of *"actual human self-consciousness, logical explications
of the same."*

In this sense—as Marx concluded with a kind of subtle reasoning
which his Talmudic ancestors might have appreciated—all proofs of the
existence of God are proofs of nonexistence, that is, refutations of
all conceptions of a god:

> Real proofs would sound the reverse of this: "Because nature is
> badly contrived, God is." "Because the world is irrational, God is."
> "Because thought is not, God is." However, what does all this say
> except that *to him to whom the world is irrational, and who is
> therefore himself irrational, God is? Or irrationality is the ex-
> istence of God.*

Marx thus philosophically disposed of God. Pastor Küpper's teachings, in other words, turned out to be a vain effort.

In a preface written when he hoped to publish his dissertation,
Marx explained the reason for his choice of subject. It was, he stated,
to help liberate philosophy, which had been "theologized" by having
been dragged into the "forum of religion." He wanted to restore the
"sovereign character" (in the words of David Hume, which Marx
quoted) of philosophy as the reigning science. The preface ended with
a eulogy of philosophy and an eloquent invocation of the names of
two of the greatest Greek philosophers who abominated the gods:

> Philosophy, so long as a drop of blood still pulsates in its world-
> conquering, absolutely free heart, will always call out to its op-
> ponents, with Epicurus:
> > Impious is not he who rejects the god of the multitude, but
> > he who attributes the conceptions of the multitudes to the
> > gods.[4]
> Philosophy makes no secret of this. Prometheus' avowal: "In simple
> truth, I bear hate for any and every god," is its own avowal, its own

---

4. From Epicurus' letter to Menoikeus.

judgment against all heavenly and earthly gods, who do not acknowledge human self-consciousness as the supreme divinity. There must be no other on a level with it.

But to the sad March hares who exult over the seemingly worsened civil position of philosophy, it answers, in the words of Prometheus to the god-attended Hermes:

With your vile slavery, this, my unhappy fate, I would never exchange, hear me clearly, Never!

Marx concluded: "Prometheus is the noblest saint and martyr in the calendar of philosophy."

The period when Marx was studying philosophy, reading Hegel, and working on his dissertation was one of ferment among the philosophers of religion. A critical tone toward Christianity and institutions connected with it was then spreading in intellectual circles in Germany. In essence, it was political radicalism, of which Germany had no historic tradition, masked as theology. An attack on the basic principles of the dominant religion was, at the same time, an effective assault on the foundations of the Christian state, such as Prussia and other Continental European monarchies then claimed to be. To change the state, it was first necessary to undermine the church. As Marx phrased it in 1844: "For Germany, the criticism of religion is the premise of all criticism."[5]

A leading figure in the religious ferment was Marx's friend Bruno Bauer, the Young Hegelian who was on the theological faculty of Bonn University. Bauer hoped that Marx, upon taking his doctorate, would join him there as a teacher of philosophy. But the government and the conservative theologians were beginning to strike back at the radicals. At Bonn University, both Protestant and Catholic theologians, although usually in doctrinal rivalry, combined against Bauer, whom they considered "godless." His lectures caused student disturbances. In Berlin, where Bauer went to deliver some lectures on Hegel, he stirred the animosity of the Prussian Government and brought upon himself the unwelcome attention of the police.

Bauer's two-volume work, *Kritik der evangelischen Geschichte der Synoptiker* (*Critique of the Evangelical History of the Synoptics*), which was published in Leipzig at about the same time that Marx completed his doctoral dissertation, caused a furor in theological circles. In subtle and Teutonically convoluted exegeses of the New Testament, Bauer, among other things, questioned the miracles imputed to Jesus. Herr Doktor Marx leaped into the controversy, after a man named O. F. Gruppe, who was also a Herr Doktor, attacked Bauer, whom he

---

5. "Toward the Critique of Hegel's Philosophy of Law. Introduction," in *Deutsch-Französische Jahrbücher.*

accused of presenting himself "as a prophet."[6] Dr. Marx, who had read Bauer's *Kritik* with relish, made a slashing counterattack on Dr. Gruppe, whom he charged with ignorance, shameless deceit, and conscienceless distortion, calling the hapless Gruppe a "comical character" and a "buffoon."[7]

Marx never became a professor at Bonn, or anywhere else, for his patron, Bauer, was soon removed from his academic position by order of Frederick William IV, the pious King of Prussia. This effectively ended Marx's hopes for an academic career in Germany, and in that year—1842—he turned to journalism for a living. This was the only profession Marx was ever to pursue.

Marx's interest in religion and its ramifications continued for two years or so after he took his doctorate. He read a number of books on the subject, in the hope of writing review articles about them.[8] Among those works were Karl Bayer's *Reflections on the Concept of the Ethical Spirit and on the Essence of Virtue*,[9] which Marx considered "weak and even unethical"; Wilhelm Vatke's *Man's Freedom in Its Relation to Sin and to Divine Grace*,[10] which he regarded as "superclever"; and Bruno Bauer's anonymously published *The Trumpet of the Latest Judgment on Hegel the Atheist and Anti-Christian*.[11] Marx also toyed with the idea of writing an article "concerning religion and art, with special reference to Christian art,"[12] but nothing came of it.

But the most important book on religion that Marx then read, and one that was clearly a turning point in his own intellectual development from idealism to materialism, was Ludwig Feuerbach's recently published *Das Wesen des Christentums* (*The Essence of Christianity*) (Leipzig, 1841).[13] In it Feuerbach undertook to humanize theology and to develop what he called a "true or anthropological essence of religion." Rejecting Hegelian idealism as disguised theology, Feuerbach denied the existence of God as an "absolute Idea" and asserted that nothing exists outside of nature and of man. Religion

---

6. Gruppe, *Bruno Bauer und die akademische Lehrfreiheit* (*Bruno Bauer and Academic Freedom of Teaching*) (Berlin, 1842).

7. Marx, in *Deutsche Jahrbücher für Wissenschaft und Kunst* (*German Annals for Science and Art*), November 16, 1842.

8. Marx to Arnold Ruge, February 10, 1842.

9. Bayer, *Betrachtungen über den Begriff des sittlichen Geistes und über das Wesen der Tugend* (Erlangen, 1839).

10. Vatke, *Die menschliche Freiheit in ihrem Verhältnis zur Sünde und zur göttlichen Gnade* (Berlin, 1841).

11. Bauer, *Die Posaune des jüngsten Gerichts über Hegel den Atheisten und Antichristen* (Leipzig, 1841).

12. Marx to Arnold Ruge, March 5, 1842.

13. It was translated by the English novelist George Eliot under the not quite accurate title *The Essence of Religion* (London, 1853). An earlier English translation, under the supervision of Frederick Engels, was being prepared in Manchester in 1844, but was never published.

existed only in man's mind; it was man's "consciousness of the infinite." God did not create man, but man created God, who is only the outward expression of man's inner nature. Since God has no existence apart from man, various aspects of existing religion merely correspond to some "feature or need of human nature." Religious beliefs were thus not divine, or even noble, and some of them, such as the sacraments, actually led to superstition and immorality. Feuerbach was critical not only of Christianity but also, like Bruno Bauer, of Judaism, which he condemned as egoistic and interested only in personal gain—a position that Marx absorbed and adopted.

Feuerbach's book had a stunning effect on Marx, as it did on Frederick Engels, who read it at about the same time (it was before the two met). In his *Ludwig Feuerbach und der Ausgang der klassischen deutschen Philosophie* (*Ludwig Feuerbach and the End of Classic German Philosophy*), published in book form in 1888,[14] Engels recalled the tremendous impact of *The Essence of Christianity* on young intellectuals like Marx and himself:

> In one blow, it . . . placed materialism back upon the throne. . . . The spell was broken . . . One must himself have experienced the liberating effect of this book to get a real idea of it. The enthusiasm was universal: We were all for the moment Feuerbachians. With what enthusiasm Marx greeted the new conception, and how much he was influenced by it—despite all critical misgivings—one may read in *The Holy Family*.

In Marx's earliest critique of religion, "Luther As Arbiter Between Strauss and Feuerbach," which he wrote in January 1842 and which was not published until a year later,[15] he suggested, with a touch of irony, that if Christian theologians and speculative philosophers wanted to liberate themselves from their preconceptions about such subjects as Providence, Omnipotence, Creation, Miracles, and Faith, they would have to turn to Feuerbach. Marx concluded with a pun on that author's name. For the theologians and the idealistic philosophers, he wrote, "there is no other road to truth and freedom for you except the one that leads through the *Feuer-bach* (stream of fire)." Feuerbach, Marx concluded his article, was "the *purgatory* of the present."

In the summer and fall of 1843, while preparing to move to Paris to publish, with Arnold Ruge, the *Deutsch-Französische Jahrbücher* there, Marx worked on two important problems. One was the philosophical-political question of civil emancipation in a "Christian" state; the other, the problem of the Jews. Still under the influence of Feuerbach,

---

14. It first appeared in the journal *Neue Zeit*, Nos. 4 and 5, 1886.
15. For a complete full chronology of Marx's life and work, see *Karl Marx on Revolution*, Vol. I of The Karl Marx Library (1971), pp. xxxi–liv.

he investigated religious questions from the political point of view. His concern was not with theology, which he had already repudiated in his doctoral dissertation, but with religion and ecclesiasticism as they affected institutions. To this end, he read and reread Hegel, particularly the *Grundlinien der Philosophie des Rechts oder Naturrecht im Umrisse* (*Base-Lines of the Philosophy of Law or Natural Law in Outline*),[16] and the classic writings of Machiavelli, Montesquieu, and Rousseau. He also read two recent publications by Bruno Bauer: a book entitled *Die Judenfrage* (*The Jewish Question*),[17] and an article, "*Die Fähigkeit der heutigen Juden und Christen, frei zu werden*" ("The Ability of Today's Jews and Christians to Become Free."[18]

The fruits of his readings were the "Critique of Hegel's Philosophy of Law," the "Introduction" to which was published in the *Deutsch-Französische Jahrbücher*,[19] and "On the Jewish Question," which appeared in the same issue of that publication.

The article on Hegel's philosophy of law opened with a sweeping formulation of the meaning of religion for men living in this, and not some other, world. Marx's discussion of the subject contained some memorable words and showed a significant development in his own shift toward materialism.

Following Feuerbach's anthropological approach, Marx asserted that "man makes religion, religion does not make man." Man himself is not some abstract creature, crouching somewhere outside this earth. He is a physical entity right here. "Man is the world of men, the state, society. This state, this society produce religion."

Religion itself is an illusion, as Marx also suggested in his doctoral dissertation in connection with the ancient gods. It is a product of the human imagination, a form of the "self-awareness and self-regard of man who has either not yet found or has already lost himself." Religion does not degrade man; rather, it is degraded man who seeks consolation in religion, as an escape from reality. It is man's search for a "supernatural being in the fantastic reality of heaven," where he finds no reality but only a "reflection of himself."

Religion is both an escape from the misery of this world and a protest against this misery. It is, Marx wrote, "the sigh of the distressed creature, the soul of a heartless world, as it is also the spirit of a spiritless condition. It is the *opium* of the people."

---

16. Vol. VIII of Hegel's *Werke,* issued by Eduard Gans (Berlin, 1833).

17. Brunswick, 1843.

18. In *Einundzwanzig Bogen aus der Schweiz* (*Twenty-one Sheets from Switzerland*), edited by Georg Herwegh (Zurich and Winterthur, 1843).

19. "Zur Kritik der Hegelschen Rechtsphilosophie. Einleitung," in *Deutsch-Französische Jahrbücher,* 1844. For part of the text, see Saul K. Padover, *Karl Marx on Revolution,* Vol. I of The Karl Mark Library (New York, 1971), pp. 422–26.

Since religion is an illusion, it cannot solve man's problems. It can only aggravate them, as Marx stated in another connection: "The more man puts into God, the less he retains in himself."[20] To achieve real happiness for man, it is necessary to abolish the illusory one of religion. This involves the elimination of conditions that require such illusions. In this connection, Marx introduced the notion of the "proletariat" as the instrument for such elimination. Thus Marx, after jettisoning theology and discarding idealism, found no other place to go except into humanism, as it is rooted in physical, and not abstract, man.

Marx's other article, "On the Jewish Question," was different in tone and content from the piece on Hegel.

Marx's first published expression of interest in the "Jewish Question" appeared in the Cologne *Rheinische Zeitung*, of which he became editor in October, 1842. When in the summer of that year Carl Heinrich Hermes, of the *Kölnische Zeitung*, a Catholic daily in Cologne, came out against granting "civil equality to Jews," Marx, then living in Trier, asked Dagobert Oppenheim, a banker connected with the *Rheinische Zeitung*, to send him "all the articles by Hermes against Judaism."[21] He then wrote an attack both on Hermes, whom he called an "ignorant," "insipid," "trivial," and mediocre prattler, and on the whole prevailing notion of the "so-called Christian state." But this was done for political reasons, not out of sympathy for Judaism.

In the last month of his editorship of the *Rheinische Zeitung*, Marx made a revealing statement in a letter to Arnold Ruge:

> Just now the chief of the local Israelites came to see me and asked me to forward a petition for the Jews to the Landtag [Diet], and I want to do it. Revolting [*widerlich*[22]] though the Israelite religion is to me, nevertheless Bauer's opinion [in *The Jewish Question*] seems to me to be too abstract.[23]

Despite his revulsion for Judaism, Marx sent the petition. The reason for his gesture was political. "The point is," he told Ruge, "to puncture as many holes as possible in the Christian state and to smuggle in, insofar as it is up to us, what is rational." Marx expected, and probably hoped, that the petition would be rejected, but as it happened, his expectations were not fulfilled. A few months later, in July, 1843, the Rhenish Diet, to everybody's surprise, voted in favor of the Jews. It was, incidentally, the first time a German parliament granted "complete equality of Jews in civil and political matters."

---

20. *Economic and Philosophic Manuscripts of 1844*, "Alienated Labor."
21. Marx to Oppenheim, *ca.* August 25, 1842.
22. The German word *widerlich* can also be translated as "disgusting," "repulsive," "loathsome," "nauseating."
23. See Marx's letter to Ruge, March 13, 1843.

Marx's essay, "On the Jewish Question," was rooted in the belief that Judaism, against which Christendom had warred for a millennium, was a degraded religion of materialism and arrogance, and its practitioners, the Jews, were thus necessarily a debased people. This was a dogma that prevailed almost universally in Marx's time. So long as Jews professed this religion, they would continue to be something less than human. To become really human and fit to be citizens in a Christian society, Jews would have to give up their religion. Such was the argument even of men who were not particularly anti-Semitic, like Bruno Bauer, who thought that Jews were victims not merely of Judaism but also of German society.

Bauer wrote in the *The Jewish Question:*

> The question is whether the Jew as such . . . is capable of accepting human rights and conceding them to others. His religion and way of life force him to eternal separation . . . for it is their essence. Their essence makes him, not a human being, but a Jew.

Bauer's argument was that religion in general was a bar to social emancipation. So long as men clung to their faith they could not be free. This was true also of Christians, for whom, however, emancipation was easier, since essentially their religion was a superior one. A Christian had to take but one step to universalize his religion, but a Jew, trapped in his primitive and egoistic faith, had first of all to get rid of Judaism altogether before he could move toward universality. Bauer simply questioned the right of Jews to claim political emancipation so long as they remained Jews.

Marx agreed with Bauer's fundamental premises about Judaism and Jews, but he differed from his friend in that he rejected all religion, both Christian and Jewish, as a condition of political emancipation or civil rights. In Marx's view, the situation should be reversed: it was the state, rather than the citizen, that ought to give up claims to any religion, which it had no business asserting or dictating: "The *political* emancipation of the Jew, the Christian, the religious man in general, is the *emancipation of the state* from Judaism, from Christianity, from *religion* generally."

In fully developed modern states, religious freedom existed alongside political freedom. This was not the case in Prussia, but was true in countries like the United States, where theological questions did not enter the arena of the political. Marx quoted Gustave-Auguste de Beaumont:[24] "In the United States there exists neither a state religion nor a religion declared to be that of the majority, nor a preeminence of one faith over another. The state is foreign to all cults."

---

24. De Beaumont, *Marie ou L'Esclavage aux États-Unis* (*Marie or Slavery in the United States*) (Brussels, 1835), p. 214.

In the states of North America, Marx continued his quotation from De Beaumont, the " 'constitution does not impose religious beliefs or sectarian practice as a condition of political rights.' " And all this, Marx added, despite the fact that the United States, "preeminently a land of religiosity," is a place where, in the words of De Beaumont, no one "believes that a man without religion can be an honest man."

Bruno Bauer, in other words, erred in bringing religious considerations into the area of civil rights.

The real problem, according to Marx, lay in religion as connected with *Schacher*—haggling, or bargaining—and it is here that the Jews come in for castigation. For their religion had not only corrupted Christian society with their materialistic spirit, but they themselves personified such corruption in practice. Here Marx reechoed the ancient anti-Semitic charges that Judaism was a Mammon-oriented religion and the Jews its money-worshiping votaries. As if to curry favor with Christian anti-Semites, Marx went far beyond Bauer in his brutal accusations against Jews and Judaism. He made his charges in apodictic sentences, as if they were self-evident truth:

> Let us consider the actual, secular Jew, not the *Sabbath Jew*, as Bauer does, but the *everyday Jew*.
>
> Let us not look for the secret of the Jew in his religion, but let us look for the secret of religion in the actual Jew.
>
> What is the secular basis of Judaism? *Practical need, self-interest*.
>
> What is the worldly cult of the Jew? *Schacher*. What is his worldly god? Money!

Marx repeated his accusations like hammer blows:

> What actually was the foundation, in and of itself, of the Jewish religion? Practical need, egoism.
>
> Hence the Jew's monotheism is in reality the polytheism of many needs, a polytheism that makes even the toilet an object of divine law. . . . The god of *practical need and self-interest* is *Money*.
>
> Money is the jealous god of Israel before whom no other god may exist. Money degrades all the gods of mankind—and converts them into commodities. . . .
>
> The god of the Jews has been secularized and has become the god of the world. The bill of exchange is the real god of the Jew. His god is only an illusory bill of exchange. . . .
>
> What is contained abstractly in the Jewish religion—contempt for theory, for art, for history, for man as an end in himself—is the *actual conscious* standpoint and virtue of the money-man. . . .
>
> The chimerical nationality of the Jew is the nationality of the merchant, of the money-man in general.

Marx concluded that so long as this Jewish spirit of money pervades society, it cannot be free. Nor can Jews be free while they worship a Mammon-religion. Both society and Jews must get rid of Judaism and the profit motive which lies at its core. "On the Jewish Question" concluded with these words: "The *social* emancipation of the Jew is the *emancipation of society from Jewishness*."

The charges Marx leveled against the people and the religion of at least twenty-five generations of his direct ancestors have rarely been exceeded by any other serious writer in the field, not even by Werner Sombart, the German economic historian who wrote, in *Die Juden und das Wirthschaftsleben* (1911)[25]: "I think the Jewish religion has the same leading ideas as capitalism." Sombart, like many another social-economic writer, was influenced by Marx.

Marx's vilification of Jews and their religion, in the long-established tradition of the systematic warp of Christian theologians, reflected nearly total ignorance, possibly willful, of the lives and faith of the people from whom he descended. An objective study of the subject would have shown him that Jews did not worship Mammon but an all-pervasive Deity, and that their religious leaders, the rabbis, were often profoundly and mystically other-worldly persons, with a total dedication of life and soul, not to money, but to the worship of the One and Only God. Far from being money-grubbers, orthodox Jews frequently evinced a practical sense as minimal as that of Marx himself (he had none). As an ethical man, he should have been impressed with the teachings of the Talmud, an ancient source of wisdom and modera-tion and humane practices (among other things, hunting and cruelty to servants and animals were taboo to Jews, at a time when they were widely practiced by Marx's non-Jewish contemporaries, high and low). Indeed, Marx's own indisputable ethical passion has often been regarded by his admirers as messianically Jewish in nature. As his-torian, Marx should have known that the founders and earliest practitioners of Judaism were not money-minded tradesmen but shepherds and simple country people who were moved by an over-whelming sense of a monotheistic Deity; and that insofar as later Jews, dispersed in Christian Europe, pursued money affairs, they did so out of desperate necessity and not out of religious compulsion, primarily in countries and in periods where virtually all other means of livelihood were closed to them—for example, Czarist Russia in Marx's day.

Marx's slander of Jews as hagglers and money-men by nature was thoroughly inaccurate. In his time, the vast majority of Europe's Jews were neither capitalists nor merchants. Most of them, where permitted, followed "normal" occupations. The vast majority of them were poor, often pitifully exploited working people. A considerable number of them were beggars. In the year 1844, when "On the Jewish Question" was published, there were, for example, 10,000 Jews in Bavaria, and of

25. Translated into English as *The Jews and Modern Capitalism* (London, 1913).

these, well over half made their living as craftsmen on the land or in some pursuit other than retail trade or the professions. In that same year, according to the historian Simon Dubnow,[26] there were some 5,000 Jews in the German cities of Breslau and Oppeln, and of these only 20 percent lived by trade. In Russia, where most of Europe's Jews lived, they were without civil rights, huddled in miserable ghettos, and often cruelly persecuted. Next to the serfs, they were the most oppressed people in Czardom. But neither then nor later did Marx, whose heart bled for the world's other poor, show the poverty-stricken Jews the slightest sympathy.

The only known instance when Marx spoke of Jews without disparagement was in an article in the *New-York Daily Tribune*,[27] wherein he discussed the religious situation in Turkish-occupied Jerusalem, where, of a total population of some 15,500, about half, or 8,000, were Jews. Marx wrote:

> Nothing equals the misery and the sufferings of the Jews at Jerusalem, inhabiting the most filthy quarter of the town, called *hareth-el-yahoud*, in the quarter of dirt, between the Zion and the Moriah, where their synagogues are situated—the constant objects of Mussulman oppression and intolerance, insulted by the Greeks, persecuted by the Latins, and living only upon the scanty alms transmitted by their European brethren. The Jews, however, are not natives, but from different and distant countries, and are only attracted to Jerusalem by the desire of inhabiting the Valley of Jehoshaphat; and to die on the very place where the redemption is to be expected.

After writing "On the Jewish Question," Marx never returned to the subject as such. Having solved the problem to his own satisfaction and having settled with his family background, he dropped the whole matter for good. Nor did he write extensively on religion in general in later years. He found it, he told Engels in 1851, a "boring theme."

Marx never retracted his defamation of the Jews and their religion. On the contrary, he harbored a lifelong hostility toward them. In his *Theses on Feuerbach* (1845), a brief compilation of pithy sayings, he thought it necessary to drag in his bias, referring to the "dirty Jewish" aspect of Christianity. His private letters—as can be seen in this volume, mostly translated here for the first time—are replete with anti-Semitic remarks, caricatures and crude epithets "Levy's Jewish nose," "usurers," "Jew-boy," "nigger-Jew," etc.). His hatred was a canker which neither time nor experience ever eradicated from his soul.

After *The Holy Family*, which he published with Engels in 1845, Marx wrote about religious subjects only briefly and intermittently.

---

26. Dubnow, *Weltgeschichte des jüdischen Volkes* (*World History of the Jewish People*) (Jerusalem, 1938), Vol. III, p. 73.
27. April 15, 1854.

When he did, it was with antipathy for church, clergy, and Christian governments. He had, as he told Ferdinand Lassalle, an "aversion" for Christianity. An example of his animosity is his savage attack on the Prussian Consistorial Council's invocation of the "social principles of Christianity." Marx wrote:

> The social principles of Christianity justified slavery in antiquity, glorified medieval serfdom. . . .
> The social principles of Christianity preach the necessity of a ruling and an oppressed class. . . .
> The social principles of Christianity transfer the . . . settlement of all infamies to heaven, and thereby justify the continuation of these infamies on earth. . . .
> The social principles of Christianity declare all vile acts of the oppressors against the oppressed to be either just punishment for original sin and other sins, or suffering that the Lord in his infinite wisdom has destined for those redeemed.
> The social principles of Christianity preach cowardice, self-contempt, abasement, submission, humility—in brief, all the characteristics of the *canaille*. . . .
> The social principles of Christianity are hypocritical. . . .[28]

As a journalist, Marx on occasion adverted to the subject of religion, but only incidentally. Religion interested him only insofar as it affected economic behavior and institutions. His research notes in the *Grundrisse* and scholarly references in *Capital* show that he read a good deal on religion, but not in its theological aspects, paying special attention to the role of the church in matters of capital and property. In *Capital*, Vol. I, Chapter 1, Section 4, for example, he noted:

> For a society of commodity producers . . . thereby reducing their individual private labor to the standard of homogeneous human labor— for such a society, Christianity with its *cultus* of abstract man, particularly in its bourgeois developments, Protestantism, Deism, etc., is the most suitable form of religion. . . . Trading nations . . . exist in the ancient world only in its interstices, like the gods of Epicurus in the Intermundia, or like Jews in the pores of Polish society.

Toward the end of his life, sometime in the late 1870s and early 1880s, Marx, then seriously ailing, read Volumes 11 through 14 of Friedrich Christoph Schlosser's monumental *Weltgeschichte für das deutsche Volk* (*World History for the German People*), from which he made voluminous notes on the German Reformation. Whatever the use for which he intended his research notes, the Reformation held an obvious fascination for him. It was, after all, Europe's first all-encompassing revolution, and Martin Luther, its German originator,

---

28. In *Deutsche-Brüsseler-Zeitung*, September 12, 1847.

was a great revolutionary figure, although he ended as a vicious political reactionary. Marx, who had mixed feelings about Luther, the
thoroughgoing rebel and fanatical monk, called him "the oldest German
national economist" and also referred to him as a *"Halunke"*—a
scoundrel.

Marx seems to have retained a lingering affection for the idealistic
strains of Christianity, as distinct from its mystical and institutionalized
forms. His daughter Eleanor said after her father's death: "Again and
again I heard him say: 'Despite everything, we can forgive Christianity
much, for it has taught to love children.'"

No major editorial changes have been made in the selections in
this volume. Among the few minor alterations is the elimination of
italics for some words and phrases, primarily those that Marx was in
the habit of underlining in nineteenth-century polemical fashion.
Brief explanations and translations of words and phrases from various
languages (Marx was multilingual and peppered his writing with
Latin, French, English, and other languages) are given in brackets.
Except when otherwise indicated, these explanations, as well as the
textual translations from the German, are by the editor. Footnotes
are the editor's except when otherwise signed.

CHRISTIANITY AND
RELIGION IN GENERAL

The Union of the Faithful with Christ*

Marx wrote the following composition on August 17, 1835, at the age of seventeen, as one of the essays on religion required for graduation from the Trier Gymnasium. Marx's religious teacher, Johann Abraham Küpper, the Protestant minister who had also prepared him for baptism, commented on it: "An essay rich in thought, glowing, forceful, deserving of every praise, even though the Essence of the Union [with Christ] under consideration is not given and the Reason for it is conceived only one-sidedly and its Necessity demonstrated only meagerly."

BEFORE we consider the Reason and Essence and the effects of the Union of Christ with the faithful, let us see whether this Union is necessary, whether it is determined by the nature of man, whether or not it may in itself achieve the goal for which God has created him out of the Void.

If we turn to history, the great teacher of humanity, we will find there engraved with an iron stylus that all nations, even those that attained the highest levels of culture, gave birth to the greatest men, produced the most splendid arts, had the most complex scientific problems—nevertheless could not shake off the fetters of superstition, had no proper conception of themselves or the Deity, could not cleanse their morality of alien admixtures and unworthy limitations. Even their virtues were more the product of a rough kind of greatness, of unrestrained egoism, of a passion for fame and bold deeds, than a striving for true perfection.

---

* "The Union of the Faithful with Christ, according to St. John 15: 1–14, presented in its Reason and Essence, in its Absolute Necessity and its Effects."

And the ancient peoples, the savages, among whom the teaching of Christ had not yet spread, show an inner unrest, a fear of the wrath of their gods, an inner conviction of their unworthiness, while at the same time they bring sacrifices to their gods to atone for their sins.

Yes, the greatest sage of antiquity, the divine Plato, in more than one passage expresses a deep yearning for a higher Being whose appearance would fulfill the unsatisfied longing for truth and light.

Thus the history of nations teaches us the necessity of the Union with Christ.

To be sure, even when we study the history of the individual and the nature of man, we always see a divine spark in his breast, an enthusiasm for the Good, a striving for perception, a longing for truth— but the sparks of the eternal are smothered by the flame of lust. The enthusiasm for virtue is stifled by the tempting voice of sin, which is made ridiculous when the full power of life is felt. The striving for perception is replaced by the inferior striving for worldly goods; the longing for truth is extinguished by the sweet-smiling power of the lie; and so man stands, the only creature that does not fulfill its goal, the only member in all Creation not worthy of the God that created him. But the benevolent Creator does not hate his handiwork; he wanted to elevate it to his own level and He sent us his Son, through whom He calls to us: "Now ye are clean through the word which I have spoken unto you. Abide in me, and I in you [John 15:3–4]."

Now that we have seen how the history of nations and the consideration of the individual prove the necessity of a union with Christ, let us consider the last and most difficult proof of all, the word of Christ himself.

And where does He express the necessity of the union more clearly than in the beautiful comparison between the vine and the branch, where He calls himself the vine and us the branch? The branch cannot bear fruit of itself, and likewise, says Christ, you can do nothing without Him. He states this even more strongly when he says: "I am the vine, ye are the branches: He that abideth in me, and I in him, the same bringeth forth much fruit: for without me ye can do nothing. If a man abide not in me, he is cast forth as a branch, and is withered [John 15:5–6]."

But it should be kept in mind that this applies only to those who have succeeded in understanding the word of Christ; as for others, who have not been able to comprehend Him, we cannot judge the decree of the Lord over such nations and individuals.

Our heart, our reason, history itself, and the word of Christ, all call to us loudly and decisively that a union with Him is an absolute necessity, that without Him we cannot attain our goal, that without Him we are rejected by God, and that only He can save us.

Thus penetrated by the conviction that this union is an absolute necessity, we are eager to learn the meaning of this high gift, this ray of light from a loftier world which falls upon our ear and ringingly raises us to heaven, and to discover its inner Being and its Essence.

Once we have comprehended the necessity of the union, the basis for it—our need for salvation, our sinfully inclined nature, our uncertain reason, our corrupted heart, our unworthiness in God's presence—is clearly revealed before our eyes, and we need search no more.

But who could express the essence of the union more beautifully than did Christ in his comparison of the vine and the branch? Who, even in great treatises, could lay before the eye the innermost parts that are at the basis of this union better than Christ did in these words: "I am the true vine, and my Father is the husbandman [John 15:1]." "I am the vine, ye are the branches [John 15:5]."

If the branch were sentient, how joyously would it look to the gardener who tends it, who anxiously clears it of weeds and ties it to the vine from which it derives nourishment and sap for its beautiful blossoms.

In the union with Christ, therefore, we turn, before everything, our loving eye toward God, feel for Him an ardent gratitude, sink joyfully on our knees before Him.

Then, after a beautiful sun has risen through our union with Christ, when we feel our total unworthiness and at the same time exult over our salvation, then only can we love God, who formerly appeared to us as an offended lord but is now a forgiving father and a benevolent teacher.

But the branch, if it were sentient, would not only look up to the vine dresser, but would also fervently cling to the vine stock and feel the closest relation to the branches around it; it would love the other branches, because a gardener tends them and a stock gives them vigor.

Thus the union with Christ means a most intimate and vital companionship with Him, keeping Him before our eyes and in our hearts, and being permeated by the highest love, so that we can turn our hearts toward our brothers, united with us through Him, and for whom He had sacrificed himself.

But this love for Christ is not fruitless; it fills us not only with the purest reverence and highest respect for Him, but also has the effect of making us keep his commandments in that we sacrifice ourselves for each other and are virtuous, but virtuous only out of love for Him: "Of sin, because they believe not on me; Of righteousness, because I go to my Father, and ye see me no more; Of judgment, because the prince of this world is judged. I have yet many things to say unto you, but ye cannot bear them now. Howbeit when he, the Spirit of truth, is come, he will guide you into all truth: for he shall not speak of himself; but whatsoever he shall hear, that shall he speak: and he will shew you things to come. He shall glorify me; for he shall receive of mine, and shall shew it unto you [John 16:9–14]."

This is the great chasm which separates and elevates Christian virtues from others; this is one of the greatest effects brought out in men by the union with Christ.

Virtue is not the gloomy caricature found in the Stoic philosophy; it is not the child of the harsh doctrines of duty found among all heathen nations. It is, rather, the consequence of the love for Christ, love for a divine Being; and when it derives from such a pure source, it appears free of everything earthly and is truly divine. Then every repulsive aspect is submerged, everything earthly suppressed, everything crude extinguished, and virtue is more enlightened as it becomes milder and more humane.

Never before had human reason been able to present it so; previously virtue had been a limited, an earthly quality.

Once a man has attained this virtue, this union with Christ, he will quietly and calmly bear the blows of fortune, bravely meet the storms of passions, and fearlessly endure the rage of evil—for who could then oppress him, who could deprive him of his Savior?

His prayers will then be answered, for he prays only for the union with Christ, that is, only for the divine, and how can it fail to elevate and to comfort when one proclaims the Savior himself? "Nevertheless I tell you the truth; it is expedient for you that I go away: for if I go not away, the Comforter will not come unto you; but if I depart, I will send him unto you [John 16:7]."

And who would not gladly endure pain, knowing that through his abiding in Christ and through his works, God Himself is honored, that his consummation elevates the Lord of Creation? "And when he is come, he will reprove the world of sin, and of righteousness, and of judgment [John 15:8]."

Thus the union with Christ imparts an inner exaltation, comfort in suffering, calm trust, and a heart full of love for humankind, open to everything noble, everything great, not out of ambition but for the sake of Christ. Thus the union with Christ imparts a joyousness which the Epicurean in his frivolous philosophy and the deep thinker in his most arcane science have vainly tried to snatch at, but which the soul can attain only through its unrestrained and childlike Union with Christ and God, which alone makes life more beautiful and exalted. "Of judgment, because the prince of this world is judged [John 16:11]."

Proof of the Existence of God*

FINALLY we remind Herr Schelling of the concluding words of the letter cited above: "It is time to announce freedom of the mind to the better part of mankind, and no longer to tolerate that it laments the loss of its fetters."[1]

If this was already true in 1795, what of the year 1841?

To take the occasion here of recalling a theme that has become almost notorious—the *proof of the existence of God*—Hegel entirely turned around, that is, rejected, these theological proofs in order to justify them. What kinds of clients are these whom the lawyer cannot save from being condemned without killing himself? For example, Hegel interprets the end of the world as God in the image: "Because the accidental is *not*, God or the Absolute is." The theological proof alone puts it in reverse: "Because the accidental has true Being, God is." God is the guarantee of the accidental world. Obviously the reverse can also be said.

The proofs of the existence of God are either nothing but hollow tautologies—for example, the ontological proof means only that "what I really conceive is a true conception for me," and has an effect on me; in this sense all the gods, heathen as well as Christian, possess a real existence. Did not the old Moloch rule? Was not the Delphic Apollo a real power in the life of the Greeks? Here Kant's *Critique* [of *Pure*

---

*From "Critique of the Plutarchian Polemic Against Epicurus' Theology," Appendix in Notes and Comments in Marx's doctoral dissertation, *Difference Between the Democritean and Epicurean Philosophy of Nature* (1841).

1. Friedrich Wilhelm Joseph von Schelling's *Philosophische Briefe über Dogmatismus und Kriticismus* (*Philosophical Letters on Dogmatism and Criticism* (1795), p. 129.

Reason] also means nothing. If somebody imagines that he possesses a hundred Taler, and if this notion is not merely a subjective wish but one he believes in, then the hundred imagined Taler have the same value as a hundred real ones. He will, for example, incur debts in his imagination and they will have the same effect as the debts that humanity has contracted with its gods. On the contrary, Kant's example could have strengthened the ontological proof. Real Taler have the same existence as imagined gods. Does a real Taler have existence elsewhere than in the imagination, even if it is in a universal or fairly common imagination of humanity? Introduce paper money into a country where its usage is not known and everybody will laugh at your subjective imagination. Bring your gods to a land where other gods prevail and it will be proved to you that you suffer from imaginings and abstractions. Rightly so. He who brought the old Greeks a different god would have had to find proof of his existence. Because for the Greeks he did not exist. *What a particular country is for particular foreign gods, that the country of reason is for god altogether—a territory in which his existence ceases to be.*

Or else the proofs of the existence of a god are nothing but the *proofs of the existence of actual human self-consciousness, logical explications of the same.* For example, the ontological proof. What is the direct Being in which this is conceived? Self-consciousness.

In this sense, all the proofs of the existence of a god are proofs of *nonexistence, refutations* of all conceptions of a god. Real proofs would sound the reverse of this. "Because nature is badly contrived, God is." "Because the world is irrational, God is." "Because thought is not, God is." However, what does all this say except that *to him to whom the world is irrational, and who is therefore himself irrational, God is? Or irrationality is the existence of God.*

Religion and Animals*

The speaker blames the Swiss press for having adopted the "beastly" party names of the "horn-and-claw men," in brief for speaking Swiss to the Swiss, who live with oxen and cows in a certain patriarchal harmony. . . .

In regard to the "beastly" party names we remark that religion itself dignifies the "beastly" as symbol of the spiritual. Our speaker will in any case reject the Indian press, which in religious enthusiasm celebrates the cow Sabala and the ape Hanuman. He will reproach the Indian press for the Indian religion, as he reproached the Swiss press for the Swiss character. But there is one press which he will hardly subject to censure; we mean the *holy press*, the Bible; and doesn't the latter divide all mankind into two great parties, the *goats* and the *sheep?* Does not God himself characterize his own relationship to the houses of Judah and Israel in the following way: I am a moth to the house of Judah and a mite to the house of Israel? Or, what is closer to us seculars, isn't there a princely literature which transforms all of anthropology into zoology—we mean the heraldic literature? That contains more curiosities than the horn-and-claw men.

---

* From "Debates on Freedom of the Press and Publication," in *Rheinische Zeitung*, May 8, 1842. For the complete text, see *Karl Marx on Freedom of the Press and Censorship*, Vol. IV of The Karl Marx Library (1974).

On the Christian State*

July 10

We have hitherto admired the *Kölnische Zeitung*[1] for being, if not the "paper of the Rhineland intelligentsia," at least the Rhineland *"Intelligenzblatt"* [Advertiser]. We saw above all in its "leading political articles" a means, as wise as it was select, of disgusting the reader with politics so that he would turn all the more eagerly to the vigorous, industriously pulsating, and often aesthetically piquant domain of advertising, so that here too the motto would be *per aspera ad astra* [through a rough (path) to the stars], through politics to oysters.[2] But the fine balance that the *Kölnische Zeitung* has so far known how to maintain between politics and advertisements has been upset of late by what could be called "political industry advertisements." In the initial uncertainty as to where the new variety should be inserted, it happened that an advertisement was transformed into a leading article and the leading article into an advertisement of the kind that is called in political language a denunciation but which, if paid for, is merely called an advertisement.[3]

It is a custom in the North to treat guests to exquisite liqueurs before meager meals. We are all the more willing to follow that custom

* "The Leading Article in No. 179 of the *Kölnische Zeitung*," in *Rheinische Zeitung*, July 10, 12, 14, 1842. Based on a translation by Progress Publishers, Moscow, 1957.
1. Cologne's influential Catholic daily.
2. The German word for oysters is *Austern*, which Marx uses here as a pun on *astra*.
3. The German word for advertisement is *Anzeige*, which also means denunciation.

in regard to our northern guests and give them spirits before the meal, since in the meal itself—the "ailing"[4] article in No. 179 of *Kölnische Zeitung*—we find no spirits at all. So first we treat the reader to a scene from Lucian's *Dialogues of the Gods* in a translation accessible to all, for among our readers there will be at least one who is no Hellene.

Lucian's *Dialogues of the Gods*
XXIV. COMPLAINTS OF HERMES
Hermes, Maia

Hermes. Is there, dear mother, in the whole heavens, a god more harassed than I?

Maia. Speak not so, my son.

Hermes. Why should I not? I, who have a multitude of affairs to attend to, must always work alone and submit to so many slavish duties? I must rise in the small hours of the morning and clean out the dining hall, arrange the couches in the Council Room, and when everything is in order attend on Jupiter, running errands all day as his messenger. Hardly am I back, covered with dust, when I must serve the ambrosia. And what is most annoying, I am the only one to whom no peace is granted even at night, for then I must escort the souls of the dead to Pluto and act as attendant at their judgment. It is not enough for me to work during the day, I must attend the gymnastics, act the herald at the assemblies of the people, and help the popular orators to learn their speeches. No, I, who am torn asunder by so many matters, must over and above attend to the whole business of the dead.

Since his expulsion from Olympus Hermes has been going on by force of habit with his "slavish duties" and the whole business of the dead.

Whether it was Hermes himself or his son Pan, the caprine god, who wrote the ailing article in No. 179, we shall leave the reader to decide, remembering that Hermes of the Greeks was the god of eloquence and logic.

"To spread philosophical and religious views by means of the newspapers or to combat them in newspapers seems to us equally inadmissible."

As the old man[5] chattered away it was easy for me to note that he was bent on a tedious litany of oracles, but I calmed my impatience, for why should I not believe the sensible man who is so impartial as to

---

4. This is a pun on the German word *leitender*, which means "leading," while *leidender* means "ailing."

5. Karl Heinrich Hermes was one of the editors of the *Kölnische Zeitung*.

speak out his opinion quite frankly in his own house, and I read on. But lo and behold! This article, which cannot be reproached with a single philosophical view, has at least a tendency to combat philosophical views and spread religious ones.

What use to us is an article which disputes its own right to exist, which introduces itself by a declaration of its own incompetence? The loquacious author will answer us. He explains how his bombastic articles are to be read. He confines himself to giving fragments whose "concatenation and interconnection" he leaves to "the ingenuity of his reader" to discover—the most appropriate method for the kind of advertisement that he deals with. So we shall "concatenate and interconnect" and it is not our fault if the rosary does not become a string of pearls.

The author states: "A party which makes use of these means" (spreading and combating philosophical and religious views in newspapers) "thereby shows, in our opinion, that its intentions are not honorable and that it is less interested in teaching and enlightening the people than in attaining ulterior aims."

This being *his* opinion, the article can have nothing else in view than the attainment of ulterior aims. These "ulterior aims" will not remain concealed.

The state, the author says, has not only the right but also the duty "to silence *nonprofessional* babblers." He means the opponents of his views, for he has long agreed with himself that he is a *professional* babbler.

It is a question, therefore, of a further tightening of censorship in religious matters, a new police measure against a press which has hardly begun to breathe freely.

"In our opinion, the state can be reproached with undue forbearance rather than with excessive rigor."

But the author of the leading article thinks better of it: it is dangerous to reproach the state, so he addresses himself to the authorities; his accusation against freedom of the press becomes an accusation against the censors; he accuses the censors of applying "too little censorship."

"A blameworthy forbearance has been shown so far, not, admittedly, by the state, but by 'individual authorities,' in allowing the new philosophical school to permit itself the most unseemly attacks upon Christianity in public papers and other printed works not intended exclusively for scientific readers."

The author pauses again and thinks better of it again: not eight days ago he found that with freedom of censorship there was too little freedom of the press; he now finds that with compulsion of censors there is too little compulsion by the censorship.

That must be set right again: "As long as censorship exists it is its most urgent duty to cut out such repulsive excrescences of boyish insolence as have repeatedly offended our eyes in recent days."

Weak eyes! Weak eyes! And the "weakest eye will be offended by an expression which can be intended only for the powers of comprehension of the broad masses."

If relaxed censorship allows repulsive excrescences to appear, what can be expected of freedom of the press? If our eyes are too weak to bear the "insolence" [*Übermut*] of what has been censored, how can they be strong enough to bear the "audacity" [*Mut*] of the free press?

"As long as censorship exists it is its most urgent duty to . . ." And once it no longer exists? The sentence must be interpreted: It is the most urgent duty of the censorship to exist as long as possible.

And again the author thinks better of it: "It is not our function to act as public prosecutor and therefore we refrain from any mo e precise specification."

What heavenly kindness the man has! He refrains from more precise "specification" whereas only by quite precise, quite distinct signs could he prove and show what *his* views aim at; he utters only vague, half-whispered words of suspicion; it is not his function to act as *public* prosecutor: his function is to be a *concealed accuser*.

For the last time the wretched man thinks better of it: his function is to write liberal leading articles, to play the "loyal supporter of freedom of the press." He therefore springs to his last position: "We could not refrain from protesting against a procedure which, if it is not a result of casual negligence, can have no other aim than to discredit a freer press movement in the public eye and to give the game to its opponents who fear to lose by playing fair."

The censorship, says this champion of freedom of the press, who is as daring as he is penetrating, if it is not merely the English leopard with the inscription "I sleep, wake me not!" has engaged in this "godless" procedure to discredit a freer press movement in the public eye.

Is there still any need to discredit a press movement which draws the censorship's attention to "casual negligences" and which expects to get its renown in the public eye from the "censor's penknife"?

This movement can be called "free" only to the extent that the license of shamelessness is sometimes called "free." And is it not the shamelessness of absurdity and hypocrisy to try to pass as a champion of the freer press movement and at the same time to teach that the press will fall into the gutter the moment two gendarmes stop holding its arms?

What do we need the censorship for, what do we need this leading article for, when the philosophical press discredits itself in the public eye? The author, of course, does not want to limit in any way "the freedom of scientific research." "In our day, scientific research is rightly allowed the widest and most boundless scope."

But the following pronouncement will show what a conception this gentleman has of scientific research: "A sharp distinction must be made between what is required by the freedom of scientific research, which can but benefit Christianity itself, and what is beyond the bounds of scientific research."

Who should decide on the bounds of scientific research if not scientific research itself! According to the leading article, bounds should be prescribed to scientific research. The leading article, therefore, knows an "official reason" which does not learn from scientific research but teaches it, and which, like a learned providence, prescribes the length every hair should have to transform a scientific beard into one of world significance. The leading article believes in the scientific inspiration of the censorship.

Before further pursuing these "silly" explanations of the leading article on "scientific research," let us regale ourselves awhile with Mr. H.'s "philosophy of religion," his "own science":

"Religion is the foundation of the state, as it is the most necessary condition for every social association not aimed merely at attaining some ulterior aim."

Proof: "In its crudest form as childish fetishism it raises man to a certain extent above sensuous appetites, which, if he lets himself be dominated exclusively by them, debase him to an animal and make him incapable of fulfilling any more elevated purpose."

The leading article calls fetishism the "crudest form" of religion. It therefore admits something which is recognized as established by all men of "scientific research" even without his consensus, that "animal worship" is a higher religious form than fetishism; but does not animal worship debase man below the animal, does it not make the animal man's god?

Now this talk about "fetishism"! Real penny-paper learning! Fetishism is so far from raising man above the appetites that it is on the contrary "the religion of sensuous appetites." The fantasy of the appetites tricks the fetish worshiper into believing that an "inanimate object" will give up its natural character to gratify his desires. The crude appetite of the fetish worshiper therefore smashes the fetish when the latter ceases to be its most devoted servant.

"In those nations which attained a higher historic significance, the prime of national life coincides with the highest development of their sense of religion, and the decline of their greatness and power coincides with the decline of their religious culture."

The truth will be obtained by exactly reversing the assertion of the author; he has turned history upside down. Greece and Rome are certainly the countries of the highest "historical culture" among the peoples of antiquity. The peak of Greece's greatest internal progress coincides with the time of Pericles, its external zenith with the time of Alexander. In Pericles' time the sophists, Socrates—who may be called philosophy incarnate—art, and rhetoric had superseded religion. Alexander's time was the time of Aristotle, who rejected the eternity of the "individual" spirit and the god of the positive religions. And then Rome! Read Cicero! Epicurean, Stoic, or Skeptic philosophy was the religion of the Romans of culture when Rome reached the zenith of its career. If with the downfall of the old states the religions of the old states disappear, this needs no further explanation than that the "true religion" of the people of antiquity was the cult of their "nationality," of their "state." It was not the downfall of the old religions that brought the downfall of the old states, but the downfall of the old states that brought the downfall of the old religions. And ignorance like that of the leading article proclaims itself the "legislator of scientific research" and writes "decrees" for philosophy.

"The whole ancient world was bound to collapse because the progress that the peoples made in their scientific development necessarily involved the discovery of the errors on which their religious views were based."

So, according to the leading article, the whole ancient world perished because scientific research disclosed the errors of the antique religions. Would the ancient world not have perished if research had passed over in silence the errors of the religions, if the author of the leading article had recommended to the Roman authorities that they cut out Lucretius' and Lucian's works? ...

July 12

Just as the downfall of the ancient world was approaching there arose the school of Alexandria, which strove to prove by force "the eternal truth" of Greek mythology and its thorough agreement "with the data of scientific research." The Emperor Julian also belonged to that trend, which thought it would cause the new spirit of the times that was asserting itself to disappear if it kept its eyes closed so as not to see it. But let us keep to Mr. H.'s results! In the religions of antiquity "the faint notions of the divine were veiled in the deepest night of error" and could therefore not resist scientific research. With Christianity the situation is reversed, as any thinking machine will conclude. Indeed, Mr. H.'s says: "The best conclusions of scientific research have so far served only to confirm the truths of the Christian religion."

Apart from the fact that every philosophy of the past without exception was accused by the theologians of apostasy, not excepting even the pious Malebranche and the inspired Jakob Böhme, that Leibniz was accused by the Brunswick peasants of being a *"Löwenix"* (*Glaubenichts*—one who believes in nothing) and by the Englishman Clarke and Newton's other followers of being an atheist: apart from the fact that Christianity, as the most capable and consistent of the Protestant theologians affirm, cannot agree with reason because "worldly" and "religious" reason contradict each other, which Tertullian classically expressed: *"verum est, quia absurdum est";* apart from all this, how can the agreement of scientific research with religion be proved except by forcing research to resolve itself into religion by letting it follow its own course? The least we can say is that further compulsion is no proof.

If, of course, you acknowledge beforehand as scientific research only what conforms to your own view, it is not difficult for you to make prophecies, but then what advantage has your assertion over that of the Indian Brahmin who proves the holiness of the Vedas by reserving for himself alone the right to read it!

Yes, says H.'s "scientific research." But any research that contradicts Christianity "stops halfway" or "takes a wrong road." Can one make the argument easier for oneself?

Once scientific research "has 'made clear' to itself the content of what it has found, it will never clash with the truths of Christianity" but at the same time the state must insure that this "making clear" is impossible, for research must never appeal to the powers of comprehension of the masses, i.e., must never become popular and clear *to itself*. Even if it is attacked by all the unscientific papers of the monarchy it must be modest and keep silence.

Christianity precludes the possibility of "any new decadence," but the police must be on its guard so that the philosophizing newspaper writers do not lead to decadence; it must keep an extremely strict guard. Error will be recognized as such of itself in the struggle with truth, without any need for suppression by external force; but the state must make the struggle of truth easier by depriving the champions of "error," not indeed of internal freedom, which it cannot take away from them, but of the possibility of that freedom, the possibility of existence.

Christianity is sure of victory, but according to Mr. H. it is not so sure of victory that it can scorn the help of the police.

If from the outset everything which contradicts your faith is error and must be dealt with as such, what is there to distinguish your claims from those of the Mohammedans, from the claims of any other religion? Must philosophy adopt different principles for every country, according to the saying "different countries, different customs," in order not to contradict the basic truths of dogma? Must it believe in one country that $3 \times 1 = 1$, in another that women have no soul, and in yet another that beer is drunk in heaven? Is there not a *universal human* nature just as there is a universal nature of plants and heavenly bodies? Philosophy asks what is true, not what is acknowledged as such, what is true for all men, not what is true for individuals: philosophy's metaphysical truths do not know the boundaries of political geography; its political truths know too well where the "boundaries" begin to confuse the illusory horizon of particular world and national outlooks with the true horizon of the human mind. H. is the weakest of all the champions of Christianity.

His only proof in favor of Christianity is Christianity's *long existence*. Has not philosophy also existed from Thales down to our time and has it not precisely now, according to H. himself, greater claims and a greater opinion of its own importance than ever?

How, finally, does H. prove that the state is a "Christian" state, that instead of being a free association of moral human beings it is an association of believers, that its purpose, instead of to make freedom a reality, is to make dogma a reality? "Our European states all have Christianity as their foundation."

The *French* state too? The *Charte*,[6] Article 3, does not say that "every Christian" or "only the Christian" but "*tous les français*" are equally eligible for civil and military posts.

The Prussian *Landrecht* [common law] also says, Part II, Section XIII: "The primary duty of the Supreme Head of the State is to maintain both internal and external peace and security and to safeguard each and every one in what is his from violence and interference."

But according to §1 the Supreme Head of the State combines in his person all "duties and rights of the State." It does not say that the primary duty of the state is the suppression of heretical errors and bliss in the other world.

If, however, some European states are in fact founded upon Christianity, do those states conform to their conception, is the "pure existence" of a condition the right of that condition?

In the view of our H. it is so, for he reminds the supporters of Young Hegelianism "that according to the laws in force in the greater part of the state, marriage not consecrated by the Church is declared concubinage and as such is punished by the police courts."

---

6. The French *Charte Constitutionnelle* (Constitutional Charter), adopted after the 1830 revolution.

If, therefore, "marriage not consecrated by the Church" is considered on the Rhine according to the Napoleonic Code as "marriage" and on the Spree according to the Prussian *Landrecht* as "concubinage," the "police court" punishment must be an argument for the philosophers that what is right in one place is wrong in another, that not the Napoleonic Code but the *Landrecht* has the scientific and moral, the reasonable conception of marriage. This "philosophy of police court punishment" may be convincing in other places; it is not convincing in *Prussia*. For the rest, how little inclined the Prussian *Landrecht* is to "holy" marriage is shown by §12, Part II, Section 1: "However, a marriage which is allowed by the laws of the *Land* loses none of its civil validity by the fact that the dispensation of the spiritual authorities has not been requested or has been refused."

Here in Prussia, too, marriage is partly emancipated from the "spiritual authorities" and its "civil" validity is distinct from its "ecclesiastical."

It goes without saying that our great Christian state philosopher has not a very "high" view of the state.

"Since our states are not only associations based on right, but at the same time true educational institutions with the only difference that they extend their care to a broader field than the institutions intended for the education of youth," etc., "all public education" is based "on the foundation of Christianity."

The education of our schoolchildren is based just as much on the classics of old and on science in general as on the Catechism.

The state, according to H., is distinguished from a children's home not by content but by size—it extends its "care" to a broader field.

But the true "public education" of the state is rather the reasonable and public being of the state; the state itself educates its members by making them members of the state, by changing the aims of the individual into general aims, coarse urge into moral inclination, natural independence into spiritual freedom, by the individual's finding his delight in the life of the whole and the whole in the disposition of the individual.

The leading article, on the other hand, makes the state, not an association of free human beings mutually educating one another, but a crowd of adults whose destiny is to be educated from above and to pass from the "narrow" schoolroom to the "broader" one.

This theory of education and guardianship is here brought forward by a supporter of freedom of the press who, in his love for this belle, notes the "negligences of the censorship," who knows how to depict the "powers of comprehension of the masses" in the appropriate place (perhaps the powers of comprehension of the masses have seemed so precarious to *Kölnische Zeitung* of late because the masses have forgotten how to appreciate the superiorities of the "unphilosophical newspaper"?), and who advises scientists to have one view for the stage and another one for backstage!

As the leading article showed us its "short" view of the state it will now expound to us its low view of Christianity: "All the newspaper articles in the world will never convince a population that feels on the whole well and happy that it is in a wretched predicament."

We should think not! The *material* feeling of well-being and happiness is more proof against newspaper articles than the bliss-giving and all-conquering assurance of faith! H. does not sing "A Mighty Fortress Is Our God." The truly believing heart of the "masses" is probably more exposed to the rust of doubt than the refined worldly culture of the "few."

H. fears "even incitement to insurrection in a well-ordered state" less than in a "well-ordered church," although the latter may besides be led by the "spirit of God" to all truth. A fine believer, and the grounds he has! Political articles are within the comprehension of the masses, he says, but philosophical articles are beyond it!

If, finally, we contrast the leading article's hint, "the half-measures that have been taken recently against Young Hegelianism have had the consequences half-measures usually have," to the ingenuous wish that the last steps of the Hegelians might pass over "without too unfavorable consequences for them" we can understand Cornwall's words in *King Lear:*

> He cannot flatter, he,
> An honest man and plain—he must speak truth!
> An they will take it, so; if not, he's plain.
> These kind of knaves I know, which in this plainness
> Harbour more craft and more corrupter ends
> Than twenty silly-ducking observants
> That stretch their duties nicely.[7]

We would think we were insulting the readers of *Rheinische Zeitung* if we fancied they would be satisfied with the comical rather than serious show of a *ci-devant* liberal, "a young man of days gone by," being sent back to where he belongs; we wish to say a few words about "the matter itself." As long as we were engaged in a polemic with the ailing article it would not have been right to interrupt it in the process of its self-annihilation.

July 14

First the question is raised: "Should philosophy discuss religious matters also in newspaper articles?"

---

7. Act II, Scene 2.

This question can be answered only by criticizing it.

Philosophy, above all German philosophy, has a propensity to solitude, to systematic seclusion, to dispassionate self-contemplation which in its estrangement opposes it from the outset to the quick-witted and alive-to-events newspapers whose only delight is in information. Philosophy, taken in its systematic development, is unpopular; its secret weaving within itself seems to the layman to be an occupation as overstrained as it is unpractical: it is considered a professor of magic whose incantations sound pompous because they are unintelligible.

Philosophy, in accordance with its character, has never made the first step toward replacing the ascetic priestly vestments with the light, conventional garb of the newspapers. But philosophers do not grow out of the soil like mushrooms, they are the product of their time and of their people, whose most subtle, precious, and invisible sap circulates in philosophical ideas. The same spirit that builds railways by the hands of the workers builds philosophical systems in the brain of the philosophers. Philosophy does not stand outside the world any more than man's brain is outside of him because it is not in his stomach; but, of course, philosophy is in the world with its brain before it stands on the earth with its feet, whereas many another human sphere has long been rooted in the earth before it has any idea that the "head" also belongs to the world or that this world is the world of the head.

Because every true philosophy is the spiritual quintessence of its time, the time must come when philosophy not only internally by its content but externally by its appearance comes into contact and mutual reaction with the real contemporary world. Philosophy then ceases to be a definite system in presence of other definite systems, it becomes philosophy generally, in presence of the world; it becomes the philosophy of the world of the present. The formal features which attest that philosophy has achieved that importance, that it is the living soul of culture, that philosophy is becoming worldly and the world philosophical, were the same in all times: any history book will show, repeated with stereotyped fidelity, the simplest rituals which unmistakably mark philosophy's introduction into drawing rooms and priests' studies, the editorial offices of newspapers and the antechambers of courts, into the hatred and the love of the people of the time. Philosophy is introduced into the world by the clamor of its enemies, who betray their internal infection by their desperate appeals for help against the blaze of ideas. These cries of its enemies mean as much for philosophy as the first cry of a child for the anxious ear of the mother, they are the cry of life of the ideas which have burst open the orderly hieroglyphic husk of the system and become citizens of the world. The Corybantes and Cabiri, who with the roll of drums announce to the world the birth of baby Zeus, first turn against the religious section of the philosophers, partly because their inquisitorial instinct can secure a firmer hold on this sentimental side of the public, partly because the public, to which the opponents of philosophy also belong, can feel the ideal sphere of philosophy only with its ideal feelers, and the only field of ideas whose value the public believes in almost as much as in the system of material needs is that of religious ideas, and, finally, because religion polemicizes not against a definite system of philosophy but against the philosophy generally of the definite systems.

The true philosophy of the present does not differ as far as this fate is concerned from the true philosophies of the past. Indeed, this fate is a proof that history owed to the truth of philosophy.

And for six years the German papers have been drumming against the religious trend in philosophy, calumniating it, distorting it, bowdlerizing it. *Allgemeine Augsburger* sang bravuras, nearly every overture played the theme that philosophy was not worthy of being discussed by Dame Wisdom, that it was the idle bragging of youth, a fashion for blasé coteries. But in spite of all that it could not be got rid of and there was more drumming, for in its antiphilosophical caterwauling the *Augsburger* plays but one instrument, the monotonous kettledrum. All German papers, from *Berliner Politisches Wochenblatt* and *Hamburger Correspondenten* to the obscure local papers, down to *Kölnische Zeitung*, blared out about Hegel and Schelling, Feuerbach and Bauer, *Deutsche Jahrbücher*, etc. Finally the curiosity of the public was aroused and it wanted to see the Leviathan with its own eyes, all the more as semiofficial articles threatened philosophy that it would have a legal syllabus officially prescribed for it. And that was when philosophy appeared in the papers. Long had it kept silence before the self-complacent superficiality which boasted in a few stale newspaper phrases that it could blow away like soap bubbles years of study by genius, the hard-won fruits of self-sacrificing solitude, the results of that invisible but slowly extenuating struggle of contemplation; philosophy had even *protested against the newspapers* as being an inappropriate field, but in the end it had to break its silence, it became a newspaper correspondent and—unheard-of diversion!—it suddenly occurred to the garrulous newspaper purveyors that philosophy is no food for the newspaper public and they could not refrain from drawing the attention of the governments to the dishonesty of bringing questions of philosophy and religion into the sphere of the newspapers, not to enlighten the public but to attain ulterior aims.

What is there so bad that philosophy could say about religion or about itself that your newspaper clamor had not long ago imputed to it in far worse and more frivolous terms? It only needs to repeat what you unphilosophical Capuchins have preached about it in thousands and thousands of polemics, and it has said the worst.

But philosophy speaks differently of religious and philosophical objects than you have. You speak without having studied them, it speaks after study; you appeal to the emotions, it appeals to reason; you curse, it teaches; you promise heaven and earth, it promises nothing but truth; you demand faith in your faith, it demands not faith in its results but the test of doubt; you frighten, it calms. And truly, philosophy is world-wise enough to know that its results flatter the desire for pleasure or the egoism neither of the heavenly nor of the earthly world; but the public that loves truth and knowledge for their own sakes will be able to measure itself in judgment and morality with ignorant, servile, inconsistent, and mercenary scribes.

Admittedly somebody or other, by reason of the worthlessness of his intellect or views, may misinterpret philosophy, but do not you Protestants believe that the Catholics misinterpret Christianity, do you not reproach the Christian religion with the disgraceful times of the eighth and ninth centuries, the night of St. Bartholomew, and the Inquisition? There are conclusive proofs that the hatred of the Protestant theology for philosophers arises largely out of philosophy's tolerance toward the particular confession as such. Feuerbach and Strauss were reproached more for maintaining that Catholic dogmas were Christian than for stating that the dogmas of Christianity were not dogmas of reason.

But if occasional individuals cannot digest modern philosophy and die of philosophical indigestion, that proves no more against philosophy than the occasional blowing up of a few passengers by the bursting of a boiler proves against mechanics.

The question whether philosophical and religious matters should be discussed in newspapers resolves itself in its own emptiness.

If such questions already have an interest for the public as *newspaper questions*, they have become *questions of the day;* then the point is not whether they should be discussed but where and how they should be discussed, whether within the bounds of the family and the hotels, of the schools and the churches, but not by the press; by the opponents of philosophy but not by the philosophers; whether in the obscure language of private opinion but not in the clarifying language of public reason. Then the point is whether what lives in reality belongs to the realm of the press; it is no longer a question of a particular content of the press, the question is the general one whether the press must be really the press, i.e., a free press.

From the first question we completely separate the second: "Should politics be dealt with philosophically by the newspapers in a so-called Christian state?"

If religion becomes a political quality, an object of politics, there seems to be hardly any need to mention that the newspapers not only may, but must, discuss political objects. It seems from the start that the wisdom of this world, philosophy, has more right to bother about the kingdom of this world, about the state, than the wisdom of the other world, religion. The point here is not whether the state should be philosophized about, but whether it should be philosophized about well or badly, philosophically or unphilosophically, with prejudice or without, with consciousness or without, consistently or inconsistently, in a completely rational or half-rational way. If you make religion a theory of state right, then you make religion itself a kind of philosophy.

Was it not Christianity before anything else that separated church and state?

Read Saint Augustine's *De Civitate Dei*, study the Fathers of the Church and the spirit of Christianity, and then come back and tell us which is the "Christian state," the church or the state! Does not every minute of your practical life give the lie to your theory? Do you consider it wrong to appeal to the courts when you are cheated? But the Apostle writes that that is wrong. Do you offer your right cheek when you are struck on the left, or do you not institute proceedings for assault? Yet the Gospel forbids that. Do you not claim your reasonable rights in this world? Do you not grumble at the slightest raising of a tax? Are you not furious at the slightest infringement of your personal liberty? But you have been told that the sufferings of this life are not to be compared with the bliss of the future, that suffering in patience and the bliss of hope are cardinal virtues.

Are not most of your court proceedings and the majority of civil laws concerned with property? But you have been told that your treasure is not of this world. If you base yourselves on giving to Caesar the things which are Caesar's and to God the things which are God's, do not consider the mammon of gold alone but at least just as much free reason the Caesar of this world, and the "action of free reason" is what we call philosophizing.

When at first in the Holy Alliance a quasi-religious alliance of states was to be formed and religion was to be the state motto of Europe, the Pope showed profound sense and perfect consistency in refusing to join it, for in his view the universal Christian link between nations was the Church and not diplomacy, not a worldly alliance of states.

The truly religious state is the theocratic state; the prince of such states must be either the God of religion, Jehovah himself, as in the

Jewish state, God's representative, the Dalai Lama, as in Tibet, or finally, as Görres correctly demands of Christian states in his last work, they must all submit to a church which is an "infallible church." For if, as in Protestantism, there is no supreme head of the church, the domination of religion is nothing but the religion of domination, the cult of the will of the government.

Once a state includes several confessions with equal rights, it cannot be a religious state without violating particular confessions; it cannot be a church which condemns adherents of another confession as heretics, which makes every piece of bread dependent on faith, which makes dogma the link between separate individuals and existence as citizens of the state. Ask the Catholic inhabitants of "poor green Erin," ask the Huguenots before the French Revolution: they did not appeal to religion, for their religion was not the religion of the state; they appealed to the "Rights of Humanity," and philosophy interprets the Rights of Humanity and demands that the state be the state of human nature.

But the half, the limited, rationalism, which is as unbelieving as it is theological, says that the universal Christian spirit, irrespective of confessional differences, must be the spirit of the state! It is the greatest irreligiousness, the wantonness of worldly reason, to separate the general spirit of religion from the positive religion; this separation of religion from its dogmas and institutions is equal to asserting that the universal spirit of right must reign in the state irrespective of the definite laws and the positive institutions of right.

If you presume to stand so high above religion as to have the right to separate the general spirit of religion from its positive definitions, what reproach have you to make to the philosophers if they want to make the separation complete and not a halfway one, if they proclaim not the Christian, but the human, spirit the universal spirit of religion?

Christians live in states with differing constitutions, some in a republic, some in an absolute, some again in a constitutional monarchy. Christianity does not decide on the *correctness* of the constitutions, for it knows no distinction between constitutions; it teaches, as religion must: Submit to the authority, for *all authority* is ordained by God. The correctness of state constitutions is therefore to be judged not according to Christianity, not according to the nature, the essence of the state itself, not according to the nature of Christian society, but according to the nature of human society.

The Byzantine state was the properly religious state, for there dogmas were matters of state, but the Byzantine state was the worst of all states. The states of the *ancien régime* were the most Christian states, nonetheless they were states of "the will of court."

There is a dilemma that "sound" common sense cannot solve. Either the Christian state corresponds to the concept of the state as a realization of rational freedom, and then nothing else can be demanded for it to be a Christian state than that it be a reasonable state; then it is enough to develop the state out of the reason of human relations, a work accomplished by philosophy. Or the state of rational freedom cannot be developed out of Christianity: then you will yourselves concede that this development does not lie in the tendency of Christianity, for Christianity does not wish for a bad state, and any state which is not the embodiment of rational freedom is a bad state.

Answer the dilemma as you like, you will have to concede that the state is not to be constituted from religion but from the reason of freedom. Only the crassest ignorance can assert that the theory of making the state concept independent is a passing whim of modern philosophers.

Philosophy has done nothing in politics that physics, mathematics, medicine, every science, has not done within its own sphere. Bacon of Verulam declared theological physics to be a virgin vowed to God and barren; he emancipated physics from theology and she became fruitful. You no more have to ask the politician if he has faith than the doctor. Immediately before and after the time of Copernicus' great discoveries on the true solar system, the law of gravitation of the state was discovered: the center of gravity of the state was found within the state itself. As various European governments tried to apply this result with the initial superficiality of practice to the system of equilibrium of states, similarly Machiavelli and Campanella began before them, and Hobbes, Spinoza, and Hugo Grotius afterward, down to Rousseau, Fichte and Hegel, to consider the state with the eye of man and to develop its natural laws from reason and experience, not from theology, any more than Copernicus let himself be influenced by Joshua's supposed command to the sun to stand still over Gideon and the moon over the vale of Ajalon. Modern philosophy has only continued a work already started by Heraclitus and Aristotle. So it is not the reason of modern philosophy that you are polemicizing against, but the ever modern philosophy of reason. Naturally, the ignorance that yesterday or perhaps the day before discovered the age-old ideas on the state in *Rheinische* or *Königsberger Zeitung* considers the ideas of history notions which occurred overnight to certain individuals because they appear new to it and came to it overnight; it forgets that it has assumed the old role of the doctor of Sorbonne who considered it his duty to accuse Montesquieu in public because the latter was frivolous enough to maintain that the political quality, not the virtue of the Church, was the highest quality in the state; it forgets that it has assumed the role of Joachim Lange, who denounced Wolff because his doctrine of predestination would lead to desertion among soldiers and thereby to a relaxation of military discipline and finally to the collapse of the state; lastly it forgets that the Prussian *Landrecht* comes from the very school of philosophy of "that Wolff" and the Napoleonic Code comes not from the Old Testament but from the school of ideas of Voltaire, Rousseau, Condorcet, Mirabeau, and Montesquieu and from the French Revolution. Ignorance is a demon and we are afraid it will yet play us more than one tragedy; the greatest Greek poets were right when they represented it in the terrible dramas of the royal houses of Mycenae and Thebes as tragic fate.

Whereas the earlier teachers of state law construed the state out of ambition or sociability, or even reason, though not out of the reason of society but rather out of the reason of the individual, the more ideal and profound view of modern philosophy construes it out of the idea of the whole. It considers the state the great organism in which freedom of right, of morals, and of politics has to be implemented and in which in the laws of the state the individual citizen merely obeys the natural laws of his own reason, human reason. *Sapienti sat.* [Sufficient for the wise man.]

We shall conclude with a further philosophical farewell to *Kölnische Zeitung*. It was reasonable of it to take to itself a liberal "of times gone by." One can most comfortably be both liberal and reactionary at the same time, if only one is always skillful enough to address only liberals of the recent past who know no other dilemma than that of Vidocq—"prisoner or jailer." It was still more reasonable that the liberal of the recent past combated the liberals of the present. Without parties there is no development, without a parting there is no progress. We hope that with the leading article of No. 179 *Kölnische Zeitung* there has begun a new era, the era of character.

In Defense of Bauer's Theology*

If one wanted to write a comedy of dilettantism in Germany, Herr Dr. O. F. Gruppe would be the indispensable person. Fate has equipped him with that iron perseverance which great men could not do without, at least the great men of dilettantism. If most of his adventures, like those of Sancho Panza, end in ambiguous signs of recognition, this monotony of success is diversely enlivened and varied by the comical lack of embarrassment and touching naïveté with which Herr Gruppe receives his laurels. One cannot even fail to recognize a certain greatness of soul in the consistency which leads Herr Gruppe to conclude: While I have been ousted from the schoolroom of philosophy, it will be my mission to be thrown out also from the ballroom of aesthetics and the halls of philosophy. This is much, but not everything. My role is played out only when I have also been ejected from the temple of theology. And Herr Gruppe is conscientious enough to play out his role.

Still, in his latest appearance Herr Gruppe has to some extent denied the height of his vantage point. We do not doubt for a moment that his latest work, *Bruno Bauer und die akademische Lehrfreiheit*, was in no way written "in the service of one party or another or under some influence." Herr Gruppe experienced the necessity of

---

* "One More Word on *Bruno Bauer und die akademische Lehrfreiheit (Bruno Bauer and Academic Freedom of Teaching)* by Dr. O. F. Gruppe" (Berlin, 1842). Published in *Deutsche Jahrbücher für Wissenschaft und Kunst*, November 16, 1842. This literary-philosophical journal of the Young Hegelians, edited by Arnold Ruge and Theodor Echtermeyer, appeared in Leipzig from July, 1841, to January, 1843; its previous title, from 1838 to June, 1841, was *Hallische Jahrbücher für deutsche Wissenschaft und Kunst*. This article is the only one that Marx contributed to the *Deutsche Jahrbücher*.

being thrown out of theology, but here worldly wisdom gripped his comical instinct under the arms. Herr Gruppe has hitherto labored, as befits a comical character, with the most amusing earnestness and most singular pomposity. The incompleteness, the superficiality, the misunderstandings have been his *destiny*, but they have not been his *tendency*. The great man played according to his nature, but only for himself and not for others. He was a *buffoon by profession:* we cannot doubt that in his latest appearance he is a *buffoon for hire and pay.* The bad intention, the conscienceless distortion, the base perfidy will leave no doubt in the reader either.

It would be against our views to waste time over Herr Gruppe's comical nature and far-reaching critical apparatus. Who wants a critical history of an Eulenspiegel [practical joker]? One demands anecdotes, and we will give an anecdote from Herr Gruppe which is the anecdote from his pamphlet. It concerns Bauer's exegesis of Matthew 12: 38–42. The good reader must for a moment trouble himself with theologicalism but he will not forget that Herr Gruppe and not theology is our aim. He [the reader] will find it reasonable that the character of Bauer's opponents be brought out before the newspaper public, since Bauer's character and doctrines have been made into a newspaper myth.

We give the Matthew passage in question in its entirety:

> Then certain of the scribes and of the Pharisees answered, saying, Master, we would see a sign from thee.
>
> But he answered and said unto them, An evil and adulterous generation seeketh after a sign: and there shall no sign be given to it, but the sign of the prophet Jonas.
>
> For as Jonas was three days and three nights in the whale's belly; so shall the Son of man be three days and three nights in the heart of the earth.
>
> The men of Nineveh shall rise in judgment with this generation, and shall condemn it; because they repented at the preaching of Jonas; and, behold, a greater than Jonas is here.
>
> The queen of the south shall rise up in the judgment with this generation, and shall condemn it: for she came from the uttermost parts of the earth to hear the wisdom of Solomon; and, behold, a greater than Solomon is here.

The Protestant theologians were struck by the contradiction that Jesus here rejects miracles, whereas he elsewhere accomplishes miracles. A still greater contradiction struck them, that at the same moment that he rejects the demand for miracles, the Lord promises a miracle, and a great miracle at that: his three days' sojourn in the nether world.

Since the Protestant theologians are too godless to admit a contradiction between the [Holy] Writ and their reason, and too sanctimonious to admit a contradiction between their reason and the Writ, they falsify, distort, and twist the clear words and simple sense of the Writ. They maintain that in the demand for a sign Jesus has here not counterposed his *doctrine* with his *spiritual personality;* they maintain that "he speaks of the totality of his appearance, which is more than the appearance of Solomon and Jonah, and to which 'especially' his miracles belonged."[1]

Bauer shows by the most solid exegesis the absurdity of this explanation. Then he quotes to them Luke (11: 29–30), in which the vexatious passage about the whale and the three days' sojourn within the earth is missing. Luke writes:

> And when the people were gathered thick together, he began to say, This is an evil generation: they seek a sign; and there shall no sign be given it, but the sign of Jonas the prophet.
>
> For as Jonas was a sign unto the Ninevites, so shall also the Son of man be to this generation.

Whereupon Luke has the Lord say, as the Ninevites repented at the preaching of Jonah and the queen of the south came from the uttermost parts of the earth to hear the wisdom of Solomon. Even simpler, Bauer shows, is the kernel in Mark (8: 12–13):

> And he sighed deeply in his spirit, and saith, Why doth this generation seek after a sign? verily I say unto you, There shall no sign be given unto this generation.
>
> And he left them, and entering into the ship again departed to the other side.

Thus Bauer rises up against the false interpretation and arbitrary distortion of the Writ by theologians and refers them to what is *written,* and once again he summarizes the *sense* of Jesus' preaching in the following words:

> Get thee away from me, theologian! For it is written: Here is more than Jonah, more than Solomon, that is, that the Ninevites have repented at the preaching of Jonah, the queen of the south came from the uttermost parts of the earth to hear the *wisdom* of Solomon, but you have not lent credence to my words and my preaching, and yet these words are the expression of a personality whose spiritual range is infinite, while Jonah and Solomon were still limited personalities. But it should remain thus, that only the sign of Jonah should be given to you, and you should not see another sign than this my person, even if infinite in verbal expressions.

---

1. This quotation is from Bruno Bauer's *Kritik der evangelischen Geschichte der Synoptiker* (*Critique of the Evangelical History of the Synoptics*) (Leipzig, 1841), Vol. II, p. 296.

After Bauer thus explains Jesus' preaching, he adds: "Where in particular thus remain the miracles?"

And Herr Gruppe? Herr Gruppe says: "The most peculiar thing in this is that Bauer in his baroque way presents himself as a prophet. On page 296 we read the emphatic passage: 'Get thee away from me, theologian!'" (p. 20).

Herr Gruppe's shamelessness will imply to the reader that Bauer speaks of *himself*, that he presents himself as the *infinite personality*, whereas Bauer only *exegesizes Jesus' preaching*. Much as we wish, we cannot excuse this quid pro quo, this tomfoolery, as Herr Gruppe's mental infirmity and dilettantish ignorance. The *deceit* is clear. What is involved is not that which Herr Gruppe keeps from the reader! We could always believe that the dilettante had accidentally opened to page 296 of Bauer's book, and in the cheerful hastiness of his own book producing had no time to read the preceding and following development. But Herr Gruppe suppresses the conclusion of the "emphatic passage," the conclusion that stands above all misunderstanding: "But it should remain thus, that only the sign of Jonah should be given to you, and you should not see another sign than this my person, even if infinite in verbal expression. Where thus remain the 'special' miracles?"

Herr Gruppe saw: even the embarrassed reader—the reader who was silly enough to seek Bauer not in Bauer's writings but in the writings of Herr Gruppe—he too must be convinced by these words that Bauer does not speak of himself but speaks of what has been *written down*. Apart from all other tritenesses, what else would the words mean: "Where thus remain the 'special' miracles?"

We doubt whether German literature can show a comparable shamelessness.

Herr Gruppe says in his preface: "In the course of my work it has become ever more clear to me that we live in a time of rhetoricians and sophists" (p. iv).

If this is a *personal confession*, then we must earnestly protest against it. Herr Gruppe is neither a rhetorician nor a sophist. Until the time of his pamphlet against Bauer he was a comical character, a rogue in the naïve sense, and since then he has lost nothing except his naïveté and thus is now—but let his conscience tell him. For the rest, Bauer may consider it a recognition of his intellectual superiority that they can send against him only men who are beneath all intellect and outside of any superiority, whom he would meet only if he let himself fall.

The Koran and the Bible*

WE have to tell our neighbor [the *Kölnische Zeitung*] an anecdote. In Rome, publication of the Koran is prohibited. A wily Italian knew how to get around it. He published a *refutation* of the Koran, that is, a book which bore on its title page *Refutation of the Koran*, but the content was simply the text of the Koran. And did not all heretics know how to play this trick? And wasn't Vanini burned, although in his proclamation of atheism in his book, *Theatrum mundi*,[1] he carefully and ostentatiously presented all counterarguments against it? Did not Voltaire himself, in his *Bible enfin expliquée* [*The Bible Explained at Last*], teach religious unbelief in the text and belief in the notes, and did anybody trust the purifying efficacy of these notes?

---

* From "The Denunciation of the *Kölnische Zeitung* and the Polemic of the *Rhein- und Mosel-Zeitung*"; published in the *Rheinische Zeitung*, January 13, 1843. For the complete text, see *Karl Marx on Freedom of the Press and Censorship*, Vol. IV of The Karl Marx Library (1974).

1. Lucilio Vanini, *Amphiteatrum aeternae providentiae* (*Amphitheater of Eternal Divine Providence*) (1615).

Luther As Arbiter Between
Strauss and Feuerbach*

STRAUSS and Feuerbach! Which of the two is right in the recently stirred up question of the concept of miracles?[1] Strauss, who still views the subject as a theologian, and hence with preconceptions, or Feuerbach, who considers it as a nontheologian, and hence without bias? Strauss, who looks at things as they *appear* to the eyes of a speculative theologian, or Feuerbach, who sees them as they *are?*

Is it Strauss, who does not arrive at a final judgment about the miracle and yet assumes a special power of the spirit through the miracle, distinct from wish—as if wish were not this assumed power of the spirit of man; as if, for example, wish, in order to be free, were not the first act of freedom? Or is it Feuerbach, who makes short shrift and says: Miracle is the realization of a natural or human wish in a supranaturalistic way? Which one of the two is right? Luther—a very good authority, an authority that infinitely predominates over all Protestant dogmas together, because with Luther religion was *literal truth, nature,* so to speak—let Luther decide.

Luther says, for example—and innumerable similar quotations from him can be cited—about the resurrection of the dead in Luke 7 . . .[2]

---

* Written late January, 1842; published in *Anekdota zur neuesten deutschen Philosophie und Publicistik,* II (1843).

1. The Young Hegelian journal, *Deutsche Jahrbücher für Wissenschaft und Kunst,* November 1, 1841, and January 7, 8, 10, and 11, 1842, published a series of articles on religious criticism, with reference to Ludwig Feuerbach and David Friedrich Strauss; the articles (probably written by Max Stirner) were signed "*Ein Berliner*" (A Berliner). Marx therefore signed this article "*Kein Berliner*" (No Berliner).

2. Luke 7: 12–15: "Now when he came nigh to the gate of the city, behold, there was a dead man carried out, the only son of his mother, and she was a widow: and much people of the city was with her. And when the Lord saw her,

In these few words you have an apology for Feuerbach's whole book[3]—an apology for the definitions of Providence, Omnipotence, Creation, Miracle, and Faith as given in that book. Oh, shame on you, you Christians, noble and common, educated and uneducated Christians, shame on you, that an Antichrist had to show you the essence of Christianity in its true, undisguised shape! And I advise you, you speculative theologians and philosophers: Free yourselves from the concepts and preconceptions of existing speculative philosophy, if you want to arrive differently at things as they are, that is, if you want to arrive at the *truth*. And there is no other road to truth and freedom for you except the one that leads through the *Feuer-bach* [stream of fire]. Feuerbach is the *purgatory* of the present.

---

he had compassion on her, and said unto her, Weep not. And he came and touched the bier: and they that bare him stood still. And he said, Young man, I say unto thee, Arise. And he that was dead sat up, and began to speak. And he delivered him to his mother." Quotations from Luther's *Sämtliche Schriften und Werke*, ed. by H. Zedler (Leipzig, 1732), Part XVI, pp. 442–45, are omitted here.

3. Ludwig Feuerbach, *Das Wesen des Christentums* (*The Essence of Christianity*) (Leipzig, 1841).

Democracy and Religion*

HEGEL proceeds from the state and makes man into the subjectified state; democracy proceeds from man and makes the state into objectified man. Just as religion does not create man, but man creates religion, so the constitution does not create the people, but the people create the constitution. In some respects democracy is related to all other forms of state as Christianity is related to all other religions. Christianity is religion χατ' 'εξοχήν [by preference], the *essence of religion*, deifying man as a *particular* religion. So also is democracy the *essence of every constitution*, with socialized man as a *particular* constitution; democracy is related to other constitutions as a species is related to its class, except that the species itself exists here as a *particular* class not corresponding to the essence of other existences. Democracy is related to all other forms of state as their Old Testament.

* From "Critique of Hegel's Philosophy of Law," written in the summer of 1843.

Criticism of Religion Is
the Presupposition of All Criticism*

For Germany, the criticism of religion has been essentially completed, and the criticism of religion is the presupposition of all criticism.

The profane existence of error is compromised when its heavenly *oratio pro aris et focis* [prayer for altar and hearth] has been refuted. Man, who in his search for a supernatural being in the fantastic reality of heaven found only a reflection of himself, will no longer be inclined to find only the semblance of his own self, a nonhuman being, where he seeks and must seek his true reality.

The basis of irreligious criticism is: *Man makes religion*, religion does not make man. And indeed, religion is the self-awareness and self-regard of man who either has not yet found or has already lost himself again. But man is not an abstract being, crouching outside the world. Man is the *world of men*, the state, society. This state, this society, produce religion, which is an inverted world consciousness because they are an inverted world. Religion is the general theory of that world, its encyclopedic compendium, its logic in popular form, its spiritual *point d'honneur* [point of honor], its enthusiasm, its moral sanction, its solemn complement, its general ground of consolation and justification. It is the fantastic realization of the human *being* because the human *being* possesses no true reality. The struggle against religion is therefore indirectly the struggle against that world whose spiritual aroma is religion.

Religious misery is in one way the expression of real misery, and in another a protest against real misery. Religion is the sigh of the

---

* From "Toward the Critique of Hegel's Philosophy of Law. Introduction," written at the end of 1843 and early 1844; published in *Deutsch-Französische Jahrbücher*, 1844.

afflicted creature, the soul of a heartless world, as it is also the spirit of spiritless conditions. It is the *opium* of the people.

The abolition of religion as the *illusory* happiness of the people is the demand for their *real* happiness. The demand to abandon the illusions about their condition is the *demand to give up a condition that requires illusions*. Hence criticism of religion is in embryo a *crticism of this vale of tears* whose halo is religion.

Criticism has plucked the imaginary flowers from the chain, not for the purpose of enabling man to wear the existing chain without fantasy or consolation, but to make him cast off the chain and pluck the living flower. The criticism of religion disillusions man so that he thinks, acts, and shapes his reality like a disillusioned man who has come to his senses, so that he revolves around himself and thereby around his real sun. Religion is only the illusory sun that revolves around man so long as he does not revolve around himself.

It is, therefore, the task of history, after the otherworldly truth has disappeared, to establish *the truth of this world*. It is the immediate task of philosophy, which stands in the service of history, to expose human self-alienation in its *unholy form* after it has been unmasked in its *holy form*. Criticism of heaven thus is transformed into criticism of earth, *criticism of religion* into *criticism of law*, and *crticism of theology* into *criticism of politics.* . . .

The weapon of criticism, to be sure, cannot replace the criticism of weapons; material force must be overthrown by material force, but theory itself also becomes a material force as soon as the masses grip it. Theory is capable of gripping the masses when it demonstrates *ad hominem* [in man], and it demonstrates *ad hominem* when it becomes radical. To be radical is to grasp things by the root. But for man, the root is man himself. The clear proof of the radicalism of German theory, and hence of its practical energy, is that it issues from the decisive, *positive* suspension of religion. The criticism of religion ends with the doctrine that *man is the highest being for man*, hence with the *categorical imperative to overthrow all conditions* in which man is a degraded, enslaved, abandoned, contemptible being—conditions that cannot be better described than by the exclamation of a Frenchman on the occasion of a projected dog tax: "Poor dogs! They want to treat you like human beings!"

Even historically, theoretical emancipation has a specifically practical significance for Germany. For Germany's revolutionary past is theoretical—it is the Reformation. As the revolution then began in the brain of the monk, so now it begins in the brain of the philosopher.

Luther, to be sure, vanquished the bondage of *devotion* when he replaced it with the bondage of *conviction*. He shattered faith in authority while he restored the authority of faith. He transformed parsons into laymen and laymen into parsons. He freed man from outward religiosity while he made religiosity the innerness of man. He emancipated the body from its chain while he put chains on the heart.

But while Protestantism was not the true solution, it was the true formulation of the problem. It was no longer, therefore, a question of the struggle of the layman against the *parson outside himself*, but of a struggle with *his own inner parson*, his *parson nature*. And if the Protestant transformation of German laymen into parsons emancipated the lay popes, the princes with their clergy, the privileged, and the philistines, so the philosophical transformation of the priestly Germans into men will emancipate the *people*. But little as the emancipation will stop with the princes, just as little will the secularization of estates stop with the *robbery of the church* that was set in motion by hypocritical Prussia above all. At that time the Peasant War, the most radical fact of German history, was wrecked by theology. Today, when theology itself is wrecked, the most unfree fact of German history, our *status quo*, will be shattered by philosophy. On the eve of the Reformation official Germany was the most absolute vassal of Rome. On the eve of its revolution Germany is the absolute vassal of something less than Rome—of Prussia and Austria, of bumpkin-Junkers and philistines. . . .

One fine day Germany will find itself at the *niveau* [level] of European decline before ever having reached the *niveau* of European emancipation. It will then be compared to a fetishist wasting away from the diseases of Christianity.

Politics and "Christian Religious Feeling"*

NUMBER 60 of *Vorwärts!* contains an article entitled, "The King of Prussia and Social Reform," signed by: "A Prussian."[1]

The so-called Prussian sums up the contents of the Royal Prussian Cabinet Order on the revolt of the Silesian workers[2] and the view of the French journal *La Réforme*[3] on that Cabinet Order. *La Réforme* ascribes the Cabinet Order to the King's "fears and religious feeling." . . .

As an aristocrat and an absolute monarch, the King of Prussia cannot love the bourgeoisie; he can have even less cause for fear when their submission and their impotence are heightened by a strained and difficult relation to the proletariat. Furthermore, an orthodox Catholic is more hostile to an orthodox Protestant than he is to an atheist, just as a legitimist is more inimical to a liberal than he is to a communist. Not that an atheist and a communist are closer to a Catholic than a legitimist, but that they are more alien to him than the Protestant and the liberal, since they stand outside his circle. . . .

Our "Prussian" is even more unfortunate when he denies that "religious feeling" is the source of the Royal Cabinet Order.

Why is religious feeling not the source of this Cabinet Order? Be-

---

* From "Critical Marginal Notes on the Article, 'The King of Prussia and Social Reform,' " in *Vorwärts!* No. 63, August 7, 1844. For complete text, see *Karl Marx on Revolution*, Vol. I of The Karl Marx Library (1971), pp. 7-22. *Vorwärts!* was a semiweekly published in Paris for German exiles; Marx joined it as a collaborator in the summer of 1844.

1. The "Prussian" was Arnold Ruge.

2. On June 4-6, 1844, the Silesian weavers revolted against their wretched conditions.

3. *La Réforme* was a Paris republican daily.

cause it is a "very sober expression of Christian statecraft," a "sober" expression of the doctrine that "lets no obstacle stand in the way of its own medicine, the good intentions of Christian hearts."

Is not religious feeling the source of Christian statecraft? Is not a doctrine whose universal panacea lies in the good intentions of Christian hearts based on religious feeling? Does a sober expression of religious feeling cease to be an expression of religious feeling? More than that! I maintain that it must be a religious feeling greatly infatuated, even intoxicated, with itself which seeks in the "union of Christian hearts" the "remedy for great evils" that it denies to the "state and the authorities." It is a very intoxicated religious feeling that—according to the "Prussian's" admission—finds the whole evil in the lack of Christian sentiment and hence refers the authorities to "exhortation" as the only means of strengthening this sentiment. According to the "Prussian," the purpose of the Cabinet Order is Christian conviction. Obviously, when religious feeling is intoxicated, when it is not sober, it considers itself the sole good. Where it sees evil, it ascribes evil to its own absence, for as it is the only good, it alone can produce the good. The Cabinet Order dictated by religious feeling consequently dictates the religious feeling. A politician of "sober" religious feeling would not, in his "perplexity," seek "help" in the "exhortation of pious preachers to Christian sentiment."

How, then, does the so-called Prussian of *La Réforme* prove that the Cabinet Order is not an emanation of religious feeling? By everywhere depicting the Cabinet Order as an emanation of religious feeling.

From *Economic and*
Philosophic Manuscripts of 1844

Economic and Philosophic Manuscripts were written by Marx in Paris in 1844 and remained unpublished until 1932, when the Moscow Institute of Marxism-Leninism brought them out in book form, despite their incompleteness and missing pages, under the above title. The following selections are based on the edition of Progress Publishers, Moscow, 1959, translated by Martin Milligan.

Labor and the Gods*

IF my own activity does not belong to me, if it confronts me as an alien power, to whom, then, does it belong?

To a being *other* than me.

Who is this being?

The gods? To be sure, in the earliest times the principal production (for example, the building of temples, etc., in Egypt, India, and Mexico) appears to be in the service of the gods, and the product belongs to the gods. However, the gods on their own were never the lords of labor. No more was *nature*. And what a contradiction it would be if, the more man subjugated nature by his labor and the more the miracles of the gods were rendered superfluous by the miracles of industry, the more man were to renounce the joy of production and the enjoyment of the produce in favor of those powers.

The *alien* being, to whom labor and the produce of labor belong, in whose service labor is done and for whose benefit the produce of labor is provided, can only be *man* himself.

---

* From "Estranged Labor," *Economic and Philosophic Manuscripts of 1844,* p. 74.

THE LUTHER OF POLITICAL ECONOMY*

THE *subjective essence* of private property—private property as activity for itself, as *subject*, as *person*—is *labor*. It is therefore self-evident that only the political economy which acknowledged labor as its principle (Adam Smith), and which therefore no longer looked upon private property as a mere condition external to man—that it is this political economy of the real energy and the real movement of private property—as a product of modern industry—and, on the other hand, as a force which has quickened and glorified the energy and development of modern industry—that has made it a power in the realm of consciousness. To this enlightened political economy, which has discovered within private property the subjective essence of wealth, the adherents of the money and mercantile system, who look upon private property only as an objective substance confronting men, seem therefore to be idolators, fetishists, Catholics. Engels was therefore right to call Adam Smith the Luther of Political Economy.[1] Just as Luther recognized religion—*faith*—as the substance of the external world and in consequence stood opposed to Catholic paganism—just as he superseded *external* religiosity by making religiosity the *inner* substance of man—just as he negated the priests outside the layman because he transplanted the priest into laymen's hearts, just so with wealth: wealth as something outside man and independent of him, and therefore as something to be maintained and asserted only in an external fashion, is done away with; that is, this external, mindless objectivity of wealth is done away with, with private property being incorporated in man himself and with man himself being recognized as its essence. But as a result man is brought within the orbit of private property, just as in Luther he is brought within the orbit of religion.

ATHEISM*

This *material*, immediately *sensuous* private property is the material, sensuous expression of *estranged human life*. Its movement—production and consumption—is the *sensuous* revelation of the movement of all production hitherto—i.e., the realization of the reality of man. Religion, family, state, law, morality, science, art, etc., are only particular modes of production, and fall under its general law. The positive transcendence of private property as the appropriation of human life

---

* From "Private Property and Labor," *Economic and Philosophic Manuscripts of 1844*, pp. 87–88.
1. In "Outlines of a Critique of Political Economy," in *Deutsch-Französische Jahrbücher*, February, 1844.

---

* From "The Meaning of Human Requirements," *Economic and Philosophic Manuscripts of 1844*, pp. 96, 106.

is therefore the positive transcendence of all estrangement—that is to say, the return of man from religion, family, state, etc., to his *human*, i.e., *social*, mode of existence. Religious estrangement as such occurs only in the realm of consciousness, of man's inner life, but economic estrangement is that of *real life;* its transcendence therefore embraces both aspects. It is evident that the initial stage of the movement among the various peoples depends on whether the true and for them authentic life of the people manifests itself more in consciousness or in the external world—is more ideal or real. Communism begins at the outset (Owen) with atheism; but atheism is at first far from being communism; indeed, it is still mostly an abstraction.

The philanthropy of atheism is therefore at first only philosophical, abstract philanthropy, and that of communism is at once *real* and directly bent on action. . . .

But since for socialist man the entire so-called history of the world is nothing but the creation of man through human labor, nothing but the coming-to-be of nature for man, he has the visible, irrefutable proof of his birth through himself, of his process of coming-to-be. Since the real existence of man and nature has become practical, sensuous, and perceptible—since man has become for man the being of nature, and nature for man the being of man—the question about an *alien* being, about a being above nature and man—a question which implies the admission of the inessentiality of nature and of man—has become impossible in practice. Atheism, as the denial of this inessentiality, has no longer any meaning, for atheism is a *negation of God*, and postulates the existence of man through this negation; but socialism as socialism no longer stands in any need of such a mediation. It proceeds from the *practically and theoretically sensuous consciousness* of man and of nature as the *essence*. Socialism is man's *positive self-consciousness*, no longer mediated through the annulment of religion, just as *real life* is man's positive reality through communism.

ETHICS*

You must make everything that is yours *salable*, i.e., useful. If I ask the political economist: Do I obey economic laws if I extract money by offering my body for sale, by surrendering it to another's lust? (The factory workers in France call the prostitution of their wives and daughters the xth working hour, which is literally correct.) Or am I not acting in keeping with political economy if I sell my friend to the Moroccans? (And the direct sale of men in the form of a trade in conscripts, etc., takes place in all civilized countries.) Then the

---

* From "The Meaning of Human Requirements," *Economic and Philosophic Manuscripts of 1844*, pp. 111-112.

political economist replies to me: You do not transgress my laws: but see what Cousin Ethics and Cousin Religion have to say about it. My political-economic ethics and religion have nothing to reproach you with, but—but whom am I now to believe, political economy or ethics? The ethics of political economy is *acquisition*, work, thrift, sobriety—but political economy promises to satisfy my needs. The political economy of ethics is the opulence of a good conscience, of virtue, etc.; but how can I live virtuously if I do not live? And how can I have a good conscience if I am not conscious of anything? It stems from the very nature of estrangement that each sphere applies to me a different and opposite yardstick—ethics uses one and political economy another, for each is a specific estrangement of man and focuses attention on a particular round of estranged essential activity, and each stands in an estranged relation to the other. Thus M. Michel Chevalier reproaches Ricardo with having abstracted from ethics. But Ricardo is allowing political economy to speak its own language, and if it does not speak ethically, this is not Ricardo's fault. M. Chevalier abstracts from political economy insofar as he moralizes, but he really and necessarily abstracts from ethics insofar as he practices political economy. The reference of political economy to ethics, if it is other than an arbitrary, contingent, and therefore unfounded and unscientific reference, if it is not being put up as a sham but is meant to be essential, can only be the reference of the laws of political economy to ethics. If there is no such connection, or if the contrary is rather the case, can Ricardo help it? Besides, the opposition between political economy and ethics is only a sham opposition and just as much no opposition as it is an opposition. All that happens is that political economy expresses moral laws *in its own way*.

HEGEL AND "RELIGION AS ALIENATED HUMAN SELF-CONSCIOUSNESS"*

Second, this implies that self-conscious man, insofar as he has recognized and annulled and superseded the spiritual world (or his world's general spiritual mode of being) as self-alienation, nevertheless again confirms this in its alienated shape and passes it off as his true mode of being—reestablishes it, and pretends to be at home in his other-being as such. Thus, for instance, after annulling and superseding religion, after recognizing religion to be a product of self-alienation, he yet finds confirmation of himself in *religion as religion*. Here is the root of Hegel's false positivism, or of his merely apparent criticism: this is what Feuerbach designated as the positing, negating, and re-

---

* From "Critique of the Hegelian Dialectic and Philosophy as a Whole," *Economic and Philosophic Manuscripts of 1844*, pp. 148–53.

establishing of religion or theology—but it has to be grasped in more general terms. Thus reason is as much at home in unreason as unreason. The man who has recognized that he is leading an alienated life in politics, law, etc., is leading his true human life in this alienated life as such. Self-affirmation, in contradiction with itself—in contradiction both with the knowledge of and with the essential being of the object—is thus true knowledge and life.

There can therefore no longer be any question about an act of accommodation on Hegel's part vis-à-vis religion, the state, etc., since this lie is *the* lie of his principle.

If I *know* religion as alienated human consciousness, then what I know in it as religion is not my self-consciousness, but my alienated self-consciousness confirmed in it. I therefore know my own self, the self-consciousness that belongs to its very nature, confirmed not in religion but rather in annihilated and superseded religion.

In Hegel, therefore, the negation of the negation is not the confirmation of the true essence, effected precisely through negation of the pseudoessence. With him the negation of the negation is the confirmation of the pseudoessence, or of the self-estranged essence in its denial; or it is the denial of this pseudoessence as an objective being dwelling outside man and independent of him, and its transformation into the subject.

A peculiar role, however, is played by the act of superseding, in which denial and preservation—denial and affirmation—are bound together.

Thus, for example, in Hegel's *Philosophy of Right*, private right superseded equals morality, morality superseded equals the family, the family superseded equals civil society, civil society superseded equals the state, the state superseded equals world history. In the actual world, private right, morality, the family, civil society, the state, etc., remain in existence, only they have become *moments* of man—states of his existence and being—which have no validity in isolation, but dissolve and engender one another, etc. They have become *moments of motion*.

In their actual existence this mobile nature of theirs is hidden. It first appears and is made manifest in thought, in philosophy. Hence my true religious existence is my existence in the *philosophy of religion;* my true political existence is my existence within the *philosophy of right;* my true natural existence, existence in the *philosophy of nature;* my true artistic existence, existence in the *philosophy of art;* my true *human* existence, my existence in *philosophy*. Likewise the true existence of religion, the state, nature, art, is the philosophy of religion, of nature, of the state, and of art. If, however, the philosophy of religion, etc., is for me the sole true existence of religion, then, too, it is only as a *philosopher of religion* that I am truly religious, and so I deny real religious sentiment and the really religious man. But at the same time I assert them, in part within my own existence or within the alien existence which I oppose to them—for this is only their philosophic expression—and in part I assert them in their own original shape, for they have validity for me as merely the apparent other-being, as allegories, forms of their own true existence (i.e., of my philosophical existence) hidden under sensuous disguises.

In just the same way, quality superseded equals quantity, quantity superseded equals measure, measure superseded equals essence, essence superseded equals appearance, appearance superseded equals actuality, actuality superseded equals the concept, the concept superseded equals objectivity, objectivity superseded equals the absolute Idea, the absolute Idea superseded equals nature, nature superseded equals subjective mind, subjective mind superseded equals ethical objective mind, ethical mind superseded equals art, art superseded equals religion, religion superseded equals absolute knowledge.

On the one hand, this act of superseding is a transcending of the thought entity; thus private property as a thought is transcended in the thought of morality. And because thought imagines itself to be directly the other of itself, to be sensuous reality—and therefore takes its own action for sensuous, real action—this superseding in thought, which leaves its object standing in the real world, believes that it has really overcome it. On the other hand, because the object has now become for it a moment of thought, thought takes it in its reality too to be self-confirmation of itself—of self-consciousness, of abstraction.

From the one point of view the existent which Hegel supersedes in philosophy is therefore not real religion, the real state, or real nature, but religion itself already become an object of knowledge, i.e., dogmatics; the same with jurisprudence, political science, and natural science. From the one point of view, therefore, he stands in opposition both to the real thing and to immediate, unphilosophic science or the unphilosophic conceptions of this thing. He therefore contradicts their conventional conceptions.

On the other hand, the religious man, etc., can find in Hegel his final confirmation.

It is now time to lay hold of the positive aspects of the Hegelian dialectic within the realm of estrangement:

(a) Annulling as an objective movement of retracting the alienation into self. This is the insight, expressed within the estrangement, concerning the appropriation of the objective essence through the annulment of its estrangement; it is the estranged insight into the real objectification of man, into the real appropriation of his objective essence through the annihilation of the estranged character of the objective world, through the annulment of the objective world in its estranged mode of being—just as atheism, being the annulment of God, is the advent of theoretical humanism; and communism, as the annulment of private property, is the justification of real human life as man's possession and thus the advent of practical humanism (or just as atheism is humanism mediated with itself through the annulment of religion, while communism is humanism mediated with itself through the annulment of private property). Only through the annulment of this mediation—which is itself, however, a necessary premise—does positively self-deriving humanism, *positive humanism*, come into being.

But atheism and communism are no flight, no abstraction; they are not a losing of the objective world begotten by man—of man's essential powers given over to the realm of objectivity; they are not a returning in poverty to unnatural, primitive simplicity. On the contrary, they are but the first real coming-to-be, the realization become real for man, of man's essence—of the essence of man as something real.

Thus by grasping the positive meaning of self-referred negation (if even again in estranged fashion) Hegel grasps man's self-estrangement, the alienation of man's essence, man's loss of objectivity and his loss of realness as finding of self, change of his nature, his objectification and realization. In short, within the sphere of abstraction, Hegel conceives labor as man's act of self-genesis—conceives man's relation to himself as an alien being and the manifesting of himself as an alien being to be the coming-to-be of *species consciousness* and *species life*.

(b) However, apart from, or rather in consequence of, the perverseness already described, this act appears in Hegel:

First of all as a merely formal, because abstract, act, because the human essence itself is taken to be only an *abstract, thinking essence*, conceived merely as self-consciousness. And,

Second, because the conception is formal and abstract, the annulment of the alienation becomes a confirmation of the alienation; or, again, for Hegel this movement of self-genesis and self-objectification in the form of self-alienation and self-estrangement is the absolute, and hence final, *expression of human life*—of life with itself as its aim, of life at rest in itself, of life that has attained oneness with its essence.

This movement in its abstract form as dialectic is therefore regarded as truly human life, and because it is nevertheless an abstraction—an estrangement of human life—it is regarded as a divine process, but as the divine process of man, a process traversed by man's abstract, pure, absolute essence that is distinct from him.

Third, this process must have a bearer, a subject. But the subject first emerges as a result. This result—the subject knowing itself as absolute self-consciousness—is therefore God—*absolute spirit—the self-knowing and self-manifesting Idea*. Real man and real nature become mere predicates, symbols of this esoteric, unreal man and of this unreal nature. Subject and predicate are therefore related to each other in absolute inversion—a mystical subject-object or a subjectivity reaching beyond the object—the absolute subject as a process, as subject alienating itself and returning from alienation into itself, but at the same time retracting this alienation into itself, and the subject as this process; a pure, restless revolving within itself.

First, the formal and abstract conception of man's act of self-genesis or self-objectification.

Hegel having posited man as equivalent to self-consciousness, the estranged object—the estranged essential reality of man—is nothing but consciousness, the thought of estrangement merely, estrangement's abstract and therefore empty and unreal expression, negation. The annulment of the alienation is therefore likewise nothing but an abstract, empty annulment of that empty abstraction—the *negation of the negation*. The rich, living, sensuous, concrete activity of self-objectification is therefore reduced to its mere abstraction, *absolute negativity*—an abstraction which is again fixed as such and thought of as an independent activity—as sheer activity. Because this so-called negativity is nothing but the abstract, empty form of that real living act, its content can in consequence be merely a formal content begotten by abstraction from all content. As a result there are general, abstract forms of abstraction pertaining to every content and on that account indifferent to, and consequently valid for, all content—the thought forms or logical categories torn from *real* mind and from *real* nature.

From *The Holy Family*

The Holy Family, *the first book on which Marx and Engels collaborated, was published in 1845. It was a satire on the German Hegelian, Bruno Bauer, and on other writers, including the French novelist Eugène Sue, author of* The Mysteries of Paris. *In Marx's words, the book was "directed against the ideological mysticism of Hegelian and speculative philosophy in general." The text used here is based on that of the Foreign Languages Publishing House, Moscow, 1956, translated by R. Dixon.*

NOTARIES AND PRIESTS*

HERR SZELIGA[1] transforms Christianity into an individual quality, "piety," and morality into another individual quality, "probity." He combines these two qualities in one individual whom he christens Jacques Ferrand, because Jacques Ferrand does not possess these two qualities but only pretends to. And thus Jacques Ferrand becomes the "mystery of probity and piety." His "testament," on the other hand, is "the mystery of seeming probity and piety," and no longer of probity and piety themselves. . . .

The Paris college of notaries considered Jacques Ferrand a lampoon against itself and managed to get him removed from the performances of *The Mysteries of Paris*. . . .

"Notaries are in the temporal realm what priests are in the

---

* From *The Holy Family* p. 95.
1. Szeliga was the pseudonym of Franz Zychlin von Zychlinsky, a Young Hegelian journalist who reviewed Sue's *The Mysteries of Paris* in the *Allgemeine Literatur-Zeitung*, June, 1844.

spiritual: they are the *depositories of our secrets* (Monteil, *Histoire des Français des divers États*, etc., Vol. IX, p. 37).

The notary is the temporal confessor. He is a puritan by profession, and "honesty," Shakespeare says, is "no puritan."

Deism and Materialism*

"Spinozism dominated the eighteenth century in its later French variety, which made matter into substance, as well as in deism, which conferred on matter a more spiritual name. . . . Spinoza's French school and the supporters of deism were but two sects disputing over the true meaning of his system. . . . The simple fate of this Enlightenment was its sinking into romanticism after being obliged to surrender to the reaction which began after the French movement."

That is what criticism says.

To the critical history of French materialism we shall oppose a brief outline of its profane, voluminous history. We shall admit with due respect the abyss between history as it really happened and history as it happened according to the decree of "absolute criticism," the creator equally of the old and of the new. And finally, obeying the prescriptions of criticism, we shall make the "Why?," "Whence?," and "Whither?" of critical history the "objects of a persevering study."

"Speaking exactly and in the prosaic sense," the French Enlightenment of the eighteenth century, in particular French materialism, was not only a struggle against the existing political institutions and the existing religion and theology; it was just as much an open struggle against the metaphysics of the seventeenth century, and against all metaphysics, in particular that of Descartes, Malebranche, Spinoza, and Leibniz. Philosophy was opposed to metaphysics as Feuerbach, in his first decisive attack on Hegel, opposed sober philosophy to drunken speculation. Seventeenth-century metaphysics, beaten off the field by the French Enlightenment—to be precise, by French materialism of the eighteenth century—was given a victorious and solid restoration in German philosophy, particularly in speculative German philosophy of the nineteenth century. After Hegel linked it in so masterly a fashion with all subsequent metaphysics and with German idealism, and founded a metaphysical universal kingdom, the attack on speculative metaphysics and metaphysics in general again corresponded, as in the eighteenth century, to the attack on theology. It will be defeated forever by materialism, which has now been perfected by the work of speculation itself and coincides with humanism. As Feuerbach represented materialism in the theoretical domain, French and English

---

* From *The Holy Family*, pp. 167–77. This selection is by Marx.

socialism and communism in the practical field represented materialism which coincided with humanism.

"Speaking exactly and in the prosaic sense," there are two trends in French materialism; one traces its origin to Descartes, the other to Locke. The latter is mainly a French development and leads directly to socialism. The former, mechanical materialism, merges with what is properly French natural science. The two trends cross in the course of development. We have no need here to go deep into the French materialism which comes direct from Descartes, any more than into the French Newton school or the development of French natural science in general.

We shall therefore just note the following:

Descartes in his physics endowed matter with self-creative power and conceived mechanical motion as the act of its life. He completely separated his physics from his metaphysics. Within his physics matter is the only substance, the only basis of being and of knowledge.

Mechanical French materialism followed Descartes' physics in opposition to his metaphysics. His followers were by profession anti-metaphysicists, i.e., physicists.

The school begins with the physician Leroy, reaches its zenith with the physician Cabanis, and the physician Lamettrie is its center. Descartes was still living when Leroy, like Lamettrie in the eighteenth century, transposed the Cartesian structure of animals to the human soul and affirmed that the soul is a modus of the body and ideas are mechanical motions. Leroy even thought Descartes had kept his real opinion secret. Descartes protested. At the end of the eighteenth century Cabanis perfected Cartesian materialism in his treatise, *Rapport du physique et du moral de l'homme*.

Cartesian materialism still exists today in France. It had great success in mechanical natural science which, "speaking exactly and in the prosaic sense," will be least of all reproached with romanticism.

Metaphysics of the seventeenth century, represented in France by Descartes, had materialism as its antagonist from its very birth. It personally opposed Descartes in Gassendi, the restorer of Epicurean materialism. French and English materialism was always closely related to Democritus and Epicurus. Cartesian metaphysics had another opponent in the English materialist Hobbes. Gassendi and Hobbes were victorious over their opponent long after their death, when metaphysics was already officially dominant in all French schools.

Voltaire observed that the indifference of Frenchmen to the disputes between Jesuits and Jansenists in the eighteenth century was due less to philosophy than to Law's financial speculation. And, in fact, the downfall of seventeenth-century metaphysics can be explained by the materialistic theory of the eighteenth century only as far as that theoretical movement itself is explained by the practical nature of French life at the time. That life was turned to the immediate present, worldly enjoyment and worldly interests, the *earthly* world. Its antitheological, antimetaphysical, and materialistic practice demanded corresponding antitheological, antimetaphysical, and materialistic theories. Metaphysics had in practice lost all credit. Here we have only to indicate briefly the theoretical process.

In the seventeenth century, metaphysics (cf. Descartes, Leibniz, and others) still had an element of positive, profane content. It made discoveries in mathematics, physics, and other exact sciences which seemed to come within its pale. This appearance was done away with as early as the beginning of the eighteenth century. The positive sciences broke off from it and determined their own separate fields. The whole wealth of metaphysics was reduced to beings of thought and heavenly things, although this was the very time when real beings and earthly things began to be the center of all interest. Metaphysics had gone stale. In the very year in which Malebranche and Arnauld, the last great French metaphysicians of the seventeenth century, died, Helvétius and Condillac were born.

The man who deprived seventeenth-century metaphysics of all credit in the domain of theory was Pierre Bayle. His weapon was skepticism, which he forged out of metaphysics' own magic formulas. He at first proceeded from Cartesian metaphysics. As Feuerbach was driven by the fight against speculative theology to the fight against speculative philosophy precisely because he recognized in speculation the last prop of theology, because he had to force theology to turn back from pretended science to coarse, repulsive faith, so Bayle too was driven by religious doubt to doubt about metaphysics which was the support of that faith. He therefore critically investigated metaphysics from its very origin. He became its historian in order to write the history of its death. He mainly refuted Spinoza and Leibniz.

Pierre Bayle not only prepared the reception of materialism and the philosophy of common sense in France by shattering metaphysics with his skepticism. He heralded atheistic society, which was soon to come to existence, by proving that a society consisting only of atheists is possible, that an atheist can be a respectable man, and that it is not by atheism but by superstition and idolatry that man debases himself.

To quote the expression of a French writer, Pierre Bayle was "the last metaphysician in the seventeenth-century sense of the word and the first philosopher in the eighteenth-century sense."

Besides the negative refutation of seventeenth-century theology and metaphysics, a positive, antimetaphysical system was required. A book was needed which would systematize and theoretically justify the practice of life of the time. Locke's treatise on the origin of human reason came from across the Channel as if in answer to a call. It was welcomed enthusiastically, like a long-awaited guest.

To the question: Was Locke perchance a follower of Spinoza? "profane" history may answer: Materialism is the native son of Great Britain. Even Britain's scholastic Duns Scotus wondered: "Can matter think?"

In order to bring about that miracle he had recourse to God's omnipotence, i.e., he forced theology itself to preach materialism. In addition he was a nominalist. Nominalism is a main component of English materialism and is in general the first expression of materialism.

The real founder of English materialism and all modern experimental science was Bacon. For him natural science was true science and physics based on perception was the most excellent part of natural science. Anaxagoras with his *homoeomeria* and Democritus with his atoms are often the authorities he refers to. According to his teaching the senses are infallible and are the source of all knowledge. Science is experimental and consists in applying a rational method to the data provided by the senses. Induction, analysis, comparison, observation, and experiment are the principal requisites of rational method. The first and most important of the inherent qualities of matter is motion, not only mechanical and mathematical movement, but still more impulse, vital life spirit, tension, or, to use Jakob Böhme's expression, the throes of matter. The primary forms of matter are the living, individualizing forces of being inherent in it and producing the distinctions between the species.

In Bacon, its first creator, materialism contained latently and still in a naïve way the germs of all-round development. Matter smiled at man with poetical sensuous brightness. The aphoristic doctrine itself, on the other hand, was full of the inconsistencies of theology.

In its further development materialism became one-sided. Hobbes was the one who systematized Bacon's materialism. Sensuousness lost its bloom and became the abstract sensuousness of the geometrician. Physical motion was sacrificed to the mechanical or mathematical, geometry was proclaimed the principal science. Materialism became hostile to humanity. In order to overcome the antihuman incorporeal spirit in its own field, materialism itself was obliged to mortify its flesh and become an ascetic. It appeared as a *being of reason*, but it also developed the implacable logic of reason.

If man's senses are the source of all his knowledge, Hobbes argues, proceeding from Bacon, then conception, thought, imagination, etc., are nothing but phantoms of the material world more or less divested of its sensuous form. Science can only give a name to these phantoms. One name can be applied to several phantoms. There can even be names of names. But it would be a contradiction to say, on the one hand, that all ideas have their origin in the world of the senses and to maintain, on the other hand, that a word is more than a word, that besides the beings represented, which are always individual, there exist also general beings. An incorporeal substance is just as much a contradiction as an incorporeal body. Body, being, substance are one and the same real idea. One cannot separate the thought from matter which thinks. Matter is the subject of all changes. The word "infinite" is meaningless unless it means the capacity of our mind to go on adding without end. Since only what is material is perceptible, knowable, nothing is known of the existence of God. I am sure only of my own existence. Every human passion is a mechanical motion ending or beginning. The objects of impulses are what is called good. Man is subject to the same laws as nature; might and freedom are identical.

Hobbes systematized Bacon, but did not give a more precise proof of his basic principle that our knowledge and our ideas have their source in the world of the senses.

Locke proved the principle of Bacon and Hobbes in his essay on the origin of human reason.

Just as Hobbes did away with the theistic prejudices in Bacon's materialism, so Collins, Dodwell, Coward, Hartley, Priestley, and others broke down the last bounds of Locke's sensualism. For materialists, at least, deism is no more than a convenient and easy way of getting rid of religion.

We have already mentioned how opportune Locke's work was for the French. Locke founded the philosophy of *bon sens*, common sense; i.e., he said indirectly that no philosopher can be at variance with the healthy human senses and reason based on them.

Locke's immediate follower, Condillac, who also translated him into French, at once opposed Locke's sensualism to seventeenth-century metaphysics. He proved that the French had quite rightly rejected metaphysics as the mere bungling of fancy and theological prejudice. He published a refutation of the systems of Descartes, Spinoza, Leibniz and Malebranche.

In his *Essai sur l'origine des connaissances humaines* he expounded Locke's ideas and proved that not only the soul, but the senses too, not only the art of creating ideas, but also the art of sensuous perception, are matters of experience and habit. The whole development of man therefore depends on education and environment. It was only by eclectic philosophy that Condillac was ousted from the French schools.

The difference between French and English materialism follows from the difference between the two nations. The French imparted to English materialism wit, flesh and blood, and eloquence. They gave it the temperament and grace that it lacked. They civilized it.

In Helvétius, who also based himself on Locke, materialism became really French. Helvétius conceived it immediately in its application to social life (Helvétius, *De l'homme, de ses facultés intellectuelles et de son éducation*). Sensuous qualities and self-love, enjoyment and correctly understood personal interests, are the bases of morality. The natural equality of human intelligence, the unity of progress of reason and progress of industry, the natural goodness of man, and the omnipotence of education are the main points in his system.

In Lamettrie's works we find a combination of Descartes' system and English materialism. He makes use of Descartes' physics in detail. His *Man Machine* is a treatise after the model of Descartes' beast-machine. The physical part of Holbach's *Système de la nature, ou des lois du monde physique et du monde moral* is also a result of the combination of French and English materialism, while the moral part is based substantially on the moral of Helvétius. Robinet (*De la Nature*), the French materialist who had the most connection with metaphysics and was therefore praised by Hegel, refers explicitly to Leibniz.

We need not dwell on Volney, Dupuis, Diderot, and others any more than on the physiocrats, having already proved the dual origin of French materialism from Descartes' physics and English materialism and the opposition of French materialism to seventeenth-century metaphysics and to the metaphysics of Descartes, Spinoza, Malebranche, and Leibniz. The Germans could not see this opposition before they came into the same opposition with speculative metaphysics.

As Cartesian materialism merges into natural science proper, the other branch of French materialism leads direct to socialism and communism.

There is no need of any great penetration to see from the teaching of materialism on the original goodness and equal intellectual endowment of men, the omnipotence of experience, habit, and education, and the influence of environment on man, the great significance of industry, the justification of enjoyment, etc., how necessarily materialism is connected with communism and socialism. If man draws all his knowledge, sensation, etc., from the world of the senses and the experience gained in it, the empirical world must be arranged so that in it man experiences and gets used to what is really human and that he becomes aware of himself as man. If correctly understood interest is the principle of all morality, man's private interest must be made to coincide with the interest of humanity. If man is not free in the materialist sense, i.e., free not through the negative power to avoid this or that, but through the positive power to assert his true individuality, crime must not be punished in the individual, but the antisocial source of crime must be destroyed, and each man must be given social scope for the vital manifestation of his being. If man is shaped by his surroundings, his surroundings must be made human. If man is social by nature, he will develop his true nature only in society, and the power of his nature must be measured not by the power of separate individuals but by the power of society.

This and similar propositions are to be found almost literally even in the oldest French materialists. This is not the place to assess them. *Fable of the Bees; or, Private Vices, Public Benefits*, by Mandeville, one of the early English followers of Locke, is typical of the social tendencies of materialism. He proves that in modern society vice is indispensable and useful. This was by no means an apology for modern society.

Fourier proceeds immediately from the teaching of the French materialists. The Babouvists were coarse, uncivilized materialists, but mature communism too comes directly from French materialism. The latter returned to its mother country, England, in the form Helvétius gave it. Bentham based his system of correctly understood interest on Helvétius' morality, and Owen proceeded from Bentham's system to found English communism. Exiled to England, the Frenchman Cabet came under the influence of communist ideas there and on his return to France became the most popular, although the most superficial, representative of communism. Like Owen, the more scientific French communists, Dézamy, Gay, and others, developed the teaching of materialism as the teaching of real humanism and the logical basis of communism.

FLEUR DE MARIE*

We come across Marie surrounded by criminals; a prostitute, a serf to the proprietress of a criminals' tavern. In this debasement she preserves a human nobleness of soul, a human unaffectedness and a human beauty that impress those around her, raise her to the level of a poetical flower of the criminal world, and win for her the name of Fleur de Marie.

We must observe Fleur de Marie attentively from her first appearance in order to be able to compare her original form with her "Critical" transformation.

In spite of her frailty Fleur de Marie shows great vitality, energy, cheerfulness, elasticity of character, qualities which alone explain her human development in her inhuman situation.

When Chourineur ill treats her, she defends herself with her scissors. That is the situation in which we first find her. She does not appear as a defenseless lamb who surrenders without any resistance to

* From *The Holy Family*, pp. 225–35. This section is by Marx.

overwhelming brutality; she is a girl who can vindicate her rights and put up a fight.

In the criminals' tavern in Rue aux Fèves she tells Chourineur and Rudolph her life's story. As she does so she laughs at Chourineur's wit. She accuses herself of not having looked for work after her release from prison and of having spent on amusements and dresses the three hundred francs she had earned. "But," she said, "I had no one to advise me." The memory of the catastrophe of her life—her selling herself to the proprietress of the criminals' tavern—rouses melancholy in her. It is the first time since her childhood that she has recalled these events. "The fact is that it grieves me when I look back . . . it must be lovely to be honest." When Chourineur makes fun of her and tells her she must become honest, she exclaims, "Honest! My God! What do you want me to be honest with?" She insists that she is not the one "to have fits of tears" ("*je ne suis pas pleurnicheuse*"); but her position in life is sad—"*ce n'est pas gai.*" In the end, contrary to Christian repentance, she expresses the stoic and at the same time epicurean human principle of a free and strong nature:

"*Enfin ce qui est fait, est fait.*"

Let us go with Fleur de Marie on her first outing with Rudolph.

"The consciousness of your terrible situation probably often distressed you," Rudolph says, itching to moralize. "Yes," she answers, "more than once I looked over the parapet of the Seine; but then I would gaze at the flowers and the sun and think the river would always be there and I was only seventeen years old. Who could tell? On such occasions I thought I had not deserved my fate, that I had something good in me. People have tormented me enough, I used to say to myself, but at least I have never done any harm to anybody."

Fleur de Marie considers her situation not as a free creation, not as the expression of her own person, but as a fate she has not deserved. Her bad fortune can change. She is still young.

Good and evil, in Marie's mind, are not the moral abstractions of good and evil. She is good because she has never caused suffering to anybody, she has always been human toward her inhuman surroundings. She is good because the sun and the flowers reveal to her her own sunny and blossoming nature. She is good because she is still young, full of hope and vitality. Her situation is not good because it does her unnatural violence, because it is not the expression of her human impulses, the fulfillment of her human desires; because it is full of torment and void of pleasure. She measures her situation in life by her *own individuality*, her *natural* essence, not by the *ideal of good*.

In *natural* surroundings the chains of bourgeois life fall off Fleur de Marie; she can freely manifest her own nature and consequently is bubbling with love of life, with a wealth of feeling, with human joy at the beauty of nature; these show that the bourgeois system has only grazed the surface of her and is a mere misfortune, that she herself is neither good nor bad, but *human*.

"Monsieur Rudolph, what happiness! . . . grass, fields! If you would only let me get out, the weather is so fine. . . . I should love to run over those meadows."

Alighting from the carriage she plucks flowers for Rudolph, "can hardly speak for joy," etc.

Rudolph tells her that he is going to take her to Madame Georges' farm: There she sees dovecotes, cow stalls and so forth; there they have milk, butter, fruit, etc. Those are real blessings for that child. She will be merry, that is her main thought. "You just can't believe how I am longing for some fun!" She explains to Rudolph without the least constraint how far she was to blame for her fate. "The cause of my whole fate was that I did not save up my money." Consequently she advises him to be thrifty and to put money in the savings bank. Her fancy runs wild in the castles in the air that Rudolph builds for her. She becomes sad only because she is "forgetting the present" and "the contrast of that present with the dream of a pleasant and laughing existence reminds her of the cruelty of her situation."

So far we have seen Fleur de Marie in her original un-Critical form. Eugène Sue has here risen above the horizon of his own narrow world outlook. He has slapped bourgeois prejudice in the face. He will hand over Fleur de Marie to the hero Rudolph to make up for his own rashness and to reap applause from all old men and women, from the whole of the Paris police, from the current religion and from "Critical Criticism."

Madame Georges, with whom Rudolph leaves Fleur de Marie, is an unhappy, hypochondriacal, religious woman. She immediately welcomes the child with the unctuous words: "God blesses those who love and fear him, who have been unhappy and repenting." Rudolph, the man of "pure Criticism," has the wretched priest Laporte, whose hair has grayed in superstition, called in. He has the mission of accomplishing Fleur de Marie's Critical reform.

Joyfully and without constraint, Marie comes to the old priest. In his Christian brutality Eugène Sue makes a "marvelous instinct" at once whisper in her ear that "shame ends where repentance and penance begin," that is, in the church, which alone can give happiness. He forgets the unconstrained merriness of the outing, a merriness which the graces of nature and Rudolph's friendly sympathy had produced, and which was troubled only by the thought of having to go back to the proprietress of the criminals' tavern.

The priest immediately adopts a supermundane attitude. His first words are:

"God's mercy is infinite, my dear child! He has proved it to you by not abandoning you in your severe trials. . . . The magnanimous man who saved you fulfilled the word of the Scriptures" (note—the word of the Scriptures, not a human purpose!): "Verily the Lord is nigh to those who invoke him; he will fulfill their desires . . . he will hear their voice and will save them . . . the Lord will accomplish his work."

Marie cannot yet understand the wicked meaning of the priest's exhortations. She answers: "I shall pray for those who pitied me and brought me back to God."

Her first thought is not for God, it is for her human saver and it is he that she prays for, not for her own absolution. She attributes to her prayer some influence on the salvation of others. Indeed, she is so naïve that she supposes she has already been brought back to God. The priest feels it his duty to destroy this unorthodox belief.

"Soon," he says, interrupting her, "soon you will deserve absolution, absolution from your great errors . . . for, to quote the prophet once more, the Lord holdeth up those who are on the brink of the abyss."

One must not fail to see the inhuman expressions the priest uses. You will soon deserve absolution. Your sins are not yet forgiven.

As Laporte, when he receives the girl, tries to arouse in her the consciousness of her sins, so Rudolph, as he leaves, presents her with a golden cross, the symbol of the Christian crucifixion awaiting her.

Marie has already been living for some time on Madame Georges' farm. Let us now listen to a dialogue between the old priest Laporte and Madame Georges. He considers "marriage" out of the question for the girl "because no man, in spite of the priest's guarantee, will have the courage to face the past that has soiled her youth." He adds: "She has great errors to atone for, she should have been sustained by a moral sense." He proves that she could have remained good just like the commonest of bourgeois: "There are many virtuous people in Paris today." The hypocritical priest knows quite well that every hour of the day, in the busiest streets, those virtuous people of Paris go past little girls of seven or eight selling matches and the like up to midnight as Marie herself used to do and who, almost without exception, will have the same fate as Marie.

The priest has decided to make Marie repent; inside himself he has already condemned her. Let us go with Marie when she is accompanying Laporte home in the evening.

"See, my child," he begins with unctuous eloquence, "the boundless horizon the limits of which are not to be seen" (remember it is in the evening); "it seems to me that the calm and the vastness almost give us the idea of eternity. . . . I am telling you this, Marie, because you are sensitive to the beauty of creation. . . . I have often been moved by the religious fascination which they inspire you with, you who for so long were deprived of the sentiment of religion."

The priest has already succeeded in changing Marie's immediate naïve pleasure in the beauties of nature into religious fascination. For her, nature has already become a devout, christianized nature, debased to creation. The transparent sea of space is desecrated and turned into a dark symbol of stagnant eternity. She has already learned that all human manifestations of her being were "profane," devoid of religion, the real consecration, that they were impious and godless. The priest must soil her in her own eyes, he must trample underfoot her moral capacities and gifts to make her receptive to the supernatural grace he promises her, baptism.

When Marie wants to make a confession and asks him to be lenient he answers:

"The Lord has shown you that he is merciful." In the clemency of which she is the object Marie must not see a natural unquestioned relation of one human being to her, another human being. She must see in it a transcendent, supernatural, superhuman mercy and condescension; in human lenience she must see divine mercy. She must see all human beings and human relations in the transcendental plane of relations to God. The way Fleur de Marie in her answer accepts the priest's prattle about divine mercy shows how far she has been spoiled by religious doctrine.

As soon as she entered upon her improved situation, she said, she felt new happiness.

"I kept thinking of Monsieur Rudolph. I often raised my eyes to heaven, to look, not for God, but Monsieur Rudolph there and to thank him. Yes, I confess, Father. I thought more of him than of God; for he did for me what God alone could have done. . . . I was happy, as happy as anybody who has escaped a great danger forever."

Fleur de Marie already finds it wrong that she took a new happy situation in life simply for what it really was, that she felt it as a new happiness, that her attitude to it was a natural, not a supernatural one. She accuses herself of seeing in the man who saved her what he really was, her saver, instead of supposing some imaginary savior, God, in his place. She is already caught in religious hypocrisy which takes away from another man what he has deserved in respect of me in order to give it to God and which considers anything and everything human in man as alien to God and everything inhuman in him as really God's own.

Marie tells us that the religious transformation of her thoughts, her sentiments, her attitude toward life was effected by Madame Georges and Laporte.

"When Rudolph took me away from the city I already had a

vague consciousness of my degradation. . . . But the education, the advice and examples I got from Madame Georges and from you made me understand . . . that I had been more guilty than unfortunate. Madame Georges and you made me realize the infinite depth of my damnation."

That means that she owes to the priest Laporte and Madame Georges the replacement of the human and therefore bearable consciousness of her debasement by the Christian and hence unbearable consciousness of eternal damnation. The priest and the bigot have taught her to judge herself from the Christian point of view.

Marie feels the depth of the moral misfortune into which she has been cast. She says:

"Since the consciousness of good and evil had to be so fatal to me, why was I not left to my wretched fate? . . . Had I not been snatched away from infamy, misery and blows would soon have killed me. At least I should have died in ignorance of a purity that I shall always regret not to have."

The heartless priest answers: "The most generously gifted nature, were it to be plunged only for a day in the filth from which you have been saved, would be indelibly branded. That is the immutability of divine justice!"

Deeply wounded by the priest's smooth honeyed curse Fleur de Marie exclaims: "You see yourself, I must despair!"

The gray-headed slave of religion answers:

"You must renounce all hope of effacing this desolate page from your life, but you must trust in the infinite mercy of God. Here below, my poor child, you will have tears, remorse and penance, but one day on high forgiveness and eternal bliss!"

Marie is not yet stupid enough to be satisfied with eternal happiness and forgiveness *on high.*

"Pity, pity, my God!" she cries. "I am so young. How wretched I am!"

Then the hypocritical sophistry of the priest reaches its peak: "Happiness for you, on the contrary, Marie; happiness for you to whom the Lord sends this bitter but saving remorse! It shows the religious sensibility of your soul. . . . Each of your sufferings will be marked down to you on high. Believe me, God left you a while on the path of evil only to reserve for you the glory of repentance and the eternal reward due to penance."

From this moment Marie is a *serf of consciousness of sin.* In her unhappy situation in life she was able to become a lovable, human individual; in her exterior debasement she was conscious that her human essence was *her true essence.* Now the filth of modern society which has come into exterior contact with her becomes her innermost being;

continual hypochondriac self-torture because of that filth will be her duty, the task of her life appointed by God himself, the self-aim of her existence. Formerly she boasted: "I am not the one to have fits of tears" and knew that "what's done is done." Now self-torment will be her *good* and remorse will be her *glory*.

It turns out later that Fleur de Marie is Rudolph's daughter. We find her again as Princess of Geroldstein. We overhear a conversation she has with her father:

"It is in vain that I pray to God to deliver me from these obsessions, to fill my heart only with his pious love and his holy hopes; in a word, to take me entirely, because I wish to give myself entirely to him. . . . He does not grant my wishes, doubtless because my earthly preoccupations make me unworthy of intercourse with him."

When man has realized that his errings are *infinite* crimes against God he can be sure of *salvation* and *mercy* only if he gives himself entirely to God and dies entirely to the world and worldly occupations. When Fleur de Marie realizes that her delivery from her inhuman situation in life was a miracle of God she must become a saint herself in order to be worthy of that miracle. Her human love must be transformed into religious love, the desire for happiness into the striving for eternal bliss, worldly satisfaction into holy hope, intercourse with man into intercourse with God. God must take her entirely. She herself reveals to us why he does not take her entirely. She has not *given* herself entirely to him, her heart is still preoccupied and engaged with earthly affairs. This is the last blaze of her strong nature. She gives herself entirely up to God by dying entirely to the world and going into a *convent*.

> A monastery is no place for him
> Who has no stock of sins laid in
> So numerous and great
> That be it early, be it late,
> He may not miss the sweet delight
> Of penance for a heart contrite.[2]

In the convent Fleur de Marie is made abbess through the intrigues of Rudolph. At first she refuses to accept this appointment because she feels unworthy. The old abbess persuades her: "I shall say more, my dear daughter: if before entering the fold your life had been as prodigal as it was pure and praiseworthy . . . the *evangelical virtues* that you have given the example of since you have been here would atone for and redeem your past in the eyes of the Lord, no matter how sinful it had been."

From what the abbess says we see that Fleur de Marie's worldly

---

2. The quotation is from Goethe's "*Zahme Xenien.*"

virtues have changed into evangelical virtues, or rather that her real virtues may no longer appear otherwise than as evangelical caricatures.

Marie answers the abbess: "Holy Mother, I now believe I can accept."

Convent life does not suit Marie's individuality—she dies. Christianity consoles her only in imagination, or rather her Christian consolation is precisely the annihilation of her real life and essence—her death.

So Rudolph first changed Fleur de Marie into a repentant sinner, then the repentant sinner into a nun, and finally the nun into a corpse. Besides the Catholic priest, the Critical priest Szeliga also preaches a sermon over her grave.

Her "innocent" existence he calls her "transient" existence, opposing it to "eternal and unforgettable guilt." He praises the fact that her last breath was a "prayer for forgiveness and pardon." But as the Protestant minister, after expounding the necessity of the Lord's mercy, the participation of the deceased in universal original sin, and the intensity of his consciousness of sin, must praise the virtues of the departed in worldly terms, so, too, Herr Szeliga uses the expression: "And yet personally, she has nothing to ask forgiveness for."

Finally he throws on her grave the most faded flower of pulpit eloquence:

"Inwardly pure as human beings seldom are, she has closed her eyes to this world."

Amen!

Theses on Feuerbach*

1

THE chief defect of all hitherto existing materialism (including that of Feuerbach) is that the *Gegenstand* [subject], reality, sensuousness, is conceived only in the form of the *object* or the *Anschauung* [view], but not as *sensuous human activity, practice*, not subjectively. Hence the *active* side, in contrast to materialism, was developed by materialism—but abstractly, since, of course, idealism does not know the actual, sensuous activity as such. Feuerbach wants sensuous objects, actually differentiated from thought objects, but he does not conceive human activity itself as *gegenständliche* [objective] activity. Hence in the *Essence of Christianity* he regards the theoretical attitude as the genuinely human one, whereas practice is conceived and fixed only in its dirty Jewish aspect.

2

The question whether objective truth can be attributed to human thinking is not a question of theory but a *practical* question. In practice, man must prove the truth, i.e., reality and power, the *Diesseitigkeit* [this-sidedness] of his thinking. The conflict over the reality or non-reality of thinking—which is isolated from practice—is a purely *scholastic* question.

---

* Written in spring, 1845. Published by Frederick Engels as an appendix to his *Ludwig Feuerbach and the End of Classical German Philosophy* (1888). See Marx's letter to Feuerbach, August 11, 1844.

3

The materialist doctrine of the change of circumstances and up-bringing forgets that circumstances are changed by men and that the educator himself must be educated. It must therefore divide society into two parts—of which one is superior to society.

The coincidence of the changing of circumstances and of human activity or self-change can be understood rationally only as *revolutionary practice*.

4

Feuerbach starts out from the fact of religious self-alienation, of the duplication of the world into a religious and a secular one. His work consists in resolving the religious world into its secular basis. But the fact that the secular basis arises from its own self and establishes an independent realm in the clouds can be explained only through the self-dismemberment and self-contradiction of this secular basis. The latter, therefore, must be understood in itself as well as in its contra-diction, as revolutionized in practice. Thus, for example, once the earthly family is discovered to be the secret of the holy family, the former must then itself be destroyed theoretically and practically.

5

Feuerbach, not satisfied with *abstract thinking*, wants the *Anschauung*; but he does not conceive sensuousness as *practical*, human-sensuous activity.

6

Feuerbach resolves the religious essence into the *human* essence. But human essence is not an abstraction inherent in the single indi-vidual. In reality it is the ensemble of social relationships.

Feuerbach, who does not enter into a critique of this real essence, is therefore compelled:

1. To abstract from the historical process and to fix the religious *Gemüt* [spirit or sentiment] as something by itself, and to presuppose an abstract—*isolated*—human individual.

2. To conceive the human essence, therefore, as *Gattung* [species], as an inner, mute generality, which *naturally* encompasses the many individuals.

7

Hence Feuerbach does not see that the "religious *Gemüt*" is itself a social product and that the abstract individual he analyzes belongs to a particular form of society.

8

All social life is essentially *practical*. All mysteries which lead to the theory of mysticism find their rational solution in human practice and in the comprehension of this practice.

9

The highest point attained by *contemplative* materialism, that is, materialism which does not conceive sensuousness as practical activity, is the *Anschauung* of single individuals and of bourgeois society.

10

The standpoint of the old materialism is bourgeois society; the standpoint of the new is human society or socialized humanity.

11

The philosophers have only *interpreted* the world in various ways; the point, however, is to *change* it.

From *The German Ideology*

The German Ideology *was, in effect, a continuation of the criticism of the Hegel-Feuerbach school begun by Marx and Engels in* The Holy Family. *The main targets in their second book were Max Stirner ("Saint Max"), Karl Gruen, and the so-called "true socialists." Written in 1845–46,* The German Ideology *was first published in German, in Moscow, in 1932. The English-language edition on which this text is based, is by Progress Publishers, Moscow, 1964; it was translated from the German by S. Ryazanskaya.*

MEN ARE THE PRODUCERS OF THEIR OWN CONCEPTIONS*

The entire body of German philosophical criticism from Strauss to Stirner[1] is confined to criticism of *religious* conceptions.[2] The critics started from real religion and actual theology. What religious consciousness and a religious conception really meant was determined variously as they went along. Their advance consisted in subsuming the allegedly dominant metaphysical, political, juridical, moral, and other conceptions under the class of religious or theological conceptions; and similarly in pronouncing political, juridical, moral consciousness as religious or theological, and the political, juridical, moral man—

---

* From *The German Ideology*, pp. 29-30, 37-38, 42-43.

1. David Friedrich Strauss, *Das Leben Jesu (The Life of Jesus)* (1835-36), and Max Stirner (Johann Caspar Schmidt), *Der Einzige und sein Eigentum (The Individual and His Property)* (Leipzig, 1845).

2. The passage following this sentence is crossed out in the manuscript: ". . . claiming to be the absolute redeemer of the world from all evil. Religion was continually regarded and treated as the archenemy, as the ultimate cause of all relationships repugnant to these philosophers."

"man" in the last resort—as religious. The dominance of religion was taken for granted. Gradually every dominant relationship was pronounced a religious relationship and transformed into a cult, a cult of law, a cult of the state, etc. On all sides it was only a question of dogmas and belief in dogmas. The world was sanctified to an ever increasing extent, till at last our venerable Saint Max [Stirner] was able to canonize it *en bloc* and thus dispose of it once for all. . . .

The production of ideas, of conceptions, of consciousness, is at first directly interwoven with material activity and the material of men, the language of real life. Conceiving, thinking, the mental intercourse of men, appear at this stage as the direct efflux of their material behavior. The same applies to mental production as expressed in the language of politics, laws, morality, religion, metaphysics, etc., of a people. Men are the producers of their conceptions, ideas, etc.—real, active men, as they are conditioned by a definite development of their productive forces and of the intercourse corresponding to these, up to its furthest forms. Consciousness can never be anything but conscious existence, and the existence of men is their actual life process. If in all ideology men and their circumstances appear upside-down as in a camera obscura, this phenomenon arises just as much from their historical life process as the inversion of objects on the retina does from their physical life process.

In direct contrast to German philosophy, which descends from heaven to earth, here we ascend from earth to heaven. That is to say, we do not set out from what men say, imagine, conceive, nor from men as narrated, thought of, imagined, conceived, in order to arrive at men in the flesh. We set out from real, active men, and on the basis of their real life process we demonstrate the development of the ideological reflexes and echoes of this life process. The phantoms formed in the human brain are also, necessarily, sublimates of their material life process, which is empirically verifiable and bound to material premises. Morality, religion, metaphysics, all the rest of ideology and their corresponding forms of consciousness, thus no longer retain the semblance of independence. They have no history, no development; but men, developing their material production and their material intercourse, alter, along with this their real existence, their thinking and the products of their thinking. Life is not determined by consciousness, but consciousness by life. In the first method of approach the starting point is consciousness taken as the living individual; in the second method, which conforms to real life, it is the real living individuals themselves, and consciousness is considered solely as *their* consciousness. . . .

For the animal, its relationship to others does not exist as a relationship. Consciousness is therefore from the very beginning a social product, and remains so as long as men exist at all. Consciousness is at first, of course, merely consciousness concerning the *immediate* sensuous environment and consciousness of the limited connection with other persons and things outside the individual who is growing self-conscious. At the same time it is consciousness of nature, which first appears to men as a completely alien, all-powerful and unassailable force, with which men's relations are purely animal and by which they are overawed like beasts; it is thus a purely animal consciousness of nature (natural religion).

We see here immediately: this natural religion or this particular relation of men to nature is determined by the form of society, and vice versa. Here, as everywhere, the identity of nature and man appears in such a way that the restricted relation of men to nature determines their restricted relation to one another, and their restricted relation to one another determines men's restricted relation to nature, just because nature is as yet hardly modified historically; and on the other hand, man's consciousness of the necessity of associating with the individuals around him is the beginning of the consciousness that he is living in society at all. This beginning is as animal as social life itself at this stage. It is mere herd consciousness, and at this point man is distinguished from sheep only by the fact that with him consciousness takes the place of instinct or his instinct is a conscious one. This sheeplike or tribal consciousness receives its further development and extension through increased productivity, the increase of needs, and, what is fundamental to both of these, the increase of population. With these there develops the division of labor, which was originally nothing but the division of labor in the sexual act, then that division of labor which develops spontaneously or "naturally" by virtue of natural predisposition (e.g., physical strength), needs, accidents, etc., etc. Division of labor becomes truly such only from the moment when a division of material and mental labor appears.[3] From this moment onward consciousness *can* really flatter itself that it is something other than consciousness of existing practice, that it *really* represents something without representing something real; from now on consciousness is in a position to emancipate itself from the world and to proceed to the formation of "pure" theory, theology, philosophy, ethics, etc. But even if this theory, theology, philosophy, ethics, etc., comes into contradiction with existing relations, this can occur only because existing social relations have come into contradiction with existing forces of production. . . .

---

3. Marginal note by Marx: "The first form of ideologists, *priests*, is concurrent."

CHRISTIANITY AND ANTIQUITY*

Just as Stirner's Ancient is ancient because he is a non-Christian, not yet a Christian or a hidden Christian, so his primitive Christian is a Christian because he is a nonatheist, not yet an atheist or a hidden atheist. Stirner, therefore, causes Christianity to be negated by the Ancients and modern atheism by the primitive Christians, instead of the reverse. Jacques le bonhomme, like all similar speculative philosophers, seizes everything by its philosophical tail. A few more examples of this childish gullibility immediately follow.

"The Christian must consider himself a 'stranger on the earth' " (Epistle to the Hebrews 11:13) (p. 23).[4]

On the contrary, the strangers on earth (arising from extremely natural causes, e.g., the colossal concentration of wealth in the whole Roman world, etc., etc.) had to consider themselves Christians. It was not their Christianity that made them vagrants, but their vagrancy that made them Christians. On the same page the holy father jumps straight from Sophocles' *Antigone* and the sacredness of the burial ceremonial connected with it to the Gospel of St. Matthew 8:22 (let the dead bury their dead), while Hegel, at any rate in the *Phänomenologie*, gradually passes from the *Antigone*, etc., to the Roman Empire. With equal right Saint Max could have passed at once to the Middle Ages and, together with Hegel, have advanced this biblical statement against the Crusaders, or even, to be quite original, have contrasted the burial of Polynices by Antigone with the transfer of the ashes of Napoleon from St. Helena to Paris.

It is stated further: "In Christianity the inviolable truth of family ties" (which on page 22 is noted as one of the "truths" of the Ancients) "is depicted as an untruth which should be got rid of as quickly as possible" (Gospel of St. Mark 10:29), "and so in everything" (p. 23).

This proposition, in which reality is again turned upside-down, should be put the right way up, as follows: The actual untruth of family ties (concerning which, *inter alia*, the still existing documents of pre-Christian Roman legislation should be examined) is depicted in Christianity as an inviolable truth, "and so in everything."

From these examples, therefore, it is superabundantly evident that Jacques le bonhomme, who strives to "get rid as quickly as possible" of empirical history, stands facts on their heads, causes material his-

---

* From *The German Ideology*, pp. 142–43.

4. The passage in the Bible reads: "These all died in faith, not having received the promises, but having seen them afar off, and were persuaded of them, and embraced them, and confessed that they were strangers and pilgrims on the earth."

tory to be produced by ideal history, "and so in everything." At the outset we learn only the alleged attitude of the Ancients to their world; as dogmatists they are put in opposition to their own world, the ancient world, instead of appearing as creators of their own world; it is a question only of the relation of consciousness to the object, to truth; it is a question, therefore, only of the philosophical relation of the Ancients to their world—instead of ancient history we have the history of ancient philosophy, and this only in the form in which Saint Max imagines it according to Hegel and Feuerbach.

Thus the history of Greece, from the time of Pericles inclusively, is reduced to a struggle of abstractions: reason, spirit, heart, worldliness, etc. These are the Greek parties. In this ghostly world, which is presented as the Greek world, allegorical persons such as Madame Purity of Heart "machinate" and mythical figures like Pilate (who must never be missing where there are children) find a place quite seriously side by side with Timon of Phlius.

THE SKEPTICS*

The extent to which Saint Max's disclosures about the Skeptics follow the same line is already evident from the fact that he considers their philosophy more radical than that of Epicurus. The Skeptics reduced the theoretical relation of people to things to *appearance*, and in practice they left everything as of old, being guided by this appearance just as much as others are guided by actuality; they merely gave it another name. Epicurus, on the other hand, was the true radical Enlightener of antiquity; he openly attacked the ancient religion, and it was also from him that the atheism of the Romans, insofar as it existed, was derived. For this reason, too, Lucretius praised Epicurus as the hero who was the first to overthrow the gods and trample religion underfoot; for this reason, among all church elders, from Plutarch to Luther, Epicurus has always had the reputation of being the atheist philosopher *par excellence*, and was called a swine; for which reason, too, Clement of Alexandria says that when Paul takes up arms against philosophy he has in mind Epicurean philosophy alone. (*Stromatum*, Book 1 [Chapter XI], p. 295, Cologne edition, 1688.) Hence we see how "cunning, perfidious," and "clever" was the attitude of this open atheist to the world in directly attacking its religion, while the Stoics adapted the ancient religion in their own speculative fashion, and the Skeptics used their concept of "appearance" as the excuse for being able to accompany all their judgments with *reservatio mentalis*.

---

* From *The German Ideology*, pp. 147–48.

MAX STIRNER AND THE CHRISTIAN "HOLY SPIRIT"*

Saint Max intends to give us a phenomenology of the Christian spirit and in his usual way seizes on only one aspect. For the Christian the world was not only *turned into* spirit but equally *estranged* from spirit, as, for example, Hegel quite correctly admits in the passage mentioned, where he brings both these aspects into relation with each other, which Saint Max should also have done if he wanted to proceed historically. As against the world's estrangement from the spirit in the Christian consciousness, the Ancients, "who saw gods everywhere," can with equal justification be regarded as the spiritualizers of the world—a conception which our saintly dialectician rejects with the well-meaning warning: "Gods, my dear modern man, are not spirits" (p. 47). Pious Max recognizes only the Holy Ghost as spirit.

But even if he had given us this phenomenology (which after Hegel is moreover superfluous), he would all the same have given us nothing. The standpoint at which people are satisfied with such tales about spirits is itself a religious one, because people who adopt it are soothed by religion, they regard religion as *causa sui* [its own cause] (for both "self-consciousness" and "Man" are still religious) instead of explaining it from empirical conditions and showing how definite relations of industry and commerce are necessarily connected with a definite form of society, hence with a definite form of state, and hence with a definite form of religious consciousness. If Stirner had looked at the real history of the Middle Ages, he could have found why the Christian's notion of the world took precisely this form in the Middle Ages, and how it happened that it subsequently passed into a different one; he could have found that *"Christianity" has no history* and that all the different forms in which it was conceived at various times were not "self-determinations" and "further developments of the religious spirit," but were brought about by wholly empirical causes in no way dependent on any influence of the religious spirit.

Since Stirner "does not go like clockwork" (p. 45), then before dealing in more detail with spirit seeing, it can be said here and now that the various "transformations" of Stirner's people and their world consist merely of the transformation of the entire history of the world into the body of Hegel's philosophy; into ghosts, which only apparently are an "other being" of the thoughts of the Berlin professor. In the *Phänomenologie*, the Hegelian bible—the "Book"—individuals are first of all transformed into "consciousness" [and the] world into "object," whereby the manifold variety of forms of life and history is reduced to a different attitude of "consciousness" to the "object."

* From *The German Ideology*, pp. 161–62.

This different attitude is reduced, in turn, to three cardinal relations: (1) the relation of consciousness to the object as to truth, or to truth as mere object (for example, sensual consciousness, the religion of nature, Ionic philosophy, Catholicism, the authoritarian state, etc.); (2) the relation of consciousness as *the true* to the object (reason, spiritual religion, Socrates, Protestantism, the French Revolution); (3) the true relation of consciousness to truth as object, or to the object as truth (logical thinking, speculative philosophy, the spirit as existing for the spirit). In Hegel, too, the first relation is conceived as God the Father, the second as Christ, the third as the Holy Spirit, etc. Stirner already used these transformations when speaking of child and youth, of Ancient and Modern, and he repeats them later in regard to Catholicism and Protestantism, the Negro and the Mongol, etc., and then accepts this series of camouflages of a thought in all good faith as the world against which he has to assert and maintain himself as a "corporeal individual."

CATHOLICISM AND PROTESTANTISM*

The Economy of the Old Testament

What we here call Catholicism Stirner calls the "Middle Ages," but as he confuses (as in everything) the holy, religious essence of the Middle Ages, the religion of the Middle Ages, with the actual, profane Middle Ages in flesh and blood, we prefer to give the matter its right name at once. "The Middle Ages" were a "lengthy period, in which people were content with the illusion of having the truth" (they neither desired nor did anything else), "without seriously thinking about whether one must be true oneself in order to possess the truth." . . . "In the Middle Ages people" (that is, the whole of the Middle Ages) "mortified the flesh, in order to become capable of taking the Holy into themselves" (p. 108).

Hegel defines the attitude to the divine in the Catholic church by saying: "that people's attitude to the absolute was as to something purely external" (Christianity in the form of external being). (*Geschichte der Philosophie*, III, p. 148 and elsewhere.) True, the individual has to be purified in order to take up the truth, but "this also occurs in an external way, through redemptions, fasts, self-flagellations, visits to holy places, pilgrimages." (Ibid., p. 140.)

Stirner makes this transition by saying: "In the same way, too, as people strain their eyes in order to see a distant object . . . so they mortified the flesh," etc.

---

* From *The German Ideology*, pp. 180–83.

Since for Stirner the Middle Ages are identified with Catholicism, they naturally end with Luther (p. 109). Luther himself is reduced to the following conceptual definition, which had already been met with in connection with the youth in the conversation with Szeliga and elsewhere: "Man, if he wants to attain truth, must become as true as truth itself. Only he who already has truth in faith can participate in it."

Concerning Lutheranism, Hegel says: "The truth of the gospel . . . exists only in the true relation to it. . . . The essential relation of the spirit exists only for the spirit. . . . Hence the attitude of the spirit to the content is that the content is of course essential, but that equally essential is that the holy and consecrating spirit should stand in relation to this content." (*Geschichte der Philosophie*, III, p. 234.) "This then is the Lutheran faith—his" (i.e., man's) "faith is required of him and it alone can truly be taken into account." (Ibid., p. 230.) "Luther . . . affirms that the divine is divine only insofar as it is apprehended in this subjective spirituality of faith." (Ibid., p. 138.) "The doctrine of the" (Catholic) "church is truth as existent truth." (*Philosophie der Religion*, II, p. 331.)

Stirner continues: "Accordingly, with Luther the knowledge arises that truth, because it is thought, exists only for the thinking man, and this means that man must adopt a totally different standpoint, a pious" (per apposition) "scientific standpoint, or that of thinking as opposed to its object, the thought" (p. 110).

Apart from the repetition which Stirner again includes here, only the transition from faith to thinking deserves attention. Hegel makes the transition in the following way: "But this spirit" (namely, the holy and consecrating spirit) "is, secondly, essentially also thinking spirit. Thinking as such must also have its development in it," etc. (p. 234).

Stirner continues: "This thought" ("that I am spirit, spirit alone") "pervades the history of the Reformation down to the present day" (p. 111).

From the sixteenth century onward, no other history exists for Stirner than the history of the Reformation—and the latter only in the view of it that Hegel presents.

Saint Max has again displayed his gigantic faith. He has again taken as literal truth all the illusions of German speculative philosophy; indeed, he has made them still more speculative, still more abstract. For him there exists only the history of religion and philosophy—and this exists for him only through the medium of Hegel, who with the passage of time has become the universal crib, the reference source for all the latest German speculators about principles and manufacturers of systems.

Catholicism = attitude to truth as thing, child, Negro, the "Ancient."

Protestantism = attitude to truth in the spirit, youth, Mongol, the "Modern."

The whole scheme was superfluous, since all this was already present in the section on "spirit."

As already hinted at in *The Economy of the Old Testament*, in Protestantism it is now possible to make the child and the youth appear on the scene again in new "transformations," as Stirner actually does on page 112, where he conceives English empirical philosophy as the child, in contrast to German speculative philosophy as the youth. Here again he copies out Hegel who here, as elsewhere in the "Book," frequently appears as "one": "One"—i.e., Hegel—"expelled Bacon from the realm of philosophy. . . ." "And, indeed, what is called English philosophy does not seem to have got any farther than the discoveries made by so-called clear intellects such as Bacon and Hume" (p. 112).

Hegel expresses this as follows: "Bacon is in fact the real leader and representative of what is called philosophy in England and beyond which the English have by no means gone as yet." (*Geschichte der Philosophie*, III, p. 254.)

The people whom Stirner calls "clear intellects" Hegel (ibid., p. 255) calls "educated men of the world." Saint Max on one occasion even transforms them into the "simplicity of childish nature," for the English philosophers have to represent the child. On the same childish grounds Bacon is not allowed to have "concerned himself with theological problems and cardinal propositions," regardless of what may be said in his writings (particularly *De dignitate et augmentis scientiarum, Novum Organum*, and the *Essays*). On the other hand, "German thought . . . sees life only in cognition itself" (p. 112), for it is the youth. *Ecce iterum Crispinus!*

How Stirner transforms Descartes into a German philosopher the reader can see for himself in the "Book," p. 112.

CHRISTIANITY AND REBELLION*

Owing to this power of Christianity, during the liberation of the feudal serfs the most bloody and embittered struggles were precisely those against the *spiritual* feudal lords, and they were carried through despite all the grumbling and indignation of Christianity as embodied in the priests (cf. Eden, *History of the Poor*, Book I; Guizot, *Histoire de la civilisation en France*; Monteil, *Histoire des Français des divers*

---

* From *The German Ideology*, pp. 236–37.

états, etc.), while, on the other hand, the little priests, particularly at the beginning of the Middle Ages, incited the feudal serfs to "grumbling" and "indignation" against the temporal feudal lords (cf., *inter alia,* even the well-known capitulary of Charlemagne). Compare also what was written above about the "oppressed classes" and their revolts in the fourteenth century in connection with the "workers' disturbances which flared up here and there."

The earlier forms of workers' uprisings were connected with the degree of development of labor in each case and the resulting form of property; direct or indirect communist uprisings were connected with large-scale industry. Instead of going into this extensive history, Saint Max accomplishes a holy transition from the *patient* oppressed classes to the *impatient* oppressed classes: "Now, when everyone should develop himself into a man" (how, for example, do the Catalonian workers "know" that "everyone should develop himself into a man"?), "the constraint of man to machine labor coincides with slavery" (p. 158).

Hence, prior to Spartacus and the uprising of the slaves, it was Christianity that prevented the "constraint of man to machine labor" from "coinciding with slavery"; and in the days of Spartacus it was only the notion of "man" that removed this relation and brought about slavery. "Or, perhaps," Stirner has "even" heard something about the connection between modern labor unrest and machine production and wanted to hint it here? In that case it was not the introduction of machine labor that transformed the workers into rebels, but the introduction of the notion of "man" that transformed machine labor into slavery. "If that is so," then "it indeed really looks as though" we have here a "unique" history of the workers' movements.

DR. KUHLMANN'S FRAUDULENT *Kingdom of the Spirit Upon Earth**

"A man was needed" (so runs the preface) "who would give utterance to all our sorrows, all our longings and all our hopes, to everything, in a word, which moves our age most deeply. And it was necessary that he should emerge from the solitude of the spirit into the press and the turmoil of doubts and longings, bearing the solution of the riddle, the living symbols of which encompass us all. This man, whom our age was awaiting, has appeared. *He is Dr. Georg Kuhlmann of Holstein.*"

---

* From *The German Ideology,* pp. 586–92. Georg Kuhlmann was the author of *Die Neue Welt oder das Reich des Geistes auf Erden. Verkündigung* (*The New World, or the Kingdom of the Spirit Upon Earth. Annunciation*) (Geneva, 1845).

August Becker, the writer of these lines, thus allowed himself to be persuaded, by a person of a very simple mind and very ambiguous character, that not a single riddle has yet been solved, not a single vital energy aroused—that the communist movement, which has already gripped all civilized countries, is an empty nut whose kernel cannot be discovered; that it is a universal egg, laid by some great universal hen without the aid of a cock—whereas the true kernel and the true cock of the walk is Dr. Georg Kuhlmann of Holstein! . . .

This great cock of the walk turns out, however, to be a perfectly ordinary capon who has fed for a while on the German artisans in Switzerland and who cannot escape his due fate.

Far be it from us to consider Dr. Kuhlmann of Holstein a commonplace charlatan and a cunning fraud, who does not himself believe in the efficacy of his elixir of life and who merely applies his science of longevity to the preservation of life in his own body—no, we are well aware that the inspired doctor is a *spiritualistic* charlatan, a *pious* fraud, a *mystical* old fox, but one who, like all his kind, is none too scrupulous in his choice of means, since his own person is intimately connected with his holy mission. Indeed, holy missions are always intimately bound up with the holy beings who pursue them; for such missions are of a purely idealistic nature and exist only in the mind. All idealists, philosophical and religious, ancient and modern, believe in inspirations, in revelations, saviors, miracle workers; whether their belief takes a crude religious or a refined philosophical form depends only upon their cultural level, just as the degree of energy they possess, their character, their social position, etc., determine whether their attitude to a belief in miracles is a passive or an active one, i.e., whether they are shepherds performing miracles or whether they are sheep; they further determine whether the aims they pursue are theoretical or practical.

Kuhlmann is a very energetic person indeed, a man of some philosophical education; his attitude to miracles is by no means a passive one and the aims he pursues are very practical.

All that August Becker has in common with him is the national infirmity of mind. The good fellow pities "those who cannot bring themselves to see that the will and the ideas of an age can be expressed only by individuals." For the idealist, every movement of world importance exists only in the head of some chosen being, and the fate of the world depends on whether this head, which has made all wisdom its own private property, is or is not mortally wounded by some realistic stone before it has had time to make its revelation. "Can it be otherwise?" adds August Becker challengingly. "Put the heads of all the philosophers and theologians of the age together, let them take counsel and register their votes, and then see what comes of it all!"

The whole of historical development consists, according to the ideologist, in those theoretical abstractions which originate in the "heads" of "all the philosophers and theologians of the age," and since it is impossible to put all these heads together and induce them to "take counsel and register their votes," there must of necessity be one sacred head, the *spearhead* of all these philosophical and theological heads, in a word, the speculative unity of all these spearheads—the savior.

This "cranium" system is as old as the Egyptian pyramids, with which it has many similarities, and as new as the Prussian monarchy, in the capital of which it has recently been resurrected, as young as ever. The idealistic Dalai Lamas have this much in common with their real counterpart: they would like to persuade themselves that the world from which they derive their subsistence could not continue without their holy excrement. As soon as this idealistic folly is put into practice, its malevolent nature is apparent: its monkish lust for power, its religious fanaticism, its charlatanry, its pietistic hypocrisy, its unctuous deceit. Miracles are the asses' bridge leading from the kingdom of the idea to practice. Dr. Georg Kuhlmann of Holstein is just such an asses' bridge—he is inspired—his magic words cannot fail to move the most immovable of mountains. How consoling for those patient creatures who cannot summon up enough energy to blast the mountain with *natural powder!* What a source of confidence to the blind and timorous who cannot see the material coherence which underlies the manifold fractions of the revolutionary movement!

"There has been lacking, up to now, a rallying point," says August Becker.

Saint George overcomes all concrete obstacles with the greatest of ease by transforming all concrete things into ideas; he then assumes himself to be the speculative unity of the latter, an assumption which enables him to "rule and regulate them": "The society of ideas is the world. And its unity regulates and rules the world" (p. 138).

Our prophet wields all the power he can possibly desire in this "society of ideas." "Let us then wander, led by our own idea, hither and thither, and contemplate everything in the minutest detail, as far as our time requires" (p. 138).

What a speculative unity of nonsense!

But paper is long-suffering, and the German public, to whom the prophet issued his oracles, knew so little of the philosophical development in its own country that it did not even notice how, in his speculative prophecies, our great prophet merely reiterated the most decrepit philosophical phrases and adapted them to his practical aims.

Just as medical miracle workers and miraculous cures are made possible by ignorance of the laws of the *natural* world, so *social* miracle workers and miraculous social cures depend upon ignorance of the laws of the *social* world—and the witch doctor of Holstein is none other than the *socialistic miracle-working shepherd* of Niederempt.

The first revelation which this miracle-working shepherd makes to his flock is as follows:

"I see before me an assembly of the elect, who have gone before me to work by word and deed for the salvation of our time, and who are now come to hear what I have to say concerning the weal and woe of mankind."

"Many have already spoken and written in the name of mankind, but none has yet given utterance to the real nature of man's suffering, his hopes and his expectations, nor told him how he may obtain his desires. That is precisely what I shall do."

And his flock believes him.

There is not a single original thought in the whole work of this "Holy Spirit"; he reduces out-of-date socialistic theories to abstractions of the most sterile and general kind. There is nothing original even in the form, the style. Others have imitated more happily the sanctified style of the Bible. Kuhlmann has taken Lamennais' manner of writing as his model, but he merely achieves a caricature of Lamennais. We shall give our readers a sample of the beauties of his style:

"Tell me, firstly, how feel ye when ye think on your eternal lot?

"Many indeed mock and say: 'What have I to do with eternity?'

"Others rub their eyes and ask: 'Eternity—what may this be? . . .'

"How feel ye, when ye think of the hour when the grave shall swallow you up?"

"And I hear many voices." One among them speaks in this wise:

"Of recent years it hath been taught that the spirit is eternal, that in death it is only dissolved once more in God, from whom it proceedeth. But they who preach such things cannot tell me what then remaineth of me. Oh, that I had never seen the light of day! And assuming that I do not die—oh, my parents, my sisters, my brothers, my children, and all whom I love, shall I ever see you again? Oh, had I but never seen you!" etc.

"How feel ye, further, if ye think of infinity?" . . .

We feel very poorly, Herr Kuhlmann—not at the thought of death, but at your fantastic idea of death, at your style, at the shabby means you employ to work upon the feelings of others.

"How dost feel," dear reader, when you hear a priest who paints hell very hot to terrify his sheep and make their minds very flabby, a priest whose eloquence only aims at stimulating the tear glands of his hearers and who speculates on the cowardice of his congregation?

As far as the meager content of the "Annunciation" is concerned, the first section, or the Introduction to the "New World," can be reduced to the simple thought that Herr Kuhlmann has come from Holstein to found the "Kingdom of the Spirit," the "Kingdom of Heaven" upon earth; that he was the first to know the real heaven and the real hell—the latter being society as it has hitherto existed and the former being future society, the "Kingdom of the Spirit"—and that he himself is the "longed-for holy spirit." . . .

None of Saint George's great thoughts are exactly original and there was really no need for him to have toiled all the way from Holstein to Switzerland, nor to have descended from the "solitude of the spirit" to the level of the artisans, nor to have "revealed" himself, merely in order to present this "vision" to the "world."

However, the idea that Dr. Kuhlmann of Holstein is the "longed-for holy spirit" is his own exclusive property—and is likely to remain so.

According to Saint George's own "revelation," his Holy Scripture will progress in the following way: "It will reveal" (he says) "the Kingdom of the Spirit in its earthly guise, that ye may behold its glory and see that there is no other salvation but in the Kingdom of the Spirit, On the other hand, it will expose your vale of tears that ye may behold your wretchedness and know the cause of all your sufferings. Then I shall show the way which leads from this sorrowful present to a joyful future. To this end, follow me in the spirit to a height, whence we may have a free prospect over the beautiful landscape."

And so the prophet permits us first of all a glimpse of his "beautiful landscape," his Kingdom of Heaven. We see nothing but a misunderstanding of Saint-Simonism, wretchedly staged, with costumes that are a travesty of Lamennais, embellished with fragments from Herr Stein.

We shall now quote the most important revelations from the Kingdom of Heaven, which demonstrate the prophetic method. For example, page 37: "The choice will be free and determined by each person's inclinations. Inclinations are determined by one's natural faculties."

"If in society," Saint George prophesies, "everyone follows his inclination, all the faculties of society without exception will be developed and if this is so, that which all need will continually be produced, in the realm of the spirit as in the realm of matter. For society always possesses as many faculties and energies as it has needs." . . . "*Les attractions sont proportionelles aux destinées.*" (Cf. also Proudhon.)

Herr Kuhlmann differs here from the socialists and the communists only by reason of a misunderstanding, the cause of which must be sought in his pursuit of practical aims and undoubtedly also in his limitations. He confuses the diversity of faculties and capacities with the inequality of possessions and enjoyment conditioned by possession, and therefore inveighs against communism: "No one shall have there" (that is, under communism) "any advantage over another," declaims the prophet, "no one shall have more possessions and live better than another . . . and if you cherish doubts about it and fail to join in their outcry, they will abuse you, condemn you, and persecute you and hang you on a gallows" (p. 100).

Kuhlmann sometimes prophesies quite correctly, one must admit:

"In their ranks then are to be found all those who cry: Away with the Bible! Away, above all, with the Christian religion, for it is the religion of humility and servility! Away with all belief whatsoever! We know nothing of God or immortality! They are but figments of the imagination, exploited and continually concocted by deceivers and liars for their advantage" (it should read: which are exploited by the priests for their advantage). "In sooth, he who still believes in such things is the greatest of fools!"

Kuhlmann attacks with particular vehemence those who are on principle opposed to the doctrine of faith, humility, and inequality, i.e., the doctrine of "difference of rank and of birth."

He founds his socialism on the abject doctrine of predestined slavery—which reminds one strongly, as Kuhlmann formulates it, of Friedrich Rohmer—on the theocratic hierarchy and, in the last instance, on his *own sacred person!*

"Every branch of labor," we find on page 42, "is directed by the most skilled worker, who himself takes part in it, and in the realm of enjoyment every branch is guided by the merriest member, who himself participates in the enjoyment. But, as society is undivided and possesses only one mind, the whole system will be regulated and governed by one man—and he shall be the wisest, the most virtuous and the most blissful."

On page 34 we learn: "If man strives after virtue in the spirit, then he stirs and moves his limbs and develops and molds and forms everything in and outside himself according to his pleasure. And if he experiences well-being in the spirit, then he must also experience it in everything that lives in him. Therefore, man eats and drinks and takes delight therein; therefore, he sings, plays and dances, he kisses, weeps and laughs."

The knowledge of the influence which the vision of God exerts on the appetite, and which spiritual blissfulness exerts upon the sex impulse is, indeed, not the private property of Kuhlmannism; but it does shed light on many an obscure passage in the prophet.

For example, page 36: "Both" (possession and enjoyment) "correspond to his labor" (this is, to man's labor). "Labor is the measure of his needs." (In this way, Kuhlmann distorts the claim that a communist society has, on the whole, always as many faculties and energies as needs.) "For labor is the expression of the ideas and the instincts. And therein needs are contained. But since the faculties and needs of men are always different, and so apportioned that the former can be developed and the latter satisfied only if each continually labors for all and the product of the labor of all be exchanged and apportioned in accordance with the deserts" (?) "of each—for this reason each receives only the value of his labor."

The whole of this tautological rigmarole would be—like the following sentences and many others which we spare the reader—utterly incomprehensible, despite the "sublime simplicity and clarity" of the "revelation" so praised by A. Becker, if we had not a key in the shape of the practical aims which the prophet is pursuing. This at once makes everything comprehensible.

"Value," Herr Kuhlmann continues like an oracle, "determines itself according to the need of all" (?). "In value the work of each is always contained and for it" (?) "he can procure for himself whatever his heart desires."

"See, my friends," runs page 39, "the society of true men envisages life always as a school . . . in which man must educate himself. And thereby it wants to attain bliss. But such" (?) "must become evident and visible" (?), "otherwise it" (?) "is impossible."

What Herr Georg Kuhlmann of Holstein has in view when he says that "such" (life? or bliss?) must "become evident" and "visible," because "it" would otherwise be "impossible"—that "labor" is contained in "value" and that one can procure for it (for what?) one's heart's desire—and finally, that "value" determines itself according to "need"—it would be impossible to fathom unless one once again takes into account the point of the whole revelation, the practical basis of it all.

Let us therefore try to offer a practical explanation.

We learn from August Becker that Saint George Kuhlmann of Holstein had no success in his own country. He arrives in Switzerland and finds there an entirely "new world," the communist societies of the German artisans. That is exactly what he wants—and he attaches himself without delay to communism and the communists. He always, as August Becker tells us, "worked unremittingly to develop his doctrine further and to make it adequate to the greatness of the times," i.e., he became a communist among the communists *ad majorem Dei gloriam.* So far everything had gone well.

But one of the most vital principles of communism, a principle which distinguishes it from all reactionary socialism, is its empiric view, based on a knowledge of man's nature, that differences of *brain* and of intellectual capacity do not imply any differences whatsoever in the nature of the *stomach* and of physical *needs;* therefore the false tenet, based upon existing circumstances, "to each according to his abilities," must be changed, insofar as it relates to enjoyment in its narrower sense, into the tenet, *"to each according to his need";* in other words, a *different form* of activity, of labor, does not justify *inequality*, confers no *privileges* in respect of possession and enjoyment.

The prophet could not admit this; for the privileges, the advantages of his station, the feeling that he is one of the elect, these are the very stimulus of the prophet. "But such must become evident and visible, otherwise it is impossible." Without practical advantages, without some tangible stimulus, the prophet would not be a prophet at all, he would not be a *practical*, but only a *theoretical*, man of God, a *philosopher*. The prophet must therefore make the communists understand that different forms of *activity* or *labor* give the right to different degrees of *value* and of *bliss* (or of enjoyment, merit, pleasure, it is all the same thing), and since each determines his own bliss and his labor, therefore, *he*, the prophet—this is the practical point of the revelation—can claim a *better life* than the *common artisan*.[5]

After this, all the prophet's obscurities become clear: that the "possession" and "enjoyment" of each should correspond to his "labor"; that the "labor" of man should be the measure of his *"needs";* that, therefore, each should receive the "value" of his labor; that "value" will determine *itself* according to "need"; that the work of each is "contained" in value and that he can procure for it what his "heart" desires; that, finally, the "bliss" of the chosen one must "become evident and visible," because it is otherwise "impossible." All this nonsense now acquires a meaning.

We do not know the exact extent of the practical demands which Dr. Kuhlmann makes upon the artisans. But we do know that his doctrine is a dogma fundamental to all spiritual and temporal craving for power, a mystic veil which obscures all furtive, hypocritical pleasure seeking, we know that it serves to extenuate any infamy and that it is the source of much mental derangement.

We must not omit showing the reader the way which, according to Herr Kuhlmann of Holstein, "leads from this sorrowful present to a joyful future." This way is lovely and delightful as spring in a flowery meadow or as a flowery meadow in spring: "Softly and gently, with

---

5. The prophet moreover *openly* admits this in a lecture which has not been printed.—K.M.

sun-warmed fingers, it puts forth buds, the buds become flowers, the lark and the nightingale warble, the grasshopper in the grass is roused. Let the new world come like the spring" (p. 114 et seq.).

The prophet paints the transition from present social isolation to communal life in truly idyllic colors. We remember how he transformed real society into a "society of ideas," so that "he could wander hither and thither, led by his own idea, and contemplate everything in the minutest detail, as far as his time required"; in the same way he transforms the real social movement which already, in all civilized countries, proclaims the approach of a terrible social upheaval into a process of comfortable and peaceful conversion, a quiet life which will permit the owners and rulers of the world to slumber on in complete peace of mind. For the idealist, the theoretical abstractions of real events, their ideal signs, are reality; real events are merely "signs that the old world is going to its doom."

"Wherefore do ye strive so anxiously for the things of the moment," scolds the prophet on page 118, "they are nothing more than signs that the old world is going to its doom; and wherefore do ye dissipate your strength in strivings which cannot fulfill your hopes and expectations?"

"Ye shall not tear down nor destroy that which ye find in your path, ye shall rather go out of your way to avoid it and pass it by. And when ye have avoided it and passed it by, then it shall cease to exist of itself, for it shall find no other nourishment."

"If ye seek truth and spread light abroad, then lying and darkness will vanish from your midst" (p. 116).

"But there will be many who will say: 'How shall we build a new life as long as the old order prevails and hinders us? Must it not first be destroyed?' 'In no wise,' answers the sagest, the most virtuous and the most blissful. 'In no wise. If ye dwell with others in a house that has become rotten and is too small and uncomfortable for you, and the others wish to remain in it, then ye shall not pull it down and dwell in the open, but ye shall first build a new house, and when it is ready ye shall enter it and abandon the old to its fate' " (p. 120).

The prophet now gives two pages of rules as to how one can insinuate oneself into the new world. Then he becomes aggressive: "But it is not enough that ye should stand together and forsake the old world—ye shall also take arms against it to make war upon it and to extend your kingdom and strengthen it. Not by the use of force, however, but rather by the use of free persuasion."

But if one finds oneself forced, after all, to take up a *real* sword and hazard one's *real* life "to conquer heaven by force of arms," the prophet promises his sacred host a Russian immortality (the Russians believe that they will rise again in their respective localities if they are killed in battle by the enemy): "And they who shall fall by the wayside shall be born anew and shall rise more beauteous than they were before. Therefore" (therefore!) "take no thought for your life and fear not death" (p. 129).

Even in a conflict with *real* weapons, says the prophet reassuringly to his sacred host, you do not *really* risk your life; you merely *pretend* to risk it.

The prophet's doctrine is in every sense *sedative*. After these samples of his Holy Scripture one cannot wonder at the applause it has met with among certain drowsy and easygoing fellows.

From "Circular Against Kriege"

Marx and Engels' "Circular Against Kriege," written May, 1846, was published in the New York communist weekly, Der Volks-Tribun *(of which Hermann Kriege himself was editor), and in* Das Westphälische Dampfboot, *July, 1846. The article was an attack on Kriege for not hewing to the Marx communist party line.*

COMMUNISM AND THE HOLY GHOST*

(1) KRIEGE maintains here that he is "not accustomed to introduce logical tightrope dances into the sterile desert of abstraction." But it appears from every issue of *Der Volks-Tribun* that, if not "logical," he "dances on a tightrope" of twisted philosophical and love-happy phrases.

(2) The statement that "the single man lives as an individual" (which is already nonsense) Kriege expresses in the following unlogical "tightrope dance": "As long as the human species still finds its representation in individuals at all,"

(3) it ought to depend on the "pleasure" of the "creative spirit of mankind," which exists nowhere, "to make an end to the state of things today."

(4) The following is the ideal of communist man: "He bears the stamp of the species" (who does not now do so automatically?), "determines his own goals according to the goals of the species" (as if a species were a person who could have goals), "and seeks to become properly himself in order to dedicate himself, with what he is and

---

* From Section 3 of the "Circular."

what he could become, to the species" (total sacrifice and self-abasement before a fantastic apparition).

(5) The position of the individual person in regard to the species is also characterized in the following extravagant nonsense: "All of us, and our particular activities, are only symptoms of a great movement that goes on of itself deep inside mankind." "Deep inside mankind"—what is this? According to this sentence, actual men are only "symptoms," symbols of a "movement" that goes on "inside" a phantom thought.

(6) This country parson transforms the struggle for a communist society into a "search for that great spirit of community." He lets this "great spirit" foam "fully and beautifully out of the communion cup," and as "the Holy Ghost flaming out of the brother's eye."

After the revolutionary communist movement has been transformed into a "search" for the Holy Ghost and the Last Supper, Kriege can, of course, maintain that this ghost "has only to be recognized, to unite all men in love."

(7) This metaphysical result is preceded by the following confounding of *communism* with *communion:* "The spirit that conquers the world, the spirit that commands the storm and the tempest" (! ! ! !), "the spirit that heals the blind and the leprous, the spirit that bids all men to drink from one wine" (we prefer the manifold varieties) "and to eat from one loaf" (the French and English communists make greater claims), "the spirit that is eternal and omnipresent, that is the spirit of community." If this "spirit" is "eternal and omnipresent," then it must be clear why, according to Kriege, private property has been able to exist so long. But naturally, the spirit was not "recognized," and was therefore "eternal and omnipresent" only in his own imagination.

Thus Kriege preaches here, *in the name of communism*, the old religious and German-philosophical fantasy, which *directly contradicts communism*. Such a belief, and particularly the belief in the "holy spirit of community," he asks in order to achieve communism.

Religion and Communism*

It is understood that Kriege's drivel about love and his antithesis against egoism are nothing more than the soaring manifestations of a spirit thoroughly afloat in religion. We will see how Kriege, who in Europe always gave out that he was an atheist, here [in New York] tries to bring out various infamies of Christianity under the protective shield of communism, and quite consistently ends with the *self-desecration of man*.

---

* From Section 4 of the "Circular."

The articles *"Was wir wollen"* ["What We Want"] and *"Hermann Kriege an [to] Harro Harring,"* in No. 10 [of the *Volks-Tribun*], state the goal of the communist struggle thus:

(1) "To make the religion of love a truth, and the long-yearned-for community of blessed inhabitants of heaven a reality." Kriege merely overlooks the fact that these Christian ecstasies are only the fantasized expression of the existing world, and therefore its "reality" *already exists* in the evil conditions of this existing world.

(2) "In the name of that religion of love, we demand that the hungry be fed, the thirsty be slaked, and the naked be clad." Which demand has been repeated *ad nauseam* for eighteen hundred years, and without the slightest success.

(3) "We teach the practice of love," in order

(4) "To receive love."

(5) "In the kingdom of love, devils cannot abide."

(6) "It is his [man's] most sacred need to dissolve himself with his whole individuality into the society of loving beings, in whose presence he cannot hold fast to anything except

(7) his boundless love." One would suppose that with this boundlessness the love theory had attained its highest pinnacle, so high that nothing more could be thought of; nevertheless, it goes still higher.

(8) "This ardent outpouring of love, this surrender to everybody, this divine urge for community—what is it except the innermost religion of communism, which only lacks a corresponding outer world to express itself in the fullness of human life?" The present "outer world" seems meanwhile fully to suffice for Kriege to "express" most broadly his "innermost religion," his "divine urge," his "surrender to everybody," and his "ardent outpouring" in his "fullness of human life."

(9) "Do we not have the right to take seriously the long-delayed wishes of the religious heart, and in the name of the poor, the unfortunate, and the disinherited, go into the struggle for the realization of the beautiful kingdom of brotherly love?" Kriege thus goes into the struggle to attain the wishes, not of the actual and profane but of the religious, not of those embittered by actual misery but of the puffed-up heart of blessed fantasy. He shows his "religious heart" by going into the struggle as a priest, under an alien name, that is, the name of the "poor," making it clearly understood that for himself he has no need for communism but goes into battle for it out of purely magnanimous, dedicated, overflowing sacrifice for the poor, unfortunate and disinherited, who have need of him—a lofty sentiment that surges high in the breast of the philistine in the lonely, gloomy hours, and counterbalances all the sorrows of the wicked world.

(10) Kriege concludes his bombast: "He who does not support

such a party can rightly be treated as an enemy of humanity." This intolerant sentence seems to contradict the "surrender to everybody" of the "religion of love" for all. But this is quite a consistent conclusion of this new religion, which, like every other, mortally hates and persecutes its enemies. The enemy of the party is quite consistently transformed into a heretic, being changed from an enemy of the actually existing party, with whom one *contends*, into a sinner existing only in an imaginary humanity, who must be *punished*.

(11) The letter to Harro Harring says: "We want to bring all the poor of the world into insurrection against Mammon, under whose scourge they are condemned to torment, and when we have knocked the frightful tyrant from his throne we want to unite mankind with love, teaching it communal work and communal enjoyment, so that the long-postponed kingdom of joy is finally realized." To become angry at the modern rule of money, he must first transform it into the idol Mammon. This idol is overthrown—how, we are not informed; the revolutionary movement of the proletariat of all countries thus shrinks into an insurrection—and after the overthrow has taken place come the Prophets, the "we" who will "teach" the proletariat what is to be done next. These Prophets "teach" their young ones, who here seem remarkably ignorant of their own interests, how they should "work and enjoy communally," not in order to "work and enjoy communally" but merely to fulfill the Writ and insure that some visionaries of eighteen hundred years ago should not have prophesied in vain. This manner of prophesying is repeated elsewhere, for example:

"*Was ist das Proletariat?*" ["What Is the Proletariat?"] and "Andreas Dietsch," in No. 8, state:

(a) "Proletarians, the hour of your deliverance has come."

(b) "A thousand hearts beat exultantly in anticipation of the great day of Promise"—namely, "that great kingdom of love . . . for the long-yearned-for kingdom of love."

"*Antwort an Koch, den Antipfaffen*" ["Reply to Koch, the Antiparson"], in No. 12, states:

(c) "The evangel of endless world redemption already twitches from eye to eye" and—even—"from hand to hand." This miracle of the "twitching evangel," this nonsense of "endless world redemption," corresponds entirely to the other miracle, that the prophecies of the old Evangelists, given up long ago, will be fulfilled through Kriege, against all expectations.

(12) From such a religious viewpoint, the answer to all *actual questions* can consist only of some rapturously religious *images*, befogging all sense, under some pompous labels, such as "mankind," "humanity," "species," etc., and of a transformation of all actual fact into fantastic phrases. This is shown particularly in the article "*Was*

ist das Proletariat?" (No. 8). The answer to the question in the title is: "The proletariat is *mankind"*—a conscious lie, according to which the communists aim at the abolition of mankind. This answer, "Humanity," is supposed to be the same one Sieyès gave to the question: "What Is the Third Estate?"[1] Proof of how Kriege improves historical facts. He demonstrates it again by his sanctification of the American Anti-Rent movement: "And now finally this proletariat, in its capacity as mankind" (a necessary character mask, in which it has to appear—a little while ago the proletariat was mankind, now mankind is merely the characteristic of the proletariat), "makes a claim for the possession of the whole earth as its incontestable property for all eternity." One sees how a completely simple, practical movement becomes transformed into empty phrases, such as "mankind," "incontestable property," "all eternity," etc.—and hence is utilizable only in a mere "claim." Apart from the customary catchwords, "outlaws," etc., associated with the religious word "cursed," all of Kriege's communications about the proletariat reduce themselves to the following mythological-biblical images:

> "the bound Prometheus,"
> "the lamb of God, bearing the world's sins,"
> "the wandering Jew";

and finally he raises the extraordinary question: "Should mankind, a homeless vagabond, roam the earth unto eternity?" Even though the exclusive settlement of a portion of "mankind" on earth is a thorn in his flesh!

(13) Kriege's religion makes its most striking points in the following passage: "We have more important things to do than worry about our shabby selves, we belong to mankind." This religion, with its "shabby," servile humility, ends, like any other, with this infamous and disgusting servility in the face of a "mankind" separated and differentiated from the "self," hence a metaphysical one, and in his case even a religious fiction. Such a creed, which preaches the delight of cringing and self-contempt, is entirely appropriate for brave—*monks;* but never for energetic men, and particularly so in a period of struggle. It only remains for these brave monks to castrate their "shabby selves" and thereby sufficiently demonstrate their confidence in the ability of "mankind" to reproduce itself! If Kriege doesn't know any better than to bring forth these pitiful, stereotyped sentimentalities, he would be wiser to translate his "Father Lamennais" again and again in every issue of *Der Volks-Tribun.*

---

1. In 1789, on the eve of the French Revolution, the Abbé Emmanuel Sieyès wrote a pamphlet, *What Is the Third Estate?* His answer, in brief, was: Everything.

The practical consequences of Kriege's religion of endless pity and endless resignation are shown by the pleas for work which figure in practically every issue of *Der Volks-Tribun*. Thus we read in No. 8:

Work! Work! Work!

Is there anybody among all the rich gentlemen who does not consider it wasted effort to provide nourishment for honest families and keep helpless young people from misery and despair? There is, first of all, Johann Stern from Mecklenburg, who is still without work, and yet he asks for nothing more than to flay himself to the advantage of a capitalist and thereby to earn as much bread as would maintain him for his work—is this too much to expect in a civilized society? And then Karl Gescheidtle from Baden, a young man of most admirable disposition and not without higher education—he looks so loyal and good that I guarantee he is honesty itself. . . . And also an old man and other young people implore work for their hands and their daily bread. Whoever can help, let him not delay any longer, or his conscience may rob him of his sleep when he needs it most. Of course you can say: There are thousands who vainly cry for work, and after all we cannot help everybody. Yes, you can, but you are vassals of egoism and haven't enough heart to do anything. If you do not want to help everybody, at least show that you have retained a little bit of human feeling, and help as many individuals as you can.

Naturally, if they wanted to they could help as many as possible. Such is the practice, the actual carrying out of self-abasement and degradation, which that new religion teaches.

Kriege's Personal Public Appearance*

Kriege's personal position in his paper is already clear from the above passages; we therefore raise only a few points.

Kriege made his appearance as a *prophet*, hence necessarily as an emissary of a secret Essene Union, the "Union of Righteousness." Thus if he does not speak in the name of the "oppressed" he speaks in the name of "righteousness," not the usual righteousness but the righteousness of the "Union of Righteousness." He not only mystifies himself, he also mystifies history. He mystifies the actual historical development of communism in the various European countries, which he does not know, by peddling the origins and progress of communism as fictional, romantic, and falsifying intrigues of this Essene Union. For this, look over all the issues, specifically the answer to

---

* From Section 5 of the "Circular."

Harro Harring, which contains the most senseless fantasies about the power of this union.

As a real apostle of love, Kriege turns next to women, whose depravity he does not trust to be able to resist a heart that beats with love; then to the preexisting agitators, "filial" and "forgiving"—as "son," "brother," "heart's brother"; and finally, as *man*, to the rich. Hardly had he arrived in New York when he sent out a communication to all rich German merchants, pointed the popgun of love at their breasts, refraining very carefully from telling them what he wanted from them, signing himself now "a man," now "friend of men," now "a fool," and—"would you believe it, my friends?"—nobody fell for his high-flown tomfooleries. Nobody was more surprised by this than Kriege himself. Now and then the known, already cited love phrases were peppered with exclamations such as (*"Antwort an Koch,"* No. 12): "Hurrah! Long live the community, long live equality, long live love!" He cannot explain practical questions and doubts except as intentional malice and callousness (*"Antwort an Conze,"* No. 14). As a true prophet and exemplar of love, he speaks out with the whole hysterical irritation of his phony-beautiful soul against the scoffers, the unbelievers, and the men of the Old World who will not let themselves be bewitched by his sweet love warmth into "blessed inhabitants of heaven." In such a malcontent-sentimental mood, he calls out to them, under the label, "Spring" (No. 11): "Because you mock us today, you will soon become pious, for know ye that it is spring."

Two Kinds of Religion*

THE economists have a peculiar way of proceeding. For them, there are only two kinds of institutions, artificial and natural. The institutions of feudalism are artificial, those of the bourgeoisie natural. In this they resemble the theologians, who also distinguish between two kinds of religion. All religions that are not theirs are a human invention, whereas their own religion is an emanation from God. . . .

---

* From *The Poverty of Philosophy* (1847), "Seventh and Last Observation." Marx quoted this passage in *Capital*, Vol. I, Chapter I, Sec. 4, and added, "Hence forms of social production that preceded the bourgeois form are treated by the bourgeoisie in much the same way as the Fathers of the Church treated pre-Christian religions."

The Social Principles of Christianity*

"WHAT is the alpha and omega of the Christian faith? The dogma of original sin and salvation. And therein lies the link of solidarity among humanity at its highest potential; one for all and all for one."

Happy people! The *cardinal question* is solved forever. The proletariat will find two inexhaustible life sources under the double wings of the Prussian eagle and the Holy Ghost: first, the income tax surplus over and above the ordinary and extraordinary needs of the state, which surplus is equal to null; and second, the revenues from the heavenly domains of original sin and salvation, which are likewise equal to null. Both of these nulls provide a splendid ground for the one-third of the nation that has no land for its subsistence, and a powerful support for another third which is in decline. In any case, imaginary surpluses, original sin, and salvation will satisfy the hunger of the people in quite a different way from the long speeches of the liberal deputies!

It is said further: "In the 'Our Father' we pray: 'Lead us not into temptation.' And what we ask for ourselves we must also practice toward our neighbors. But our social conditions do indeed tempt man, and excessive misery incites to crime."

And *we*, the gentlemen bureaucrats, judges, and consistorial councilors of the Prussian State, exercise this respect [for our fellow men] by joyfully wracking people on the wheel, beheading, imprisoning, and flogging, and thereby "leading" the proletarians "into temptation," so that later they too can wrack, behead, imprison, and flog us. And that will not fail to happen.

---

* "The Communism of the *Rheinischer Beobachter*," in *Deutsche-Brüsseler-Zeitung*, September 12, 1847. The quoted material is from the *Beobachter*'s articles.

"Such conditions," the consistorial councilor declares, "a Christian State *must not* tolerate; it must find a remedy for them."

Yes, with absurd babble about society's duties of solidarity, with imaginary surpluses and blank checks drawn on God the Father, Son, and Company.

"We can also be spared the already tedious talk about communism," our observant consistorial councilor remarks. "If those whose calling it is would only develop the social principles of Christianity, the communists would soon become silent."

The social principles of Christianity have now had eighteen hundred years to develop, and need no further development by the Prussian consistorial councilors.

The social principles of Christianity justified slavery in antiquity, glorified medieval serfdom, and, when necessary, also know how to defend the oppression of the proletariat, although they may do so with a piteous face.

The social principles of Christianity preach the necessity of a ruling and an oppressed class, and for the latter they have only the pious wish that the former will be benevolent.

The social principles of Christianity transfer the consistorial councilors' settlement of all infamies to heaven, and thereby justify the continuation of these infamies on earth.

The social principles of Christianity declare all vile acts of the oppressors against the oppressed to be either just punishment for original sin and other sins, or suffering that the Lord in his infinite wisdom has destined for those redeemed.

The social principles of Christianity preach cowardice, self-contempt, abasement, submission, humility—in brief, all the qualities of the *canaille*; and the proletariat, not wishing to be treated as *canaille*, needs its courage, its self-respect, its pride, and its sense of independence even more than its bread.

The social principles of Christianity are hypocritical, but the proletariat is revolutionary.

So much for the social principles of Christianity.

Satire on the Catholic Clergy in Belgium*

SINCE Herr A. Bartels is more theocrat than democrat, it is all too natural that he should find an accomplice in the *Journal de Bruxelles*.[1] This paper accuses us of wanting to "improve the human race." It can rest assured! Fortunately, we Germans know very well that since 1640 the *Congregatio de propaganda fide*[2] has had the sole monopoly for the improvement of the human race. We are too modest and unimportant to compete with the venerable fathers devoted to the commendable cause of human welfare. They need only make the effort and compare the report in the *Deutsche-Brüsseler-Zeitung* with that in the *Northern Star*[3] to be assured that the *Northern Star* was mistaken when it ascribed to me the words: "Chartists . . . You will be celebrated as the saviors of the human race."[4]

The *Journal de Bruxelles* is animated by the spirit of more warm brotherly love when it reminds us of the example of Anacharsis Cloots, who had to mount the scaffold because he was more patriotic than the patriots of 1793 and 1794. In this respect the venerable fathers cannot be reproached. They were never more patriotic than the patriots. On the contrary, they were always and everywhere accused of wanting to be more reactionary than the reactionaries, and, what

---

* From "Remarks on Herr Adolphe Bartels' Article," published in *Deutsche-Brüsseler-Zeitung*, December 19, 1847. Adolphe Bartels was a Belgian Catholic journalist.

1. A Catholic journal.

2. A world-wide organization founded by the Pope in the seventeenth century for the propagation of the Catholic faith.

3. A Chartist weekly founded in 1837.

4. The correct version of Marx's speech (on Poland), appeared in "International Class Conflict," *Deutsche-Brüsseler-Zeitung*, December 9, 1847.

is even worse, to represent the aims of the government more than the national government itself. When we think of the sad experiences they had in Switzerland recently, we are completely prepared to recognize that their warning springs from noble-mindedness worthy of the first Christians, and for our part we will seek to avoid the opposite extreme and similar dangers. For this we thank you.

From *Manifesto of the Communist Party**

CHRISTIAN SOCIALISM

As the parson has ever gone hand in hand with the landlord, so has clerical socialism with feudal socialism.

Nothing is easier than to give Christian asceticism a socialist tinge. Has not Christianity declaimed against private property, against marriage, against the state? Has it not preached, in the place of these, charity and poverty, celibacy and mortification of the flesh, monastic life and Mother Church? Christian Socialism is but the holy water with which the priest consecrates the heartburnings of the aristocrat.

CHANGING RELIGIOUS IDEAS

When people speak of ideas that revolutionize society, they do but express the fact that within the old society the elements of a new one have been created, and that the dissolution of the old ideas keeps even pace with the dissolution of the old conditions of existence.

When the ancient world was in its last throes, the ancient religions were overcome by Christianity. When Christian ideas succumbed in the eighteenth century to rationalist ideas, feudal society fought its death battle with the then revolutionary bourgeoisie. The idea of religious liberty and freedom of conscience merely gave expression to the sway of free competition within the domain of knowledge.

---

* From *Manifesto of the Communist Party* (1848). For the complete text, see *Karl Marx on Revolution*, Vol. I of The Karl Marx Library, pp. 79–107.

The Prussian Monarchy's Bigotry*

WE have predicted to the Right what it can expect when the camarilla is victorious—a gratuity and kicks.

We were mistaken. The struggle is not yet decided, and already they get the kicks from their chiefs without receiving a gratuity. . . .

For an official newspaper, the *Neue Preussische Zeitung* is much too candid. It tells the various parties what is sealed in the records of the Santa Casa.[1]

In the Middle Ages Virgil was used for prophesying. In the Prussian Brumaire of 1848[2] the *Neue Preussische Zeitung* is used to spare the effort of prediction. We present new examples. What is the Court camarilla preparing for the Catholics?

Listen!

No. 115 of the *Neue Preussische Zeitung* says: "It is equally untrue that the state" (specifically, the Royal Prussian State, the *Landwehr*[3] and holy-cross state in its pre-March period) "has assumed a narrowly Protestant character and that it has conducted its religious affairs from this one-sided standpoint. This reproach, if true, would, to be sure, be decidedly laudatory. But it is untrue; for it is known

---

* From "Confessions of a Beautiful Soul," published in *Neue Rheinische Zeitung*, November 7, 1848. The title is the title of Book Six of Goethe's novel, *Wilhelm Meisters Lehrjahre*.

1. Holy House—the prison of the Inquisition in Madrid.

2. On the eighteenth Brumaire of the Revolutionary Year 8 (November 9, 1799), Napoleon Bonaparte took over the French Government as First Consul. Brumaire (Fog-Month: October 22 to November 22) was the second month of the French revolutionary calendar.

3. The militia, or national guard.

that our regime has definitely abandoned the old and good standpoint of an evangelical government."

It is known that Frederick William III turned religion into a branch of military discipline and had the police beat up dissenters. It is known that Frederick William IV, as one of the twelve minor Prophets, wanted, through the Eichhorn-Bodelschwingh-Ladenberg Ministry, forcibly to convert the people and science to Bunsen's religion. It is known that even under the Camphausen Ministry the Poles were plundered, ravaged, and clubbed for being *Poles* as much as for being *Catholics*. The Pomeranians in Poland always made it a point to impale pictures of the Mother of God and to hang Catholic priests.

The persecutions of dissenting Protestants under Frederick William III and Frederick William IV are equally known.

The former incarcerated in fortresses Protestant parsons who rejected the rituals and dogmas he had invented. This man was a great designer of uniforms and rituals. And the latter? The Eichhorn Ministry? It is enough to mention the Eichhorn Ministry.

But all that was nothing!

"Our regime has definitely abandoned the old and good standpoint of an evangelical government." Therefore, you Catholics of the Rhine Province and Westphalia and Silesia, await the restoration of Brandenburg-Manteuffel. Formerly you were whipped with birches, now you will be lashed with scorpions. You will definitely come to know "the old and good standpoint of an evangelical government"!

And now even the Jews, whose eminent representatives at least have, since the emancipation of their sect, *spearheaded the counterrevolution* everywhere—what awaits them?

The government has not even waited for a victory to hurl them back into their ghettos.

In Bromberg the government has renewed the restrictions on the right of free domicile; it thus robs the Jews of the first of the Rights of Man of 1789, to move freely from one place to another.

This is one aspect of the government of the wordy Frederick William IV under the auspices of Brandenburg-Manteuffel-Ladenberg.

Christianity and the
Collapse of the Ancient World*

"An otherwise very enlightened man in Nuremberg who was not insensitive to the new had a tremendous hatred for democratic activities. He admired Ronge, whose portrait hung in his room. But when he heard that Ronge had sided with the democrats he hung the portrait in the toilet. He once said: 'Oh, if only we lived under the Russian knout, how happy I would feel!' He died during the disturbances and I suppose that, although he was already old, it was despondency and grief that led him to the grave." (Vol. II, pp. 321, 322.)

If instead of dying, this pitiable Nuremberg philistine had gleaned his scraps of thought from *Correspondent von and für Deutschland*,[1] from Schiller and Goethe, from old schoolbooks and modern lending-library books, he would have spared himself the trouble of dying and Herr Daumer his acidly elaborated two volumes of combinative and aphoristic foundation. We, of course, should not then have had the edifying opportunity to become acquainted with the religion of the new age and at the same time with its first martyr.

Herr Daumer's work is divided into two parts, the "preliminary" and the "main" one. In the preliminary part the faithful Eckart of German philosophy expresses his profound concern that even thinking and educated Germans have let themselves be led astray for the past two years and have given up the inestimable achievements of

* Marx and Engels' review of Georg Friedrich Daumer's *Die Religion des neuen Weltalters. Versuch einer combinatorish-aphoristischen Grundlegung* (*The Religion of the New Age. An Attempt at a Combinative-Aphoristic Foundation*) (Hamburg, 1850); the review was published in *Neue Rheinische Zeitung. Politisch-Ökonomische Revue*, Heft 2, February, 1850.

1. A liberal Nuremberg newspaper.

thought for mere "external" revolutionary activity. He considers the present moment appropriate to appeal once more to the better feelings of the nation and points out what it means to so light-mindedly let all German culture, through which alone the German burgher was still anything at all, depart. He résumés the whole content of German culture in the pithiest sayings that the casket of his erudition contains, and thus discredits German culture no less than German philosophy. His anthology of the loftiest products of the German mind surpasses in platitude and triviality even the most ordinary reading book for young ladies in the educated walks of life. From Schiller's and Goethe's philistine sallies against the first French Revolution, from the classic "Dangerous it is to rouse the lion," down to the most modern literature, the high priest of the new religion zealously digs up every passage in which German pettifoggery stiffens with sleepy ill humor against the historical movement it loathes. Authorities of the weight of a Friedrich Raumer, Berthold Auerbach, Lochner, Moritz Carrière, Alfred Meissner, Krug, Dingelstedt, Ronge, *Nuremberger Bote*, Max Waldau, Sternberg, German Mäurer, Luise Aston, Eckermann, Noack, *Blätter für literarische Unterhaltung*, A. Kunze, Ghillany, Th. Mundt, Saphir, Gutzkow, a certain *"née* Gatterer," and the like are the pillars on which the temple of the new religion rests. The revolutionary movement, which is here declared anathema in so many voices, is confined for Herr Daumer on the one hand to the tritest prattle about politics as carried on in Nuremberg under the auspices of "Correspondent on and for Germany," and on the other hand to ruffianism, of which he has a most fantastic idea. The sources he draws on are worthy of being placed on a par with those already mentioned: side by side with the oft-named *Nuremberger Correspondent* figure *Bamberger Zeitung, Münchner Landbötin, Augsburger Allgemeine Zeitung*, and others. The same petty-bourgeois vulgarity that sees nothing in the proletarian but a disgusting, corrupt ragamuffin and which rubs its hands with satisfaction at the Paris massacres in June, 1848, when 3,000 of those "ragamuffins" are butchered—that very vulgarity is indignant at the raillery of which sentimental societies for the prevention of cruelty to animals are the object.

"The frightful tortures," Herr Daumer exclaims on page 293 of Volume I, "that unfortunate beasts suffer at the tyrannous and cruel hand of man are for these barbarians 'rubbish' that nobody should bother about!"

The entire class struggle of our times seems to Herr Daumer only a struggle of "coarseness" against "culture." Instead of explaining it by the historical conditions of these classes, he finds its origin in the seditious doings of a few malevolent individuals who incite the base appetites of the populace against the educated estates.

"This democratic reformism . . . excites the envy, the rage, the rapacity of the lower classes of society against the upper classes—a clean way of making man better and nobler and founding a higher degree of culture!" (Vol. I, p. 289.)

Herr Daumer does not know what struggles "of the lower classes against the upper classes" it took to bring forth even a Nuremberg "degree of culture" and to make possible a Moloch fighter à la Daumer.

The second, "main" section contains the positive aspect of the new religion. It voices all the annoyance of the German philosopher over the oblivion into which his struggles against Christianity have fallen, over the people's indifference toward religion, the only object worthy to be considered by the philosopher. To restore credit to his trade, which has been ousted by competition, all our worldly-wise man can do is invent a new religion after long barking against the old. But this new religion is confined, in accordance with the first section, to a continuation of the anthology of maxims, verses from genealogical registers, and *versus memoriales* of German petty-bourgeois culture. The chapters of the new Koran are nothing but a series of phrases morally palliating and poetically embellishing existing German conditions—phrases which, though divested of their immediately religious form, are still part and parcel of the old religion.

"Completely new world conditions and world relations can arise only through new religions. Examples and proofs of what religions are capable of are Christianity and Islam; a most vivid and sensible evidence of the powerlessness and futility of external and abstract politics is provided by the movements started in the year 1848." (Vol. I, p. 313.)

This proposition so full of content immediately brings out the flatness and ignorance of the German "thinker," who takes the small German and specifically Bavarian "March achievements" for the European movement of 1848 and 1849 and who demands that the first, in themselves very superficial, eruptions of a gradually developing and concentrating major revolution should bring forth "completely new world conditions and world relations."

The worldly-wise Daumer reduces all the complicated social struggle whose first skirmishes ranged from Paris to Debrecen and from Berlin to Palermo in the past two years, to the fact that in January, 1849, "the hopes of the Constitutional Societies of Erlangen were postponed indefinitely" (Vol. I, p. 312) and to fear of a new struggle that could once more be unpleasantly shocking for Herr Daumer in his preoccupations with Hafiz, Mohammed, and Berthold Auerbach.

The same shameless superficiality allows Herr Daumer to ignore completely the fact that Christianity was preceded by the complete collapse of ancient "world conditions" of which Christianity was the mere expression; that "completely new world conditions" arose not internally through Christianity but only when the Huns and the Germans "fell externally on the corpse of the Roman Empire"; that after the Germanic invasion the "new world conditions" did not adapt themselves to Christianity but Christianity itself likewise changed with every new phase of these world conditions. We should like Herr Daumer to give us an example of the old world conditions changing with a new religion without the mightiest "external and abstract" political convulsions setting in at the same time.

It is clear that with every great historical upheaval of social conditions the outlooks and ideas of men, and consequently their religious ideas, are revolutionized. The difference between the present upheaval and all earlier ones lies in the very fact that man has found out the secret of this historical upheaval and hence, instead of once again exalting this practical, "external" process to the rapturous form of a new religion, divests himself of all religion.

After the gentle moral doctrines of the new world wisdom—which are even superior to Knigge inasmuch as they contain all that is necessary not on intercourse with men only, but on intercourse with animals—after the Proverbs of Solomon comes the Song of the new Solomon.

"Nature and woman are the really divine, as opposed to the human and to man. . . . The sacrifice of the human to the natural, of the male to the female, is the genuine, the only true subjection and self-alienation, the highest, nay, the only virtue and piety." (Vol. II, p. 257.)

We see here that the superficiality and ignorance of the speculating founder of a religion are transformed into very pronounced cowardice. Herr Daumer flees before the historic tragedy that is threatening him too closely, to alleged nature, i.e., to mere rustic idyll, and preaches the cult of the female to cloak his own effeminate resignation.

Herr Daumer's cult of nature, by the way, is a peculiar one. He has managed to be reactionary even in comparison with Christianity. He tries to establish the old pre-Christian natural religion in a modernized form. Thus he achieves nothing but Christian-Germanic-patriarchal drivel on nature, expressed, for example, as follows:

Nature holy, Mother sweet,
In Thy footsteps place my feet.
My baby hand to Thy hand clings,
Hold me as in leading strings!

"Such things have gone out of fashion, but not to the benefit of culture, progress, or human felicity." (Vol. II, p. 157.)

We see that this cult of nature is limited to the Sunday walks of an inhabitant of a small provincial town who childishly wonders at the cuckoo laying its eggs in another bird's nest (Vol. II, p. 40), at tears being designed to keep the surface of the eyes moist (Vol. II, p. 73), and so on, and finally trembles with reverence as he recites Klopstock's "Ode to Spring" to his children. (Vol. II, p. 23, et seq.) There is no question, of course, of modern sciences, which along with modern industry have revolutionized the whole of nature and put an end to man's childish attitude toward nature as well as to other forms of childishness. But instead we get mysterious hints and astonished philistine notions about Nostradamus' prophecies, second sight in Scotsmen, and animal magnetism. For the rest, it would be desirable that Bavaria's sluggish peasant economy, the ground on which priests and Daumers likewise grow, should at last be plowed up by modern cultivation and modern machines.

The position as regards the worship of the female is the same as with nature worship. Herr Daumer naturally does not say a word about the present social situation of women; on the contrary, it is a question only of the female as such. He tries to console women for their social distress by making them the object of a cult in words which are as empty as they try to be mysterious. Thus he puts women at ease over the fact that marriage puts an end to their talents through their having to take care of the children (Vol. II, p. 237) by telling them that they can suckle babes until the age of sixty (Vol. II, p. 244), and so on. Herr Daumer calls this the "sacrificing of the male to the female." In order to find the necessary ideal women characters for his sacrificing of the male in his native country, he is forced to resort to various aristocratic ladies of the last century. Thus his woman cult is reduced to the depressed attitude of a man of letters to respected patronesses. (See *Wilhelm Meister*.)

The "culture" whose decay Herr Daumer laments is that of the time in which Nuremberg flourished as a free *Reichsstadt*, in which Nuremberg industry—that cross between art and craftsmanship— played an important role, the German petty-bourgeois culture which is falling with that petty bourgeoisie. If the downfall of former classes such as the knighthood could offer subjects for magnificent tragic works of art, the philistine bourgeoisie can achieve nothing but powerless expressions of fanatic spite and a collection of Sancho Panza maxims and rules of wisdom. Herr Daumer is the dry, absolutely humorless continuation of Hans Sachs. German philosophy, wringing its hands and lamenting at the deathbed of its foster father, German philistine bourgeoisie—such is the touching picture opened up to us by the religion of the new age.

Priests as Political Police*

THE bourgeoisie never tired of crying out to the revolution what St. Arsenius cried out to the Christians: *"Fuge, tace, quiesce!"* ["Flee, be silent, keep still!"] Bonaparte cries to the bourgeoisie: *"Fuge, tace, quiesce!"* ... Another "Napoleonic idea" is the domination of the priests as an instrument of government. But while at the time of their emergence the small-holding owners, in their accord with society, in their dependence on natural forces and submission to the authority which protected them from above, were naturally religious, now that they are ruined by debts, at odds with society and authority, and driven beyond their own limitations, they have become naturally irreligious. Heaven was quite a pleasing addition to the narrow strip of land just won, especially as it makes the weather; it becomes an insult as soon as it is thrust forward as a substitute for the small holding. The priest then appears as only the anointed bloodhound of the earthly police—another "Napoleonic idea." ...

When the puritans of the Council of Constance [1414–18] complained of the dissolute lives of the popes and wailed about the necessity for moral reform, Cardinal Pierre d'Ailly thundered at them: "Only the devil in person can still save the Catholic Church, and you ask for angels."

---

* From *The Eighteenth Brumaire of Louis Napoleon* (1852), Section VII. For the complete text, see *Karl Marx on Revolution*, Vol. I of The Karl Marx Library, pp. 243–328.

Kinkel's Christianity*

GOTTFRIED KINKEL was born about forty years ago. His life is found in an autobiography: *Gottfried Kinkel. Wahrheit ohne Dichtung. Biographisches Skizzenbuch* [*Truth Without Poetry. Biographical Sketch*] (Hamburg, 1850). . . . "Like his friend Paul Zeller, the young Gottfried studied theology and through diligence and piety he 'won' the respect of his famous teachers" (Sack, Nitzsch, and Bleek). . . (p. 5).

Gottfried finds himself in the "social swim" (p. 190), one of those little professorial or "honorary circles" of small German university towns which could be important in the life of a Christian-Germanic candidate. Mockel[1] sings and is applauded. At the table it is arranged that Gottfried sit next to her. . . .

Gottfried was "enchanted" by this courtesy (p. 189). He was extremely pleased to discover "that Mockel was not happy." He immediately concludes that "with his warm enthusiasm for the belief in redemption through Jesus Christ," he will "redeem . . . this sad human soul *also*." Since Mockel is Catholic, the relationship is begun under the fancied motive of winning a soul in the "service of the Almighty," a comedy in which Mockel also joins.

"In the course of the year 1840 Kinkel also received the position of *Hülfs* candidate of the Evangelical Church in Cologne, whither he journeyed every Sunday morning to preach." (P. 193.) This re-

* From Marx and Engels, *Die grossen Männer des Exils* (*The Great Men of the Exile*), written May–June, 1852, but not published during their lifetime. This polemic against middle-class critics of the 1848–49 revolution, including Gottfried Kinkel, was first published, in Russian translation, by Moscow's Marx-Engels Institute in 1930.
1. Johanna Mockel, a writer whom Kinkel married.

mark by the biographer induces us to say a few words about Kinkel's standing as a theologian. "In the course of the year 1840" criticism had already disintegrated the content of Christianity in the most relentless form, the scientific . . . ,[2] had already, with Bruno Bauer, come into open conflict with the government. Kinkel emerged in that period as a preacher, but without the energy of orthodoxy on the one hand or the intelligence to comprehend theology objectively on the other, he finds himself in a sentimental, lyrical-declamatory relation to Christianity, à la Krummacher, in that he introduces Christ as "friend and leader," seeks to strip the form of Christianity of the "unlovely," and replaces its content with a hollow phraseology. This manner, which tries to replace content with form, ideas with phrases, has been promoted nowadays by a series of declamatory parsons, whose latest incursion must naturally lead to democracy. If here and there in theology there is still a need for at least a superficial knowledge, empty phraseology, on the contrary, finds its full application in democracy, where the hollow, high-sounding declaration, the *nullité sonore*, makes the spirit and insight of relationships entirely superfluous. Kinkel, whose theological studies lead to nothing more than sentimental extracts of Christianity in Claurenian presentation, has been, in his speeches and writings, the expression of this pulpit-oratory swindle, otherwise designated "poetic prose," which he now comically makes the pretext for his "occupation as poet." And his poesy does not rest in the putting on of actual laurels, but in the planting of red Jerusalem cherries, with which he beautifies the trivial highway.

---

2. A word is unreadable here, having been crossed out in the manuscript.

From *New-York Daily Tribune* Articles

Marx's first article for the Tribune *was published August 21, 1852. He continued to be its London correspondent for a decade, during which the* Tribune *published approximately two of his articles a week. The selections reproduced here were written in English. Marx's last* Tribune *piece appeared on March 10, 1862. His* Tribune *articles about the United States appear in* Karl Marx on America and the Civil War, *Vol. II of The Karl Marx Library (1972).*

THE EMANCIPATION OF THE IRISH FROM THEIR PRIESTS*

A TRANSFORMATION is now going on in the character and position of Irish parties, the deep bearing of which neither they nor the English press appear yet to be aware. The bishops and the mass of the clergy approve of the course taken by the Catholic members, who have joined the Administration. At Carlow, the clergy afforded their entire support to Mr. Sadleir, who would not have been defeated but for the efforts of the Tenant Leaguers.

In what light this schism is viewed by the true Catholic party may be seen from an article in the French *Univers,* the European organ of Jesuitism: "The only reproach which can with good foundation be objected to Messrs. Keogh and Sadleir is that they suffered themselves to be thrown into connection with two associations" (the Tenant League and the Religious Equality Association) "which have no other object than to make patent the anarchy which consumes Ireland."

---

* From "Defense—Finances—Decrease of the Aristocracy—Politics," published February 23, 1853.

In its indignation the *Univers* betrays its secret: "We deeply regret to see the two associations put themselves in open opposition to the bishops and clergy, in a country where the prelates and dignitaries of the Church have hitherto been the safest guides of popular and national organization."

We may infer that, should the Tenant Leaguers happen to be in France, the *Univers* would cause them to be transported to Cayenne. The Repeal agitation was a mere political movement, and therefore it was possible for the Catholic clergy to make use of it, for extorting concessions from the English Government while the people were nothing but tools of the priests. The tenant-rights agitation is a deep-rooted social movement which, in its course, will produce a downright scission between the Church and the Irish revolutionary party, and thus emancipate the people from that mental thralldom which has frustrated all their exertions, sacrifices, and struggles for centuries past.

IRISH ANTICLERICALISM*

ALLUSION has been made in a former letter[1] to the probability of the Irish tenant-rights agitation becoming, in time, an anticlerical movement, notwithstanding the views and intentions of its actual leaders. I alleged the fact that the higher clergy was already beginning to take a hostile attitude with regard to the League. Another force has since stepped into the field which presses the movement in the same direction. The landlords of the North of Ireland endeavor to persuade their tenantry that the Tenant League and the Catholic Defense Association are identical, and they labor to get up an opposition to the former under the pretense of resisting the progress of popery.

While we thus see the Irish landlords appealing to their tenants against the Catholic clergy, we behold on the other hand the English Protestant clergy appealing to the working classes against the mill lords. The industrial proletariat of England has renewed with double vigor its old campaign for the Ten Hours' Bill and against the truck and shoppage system. . . .

By 1850 the wrath of the landlords had gradually subsided and they made a compromise with the mill lords, condemning the shift system but imposing at the same time, as a penalty for the enforcement of the law, half an hour extra work per diem on the working classes. At the present juncture, however, as they feel the approach of their final struggle with the men of the Manchester School, they are again trying

* From "Parliamentary Debates—The Clergy and the Struggle for the Ten-Hour Day," published March 15, 1853.
1. *New-York Daily Tribune*, February 23, 1853.

to get hold of the short-time movement; but not daring to come forward themselves, they endeavor to undermine the cotton lords by directing the popular force against them through the medium of the state church clergyman. In what rude manner these holy men have taken the anti-industrial crusade into their hands may be seen from the following few instances.

At Crampton a Ten Hours' meeting was held, the Rev. Dr. Brammell in the chair. At this meeting, Rev. J. R. Stephens, incumbent of Stalybridge, said:

> There had been ages in the world when the nations were governed by Theocracy . . . That state of things is now no more . . . Still the spirit of law was the same . . . The laboring man should, first of all, be partaker of the fruits of the earth, which he was the means of producing. The factory law was so unblushingly violated that the Chief Inspector of that part of the factory district, Mr. Leonard Horner, had found himself necessitated to write to the Home Secretary to say that he dared not and would not send any of his subinspectors into certain districts until he had police protection . . . And protection against whom? Against the factory masters! Against the richest men in the district, against the most influential men in the district, against the magistrates of the district, against the men who hold Her Majesty's commission, against the men who sat in the Petty Sessions of the Representatives of Royalty . . . *And did the masters suffer for their violation of the law?* . . . In his own district, it was a settled custom of the male, and to a great extent of the female workers in factories, to be in bed till 9, 10, or 11 o'clock on Sunday, because they were tired out by the labor of the week. Sunday was the only day on which they could rest their wearied frames . . . It would generally be found that, the longer the time of work, the smaller the wages . . . *He would rather be a slave in South Carolina than a factory operative in England.*

At the great Ten Hours' meeting at Burnley, Rev. E. A. Verity, incumbent of Habbergham Eaves, told his audience, among other things:

> Where was Mr. Cobden, where was Mr. Bright, where were the other members of the Manchester School, when the people of Lancashire were oppressed? . . . What was the end of the rich man's thinking? . . . Why, he was scheming how he could defraud the working classes out of an hour or two. That was the scheming of what he called the Manchester School. That made them such cunning hypocrites, and such crafty rascals. As a minister of the Church of England, he protested against such work.

The motive that has so suddenly metamorphosed the gentlemen of the Established Church into as many knights-errant of labor's rights, and such fervent knights too, has already been pointed out. They are not only laying in a stock of popularity for the rainy days of approaching democracy, they are not only conscious that the Established Church is essentially an aristocratic institution, which must either stand or fall with the landed oligarchy—there is something more. The men of the Manchester School are anti–State Church men, they are Dissenters, they are, above all, so highly enamored of the £13,000,000 annually abstracted from their pockets by the state church in England and Wales alone, that they are resolved to bring about a separation between those profane millions and the holy orders, the better to qualify the latter for heaven. The reverend gentlemen, therefore, are struggling *pro aris et focis* [for hearth and altar]. The men of the Manchester School, however, may infer from this diversion that they will be unable to abstract the political power from the hands of the aristocracy unless they consent, with whatever reluctance, to give the people also their full share in it.

The Religious Conflict in Prussia*

Everyone not thoroughly acquainted with the past history of Germany will be at a loss to understand the religious quarrels again and again troubling the otherwise still surface of German society. There are the remnants of the so-called German Church, persecuted now as eagerly as in 1847 by the established governments. There is the question of marriages between Catholics and Protestants setting the Catholic clergy and the Prussian Government by the ears, as in 1847. There is, above all, the fierce combat between the Archbishop of Freiburg, excommunicating the Baden Government and having the letter publicly read from the pulpits, and the Grand Duke, ordering the miscreant churches to be closed and the parish priests to be arrested; and there are the peasants assembling and arming themselves, protecting their priests and driving back the gendarmes, which they have done at Bischofsheim, Königshofen, Grünsfeld, Gerlachsheim, where the mayor of the village was forced to flee, and at many other villages.

It would be a mistake to consider the religious conflict in Baden as possessed of a purely local character. Baden is only the battleground the Catholic party has deliberately chosen for attacking the Protestant princes. The Archbishop of Freiburg represents in the conflict the whole Catholic clergy of Germany, as the Grand Duke of Baden represents all the great and small potentates confessing the Re-

---

* From "Manteuffel's Speech—The Religious Conflict in Prussia . . , etc.," published December 12, 1853.

formed creed. What then are we to think of a country renowned on the one hand for the profound, bold, and unparalleled criticism to which it has subjected all religious traditions, and surprising, on the other, all Europe, at periodically recurring epochs, with the resurrection of the religious quarrels of the seventeenth century?

The secret is simply this, that all popular commotions, lurking in the background, are forced by the government to assume at first the mystical and almost uncontrollable form of religious movements. The clergy, on their part, allow themselves to be deceived by appearances, and, while they fancy they direct the popular passions for the exclusive benefit of their corporations against the government, they are, in truth, the unconscious and unwilling tools of the revolution itself.

THE CONFLICT BETWEEN THE LATIN AND GREEK CHURCHES*

The Blue Books begin with dispatches relating to the demands put forward on the part of France with respect to the Holy Shrines—demands not wholly borne out by the ancient capitulations,[2] and ostensibly made with the view to enforce the supremacy of the Latin over the Greek Church. I am far from participating in the opinion of Mr. Urquhart, according to which the Czar[3] had, by secret influence at Paris, seduced Bonaparte to rush into this quarrel in order to afford Russia a pretext for interfering herself in behalf of the privileges of the Greek Catholics. It is well known that Bonaparte wanted to buy, *coûte qui coûte* [at any cost], the support of the Catholic party, which he regarded from the very first as the main condition for the success of his usurpation.[4] Bonaparte was fully aware of the ascendancy of the Catholic Church over the peasant population of France, and the peasantry were to make him emperor in spite of the bourgeoisie and in spite of the proletariat. M. de Falloux, the Jesuit, was the most influential member of the first ministry he formed, and of which Odilon Barrot, the *soi-disant* Voltairean, was the nominal head.[5] The first resolution adopted by this ministry, on the very day after the inauguration of Bonaparte as President, was the famous expedition against the Roman Republic. M. de Montalembert, the chief of the Jesuit party,

---

* From "Russian Diplomacy—The Blue Book on the Oriental Question—Montenegro," published February 27, 1854.

2. Documents in which Oriental countries, among them Turkey, granted Europeans special commercial privileges.

3. Nicholas I.

4. On December 2, 1851, Louis Napoleon, President of France, overthrew the Republic and declared himself Emperor Napoleon III.

5. On Odilon Barrot and Louis Bonaparte's seizure of power, see Marx, "The Class Struggles in France, 1848–50," in *Karl Marx on Revolution*, Vol. I of the Karl Marx Library (1971), pp. 155–242.

was his most active tool in preparing the overthrow of the parliamentary regime and the *coup d'état* of December 2. In 1850 the *Univers,* official organ of the Jesuit party, called day after day on the French Government to take active steps for the protection of the interests of the Latin Church in the East. Anxious to cajole and win over the Pope,[6] and be crowned by him, Bonaparte had reasons to accept the challenge and make himself appear the "most Catholic" emperor of France. *The Bonapartist usurpation, therefore, is the true origin of the present Eastern complication.*

It is true that Bonaparte wisely withdrew his pretensions as soon as he perceived the Emperor Nicholas ready to make them the pretext for excluding him from the conclave of Europe, and Russia was, as usual, eager to utilize the events which she had not the power to create, as Mr. Urquhart imagines. But it remains a most curious phenomenon in history, that the present crisis of the Ottoman Empire has been produced by the same conflict between the Latin and Greek churches which once gave rise to the foundations of that Empire in Europe.

THE PROSPECTS OF A RELIGIOUS WAR IN ASIA*

A treaty of alliance is said to have been concluded between Russia, Khiva, Bokhara, and Kabul.

As to Dost Mahomed, the Ameer of Kabul, it would be quite natural that after having proposed in 1838 to England to place forever a feud of blood between himself and Russia, if the English Government required it, by causing the agent dispatched to him by the Czar to be killed, and being renewed in 1839 on the part of England by the Afghan expedition, by his expulsion from the throne, and by the most cruel and unscrupulous devastation of his country[7]—that Dost Mahomed should now endeavor to avenge himself upon his faithless ally. However, as the population of Khiva, Bokhara, and Kabul belong to the orthodox Mussulman faith of the Sunni, while the Persians adhere to the schismatic tenets of the Shiites, it is not to be supposed that they will ally themselves with Russia, being the ally of the Persians, whom they detest and hate, against England, the ostensible ally of the Padishah, whom they regard as the supreme commander of the faithful.

There is some probability of Russia having an ally in Tibet and the Tartar Emperor of China, if the latter be forced to retire into Man-

---

6. Pius IX.

* From ". . . China," published March 18, 1854.

7. In 1838–42 the British fought to conquer Afghanistan and were finally defeated.

churia and to resign the scepter of China proper. The Chinese rebels, as you know, have undertaken a regular crusade against Buddhism, destroying its temples and slaying its bonzes. But the religion of the Tartars is Buddhism, and Tibet, the seat of the great Lama and recognizing the suzerainty of China, is the sanctuary of the Buddhist faith. T'ai-p'ing-wang, if he succeeds in driving the Manchu Dynasty out of China, will therefore have to enter a religious war with the Buddhist powers of Tartary. Now as on both sides of the Himalayas Buddhism is confessed and as England cannot but support the new Chinese dynasty, the Czar is sure to side with the Tartar tribes, put them in motion against England, and awake religious revolts in Nepal itself. By the last Oriental mails we are informed that "the Emperor of China, in anticipation of the loss of Peking, had directed the governors of the various provinces to send the imperial revenue to Getol [Jehol], their old family seat and present summer residence in Manchuria, about eighty miles northeast of the Great Wall." The great religious war between the Chinese and the Tartars, which will spread over the Indian frontier, may consequently be regarded as near at hand.

CHURCH AND STATE IN TURKEY*

Indeed, we are told explicitly that the great end aimed at by the western powers is to put the Christian religion on a footing of equal rights with the Mohammedan in Turkey. Now either this means nothing at all or it means the granting of political and civil rights to both Mussulmans and Christians, without any reference to either religion, and without considering religion at all. In other words, it means the complete separation of state and church, of religion and politics. But the Turkish state, like all Oriental states, is founded upon the most intimate connection, we might almost say the identity, of state and church, politics and religion. The Koran is the double source of faith and law for that empire and its rulers. But how is it possible to equalize the faithful and the giaour, the Mussulman and the rajah, before the Koran? To do that it is necessary, in fact, to supplant the Koran by a new civil code, in other words to break down the framework of Turkish society and create a new order of things out of its ruins.

On the other hand, the main feature that distinguishes the Greek confession from all other branches of the Christian faith is the same identification of state and church, of civil and ecclesiastical life. So intimately interwoven were state and church in the Byzantine Empire

---

* From "The Greek Insurrection," published March 29, 1854.

that it is impossible to write the history of one without writing the history of the other. In Russia the same identity prevails, although there, in contradistinction to the Byzantine Empire, the church has been transformed into the mere tool of the state, the instrument of subjugation at home and of aggression abroad. In the Ottoman Empire, in conformity with the Oriental notions of the Turks, the Byzantine theocracy has been allowed to develop itself to such a degree that the parson of a parish is at the same time the judge, the mayor, the teacher, the executor of testaments, the assessor of taxes, the ubiquitous factotum of civil life, not the servant, but the master of all work. The main reproach to be cast upon the Turks in this regard is not that they have crippled the privileges of the Christian priesthood, but, on the contrary, that under their rule this all-embracing oppressive tutelage, control, and interference of the church has been permitted to absorb the whole sphere of social existence. Mr. Fallmerayer very amusingly tells in his *Orientalische Briefe* how a Greek priest was quite astonished when he informed him that the Latin clergy enjoyed no civil authority at all, and had to perform no profane business. "How," exclaimed the priest, "do our Latin brethren contrive to kill time?"

It is plain then that to introduce a new civil code in Turkey, a code altogether abstracted from religion and based on a complete separation of state and church, would be not only to abolish Mohammedanism but also to break down the Greek Church as now established in that empire. Can anyone be credulous enough to believe in good earnest that the timid and reactionary valetudinarians of the present British Government have ever conceived the idea of undertaking such a gigantic task, involving a perfect social revolution, in a country like Turkey? The notion is absurd. They can only entertain it for the purpose of throwing dust in the eyes of the English people and of Europe.

THE DECAY OF RELIGIOUS AUTHORITY*

The days in which religious considerations were a governing element in the wars of Western Europe are, it seems, long gone by. The Treaty of Westphalia, in 1648, which wound up the Thirty Years' War in Germany, marks the epoch when such questions lost their force and disappeared as a prime cause of international strife. The attitude of the two great powers of Western Europe in the present war against Russia is a striking illustration of this truth. There we see England, professedly Protestant, allied with France, professedly Catholic ("damnably heretical" as they naturally are in each other's eyes, according to the orthodox phraseology of both), for the purpose of

---

* Published by the *Tribune* as a "leader," or editorial article, October 24, 1854.

defending Turkey, a Mohammedan power whose destruction they ought most religiously to desire, against the aggressions of "holy" Russia, a power Christian like themselves; and though the position of Austria and Prussia is more equivocal than that of England and France, the maintenance of the Mussulman Empire in its integrity against the assaults of its Christian neighbor to the north is an object that has been avowed and guaranteed equally with France and England by the two great powers of Christian Germany. Religious considerations are certainly not the influences which restrain them from action against Russia.

To perfectly appreciate this state of things we must call to mind the period of the Crusades, when Western Europe, as late as the eighteenth century, undertook a "holy war" against the "infidel" Turks for the possession of the Holy Sepulchre. Now Western Europe not only acquiesces in Mussulman jurisdiction over the Sepulchre but goes so far as to laugh at the contests and rivalries of the Greek and Latin monks for undivided possession of a shrine once so much coveted by all Christendom; and when Christian Russia steps forward to "protect" the Christian subjects of the Porte, the Western Europe of today arrays itself in arms against the czar to thwart a design which it would once have deemed highly laudable and righteous. To drive the Moslems out of Europe would once have roused the zeal of England and France; to prevent the Turks from being driven out of Europe is now the most cherished resolve of those nations. So broad a gulf stands between Europe of the nineteenth and Europe of the thirteenth century! So fallen away since the latter epoch is the political influence of religious dogma.

We have carefully watched for any expression of the purely ecclesiastical view of the European crisis, and have found only one pamphlet by a Cambridge D.D. and one North British review for England, and the Paris *Univers* for France, which have dogmatically represented the defense of a Mohammedan power by Christendom as absolutely sinful; and these pronunciamentos have remained without an echo in either country. Whence is this?

From the period of the Protestant Reformation, the upper classes in every European nation, whether it remained Catholic or adopted Protestantism—and especially the statesmen, legalists, and diplomats—began to unfasten themselves individually from all religious belief, and become so-called freethinkers. This intellectual movement in the higher circles manifested itself without reserve in France from the time of Louis XIV, resulting in the universal predilection for what was denominated philosophy during the eighteenth century. But when Voltaire found residence in France no longer safe, not because of his opinions, nor because he had given oral expression to them, but because he had communicated them by his writings to the whole reading public, he betook himself to England and testified that he found the solons of high life in London still "freer" than those of Paris. Indeed, the men and women of the court of Charles II, Bolingbroke, the Walpoles, Hume, Gibbon, and Charles Fox, are names which all suggest a prevalent unbelief in religious dogmas, and a general adhesion to the philosophy of that age on the part of the upper classes, statesmen, and politicians of England. This may be called, by way of distinction, the era of aristocratic revolt against ecclesiastical authority. Comte, in one short sentence, has characterized this situation:

"From the opening of the revolutionary period in the sixteenth century this system of hypocrisy has been more and more elaborated in practice, *permitting the emancipation of all minds of a certain bearing*, on the tacit condition that they should aid in protracting the submission of the masses. This was eminently the policy of the Jesuits."

This brings us down to the period of the French Revolution, when the masses, first of France, and afterward of all Western Europe, along with a desire for political and social freedom, began to entertain an ever growing aversion to religious dogma. The total abolition of Christianity as a recognized institution of state by the French Republican Convention of 1793, and since then the gradual repeal in Western Europe, wherever the popular voice has had power, of religious tests and political and civil disabilities of the same character, together with the Italian movement of 1848, sufficiently announce the well-known direction of the popular mind in Europe. We are still witnesses of this epoch, which may be characterized as the era of democratic revolt against ecclesiastical authority.

But this very movement among the masses since the French Revolution, bound up as it was with the movement for social equality, brought about in high quarters a violent reaction in favor of church authority. Nobility and clergy, lords temporal and lords spiritual, found themselves equally threatened by the popular movement, and it naturally came to pass that the upper class of Europe threw aside their skepticism in public life and made an outward alliance with the state churches and their systems. This reaction was most apparent in France, first under Bonaparte and during the Restoration under the older branch of the Bourbons, but it was not less the case with the rest of Western Europe. In our own day we have seen renewed on a smaller scale this patching up of an alliance offensive and defensive between the upper classes and the ecclesiastical interest. Since the epoch of the 1830s the statesmen had begun to manifest anew a spirit of independence toward ecclesiastical control, but the events of 1848 threw them back into the arms of Mother Church. Again France gave the clearest exemplification of this phenomenon. In 1849, when the terror of the democratic deluge was at its height, Messrs. Thiers, De Hauranne, and the Universitarians (who had passed for atheists with the clergy), together with the so-called Liberal Opposition, were unanimous in supporting that admirably qualified "savior of religion," M. Bonaparte,[8] in his project for the violent restoration of the Pope of Rome, while the Whig ministry of Protestant England, at whose head was a member of the ultra-Protestant family of Russell, were warm in their approval of the same expedition. This religious restoration by such processes was indeed redeemed from universal ridicule only by the extremely critical posture of affairs which for the moment, in the interest of "order," did not allow the public men of Europe to indulge in the sense of the ludicrous.

But the submission of the classes of leading social influence to ecclesiastical control, which was hollow and hypocritical at the beginning of this century after the Revolution of 1792, has been far more precarious and superficial since 1848, and is only acknowledged by those classes so far as it suits their immediate political interest. The humiliating position of utter dependence which the ecclesiastical power sustains toward the temporal arm of government has been made fully manifest since 1848. The Pope, indebted to the French Government for his present tenure of the chair of St. Peter; the French clergy, for the bulk of their salaries, blessing trees of liberty and proclaiming the sovereignty of the people, and afterward canonizing the present Emperor of France as the chosen instrument of God and the savior of religion, their old proper doctrines of legitimacy and the divine right of kings being in each case laid aside with the downfall of the corresponding political regime; the Anglican clergy, whose *ex officio* head is a temporal Queen, dependent for promotion on the recommendation of the Prime Minister, now generally a liberal, and looking for favors and support against popular encroachment to Parliament in which the liberal element is ever on the increase—constitute an *ensemble* from which it would be absurd to expect acts of pure ecclesiastical independence, except in the normally impossible case of an overwhelming popular support to fall back upon.

Such was the position of affairs in 1853, when the governing classes of England and France deemed it necessary and politic to espouse the cause of the Ottoman Porte against the Christian Czar; and that policy was not only sanctioned, but in a measure forced upon them by the popular sentiment of the two nations. Then the governments of France and England entered upon a policy totally inconsistent with religious considerations, and threw off unhesitatingly their feigned ecclesiastical

---

8. Napoleon III.

alliances. Then at length the upper-class current of revolt (which had been so long dissembled) formed a juncture with the broad popular current, and the two together, like the Missouri and the Mississippi, rolled onward a tide of opinion which the ecclesiastical power saw it would be madness to encounter. Beneath this twofold assault the pure ecclesiastical point of view has not dared to manifest itself; while, on the contrary, the state clergy of England, on the appointed day of the national fast and humiliation, had to pray and preach patriotic sermons on behalf of the success of the Crescent and its allies. These considerations seem to afford a rational explanation of two apparent anomalies with which we started; namely, the defense of the Crescent by allied Catholic and Protestant Europe against the assault of the Cross, as represented by Christian Russia, and the fact that no voice of any influence has been lifted up to denounce to Christendom the moral position in which it is placed.

The coalition between the politicians of Western Europe and the popular opinion in behalf of a purely secular policy is likely to generate ulterior consequences and to subject ecclesiastical influence to further shocks from its old accomplices, the politicians. It is doubtless owing to the ripeness of the public mind in this respect that Lord Palmerston ventured to refuse the request of the Edinburgh Presbytery for a day of public fast and humiliation to avert the divine scourge of cholera, the Home Secretary audaciously averring that prayers would be of no consequence unless they cleansed their streets and habitations, and that cholera was generated by natural causes, such as deleterious gases from decomposed vegetable matter. The vain and unscrupulous Palmerston knew that buffeting the clergy would be a cheap and easy way of acquiring popularity, otherwise he would not have ventured on the experiment.

A further evidence of the extreme incompetence of ecclesiastical policy to answer the exigencies of the European situation is found in the consideration that the ecclesiastical view, if logically carried out, would condemn Catholic Europe to total indifference to the present European crisis; for though it might be permissible for Anglican orthodoxy to side with the Greek Cross against the Turkish Crescent, Catholic Europe could not unite with so impious a denier of the authority of the successor of St. Peter and so unhallowed a pretender to the highest spiritual functions as the Czar of Russia, and would apparently have no other opinion to utter than that both the belligerent parties were inspired by Satan!

To complete the disparagement which ecclesiastical authority has undergone in the present European crisis, it is patent to the world that while the advanced communities of Western Europe are in a forward stage of ecclesiastical decay, on the other hand, in barbarian Russia the state church retains a powerful and undiminished vigor. While Western Europe, discarding religious biases, has advanced in defense of "right against might" and "for the independence of Europe," "holy" Russia has claimed for its war of might against right a religious sanction as a war of the vice-regent of God against the infidel Turks. It is true that Nesselrode, in his state papers, has never had the assurance in the face of Europe to appeal to the ecclesiastical aspect of the question, and this is in itself a remarkable symptom of the decline of the ecclesiastical sentiment; this method of treatment is reserved by the Russian Court for internal use among the ignorant and credulous Muscovites, and the miracle pictures, the relics, the crusading proclamations of the Russian generals show how much stress is there laid upon the religious phase of the struggle for inflaming the zeal of the Russian people and army. Even the St. Petersburg journals do not omit to cast in the teeth of France and England the reproach that they are fighting on behalf of the abhorred Crescent against the religion of the Cross. Such a contrast between religious Russia and secular France and England is worthy of a profound and thorough examination, which we cannot undertake to give it, our object being simply to call to these large, impressive, and novel facts a degree of attention they have not hitherto received. They are facts which perhaps the philosophic and religious historians of the future will alone be able to appreciate at their exact value. They appear, however, to constitute an important step in the great movement of the world toward abrogating absolute authority and establishing the independence of individual judgment and conscience in the religious as well as the political sphere of life. To defend or attack that movement is not our purpose; our duty is discharged in the simple attestation of its progress.

FERDINAND VII AND GOD*

Ferdinand VII showed his true character to the end. If he deceived the *Liberales* with false promises throughout his whole life, why should he not permit himself the jest of deceiving the *Serviles* on his deathbed? In religious matters he had always been a skeptic. Nothing could ever convince him that anyone—even the Holy Ghost—could be so simple as to tell the truth.

---

* From "Spain—Intervention," written (in German) November 21, 1854, for the *New-York Daily Tribune*, but unpublished. The *Liberales* were the representatives of the middle class and the liberal aristocracy, the *Serviles* the clerical champions of monarchical absolutism.

THE JUGGERNAUT*

The infamous mutilations committed by the Sepoys remind one of the practices of the Christian Byzantine Empire, or the prescriptions of Emperor Charles V's criminal law, or the English punishments for high treason as recorded by Judge Blackstone. With Hindus, whom their religion has made virtuosi in the art of self-torturing, these tortures inflicted on the enemies of their race and creed appear quite natural, and must appear still more so to the English, who only some years since still used to draw revenues from Juggernaut festivals, protecting and assisting the bloody rites of a religion of cruelty.

---

* From "The Indian Revolt," published September 16, 1857.

Sunday Closing in England*

London, January 19

AT this moment there is a lively debate in the *Morning Advertiser* over
the controversial question of whether the Coalition Ministry could
be rightly accused of "stupidity." From his standpoint, Urquhart, who
presupposes a secret understanding between the ministry and Russia,
happily defends the ministry against the accusation of incompetence.
The *Morning Advertiser* is a peculiar phenomenon of the English
press. Property of the "Society for the Protection of the Licensed
Publicans," founded for charitable purposes, specifically for the support
of orphans, veterans, and bankrupts, it undoubtedly enjoys the widest
circulation of all London dailies after the *Times*. Surely not because
of its editorship, under the direction of a certain Grant, a quondam
stenographer. This Grant married the daughter of the biggest man in
the "Protection Society," namely Homer, the great Homer, as the
United Publicans call him, and the great Homer made his little son-in-
law editor-in-chief of the *Morning Advertiser*. Since the society had it
in its power to push the *Advertiser* in every bar and even in most
"parlors," the material foundation for its greatness was established. For
its influence, however, it has to thank the circumstance that it is *not
edited* but constitutes rather a megaphone into which every publican
can speak. Not admitted into the "respectable" London journalism
because of being unequal in birth, it revenges itself on the fraternity

---

* From "The Publicans and Sunday Closing . . ." published in the *Neue
Oder-Zeitung*, January 22, 1855.

by opening its columns, in addition to the public, also to important writers who have not sold themselves to any party.

From the *Morning Advertiser* to beer and the latest beer acts of Mr. Wilson-Patten is not even one jump. This recent *coup d'état* of the church-minded has evoked much humor and has proved that the Shakespearean prototypes, etc., still flourish in the second half of the nineteenth century. The serious side, however, is the astonishment of the masses at this arrogance on the part of the church to disturb and regulate civil life with its intervention. So alienated are they from this church that its attempts at encroachment are taken as "practical jokes," which, however, are resisted when they become burdensome. The church party, which does not understand its situation, had the impudence to hold a public meeting last night [Sunday] at Nottingham, where it proposed that a petition be sent to Parliament for the closing of all pubs not only for the hours recently set by Wilson-Patten but also for all day Sunday. An immense audience of workers was present, and after a stormy session the following amendment by a factory worker named Halton was carried by a great majority: "To petition Parliament that all churches and chapels be closed on Sundays."

The Anti-Church Movement*

I

IT is an old and historic maxim that obsolete social forces, nominally
still in possession of all attributes of power and continuing to vegetate
after the basis of their existence has long rotted away under their feet,
inasmuch as the heirs are quarreling among themselves even before
the obituary notice has been printed and the will read—that these
forces once more summon all their strength before their last death
struggle, pass from the defensive to the offensive, make demands instead of retreating, and try to draw the most extreme conclusions from
premises which have not only been put in question but are already
condemned. Such is now the English oligarchy. Such is the church,
its twin sister. Countless attempts at reorganization have been made
within the Established Church, both the High and the Low, attempts
to come to an understanding with the Dissenters and thus to confront
the profane mass of the nation with a compact force. There has been
a rapid succession of religious coercive measures. The pious Earl of
Shaftesbury, formerly known as Lord Ashley, lamented in the House
of Lords the fact that in England alone five million people are altogether alienated not only from the church but also from Christianity
in general. *"Compelle intrare"* ["Force them to enter"], replies the
Established Church. It leaves it to Lord Ashley and other such dis-

---

* "Anti-Church Movement—A Demonstration in Hyde Park," published in
the *Neue Oder-Zeitung*, June 28, July 5, 1855. This text is based on a translation
in Karl Marx and Frederick Engels, *On Britain*, published by the Foreign Languages Publishing House, Moscow, 1962 (2nd ed.).

senting, sectarian, and overexcited pietists to pull out of the fire the chestnuts it means to eat.

The first measure of religious coercion was the Beer Bill, which shut down all places of public entertainment on Sundays, except between 6:00 and 10:00 P.M. The bill was smuggled through the House at the end of a sparsely attended session, after the pietists had bought the support of the big London beer-pub owners by guaranteeing them that the license system, that is, the monopoly of big capital, would continue. Then came the Sunday Trading Bill, which has now passed its third reading in the Commons and separate clauses of which have just been debated by the Committee of the Whole. This new coercive measure also had the assured support of big capital, because only small shopkeepers keep open on Sunday and the owners of the big stores are quite ready to do away with the Sunday competition of the small shops through parliamentary means. In both cases there is a conspiracy between the church and monopoly capital, but in both cases there are religious penal laws against the lower classes to assuage the consciences of the upper classes. The Beer Bill affected the aristocratic clubs as little as the Sunday Trading Bill did the Sunday pursuits of genteel society. The workers receive their wages late on Saturday; hence they are the only ones for whom shops open on Sunday. They are the only ones who are compelled to do their shopping, small as it is, on Sundays. Hence the new bill is directed only against them. In the eighteenth century the French aristocracy said: For us, Voltaire; for the people, the Mass and the Tithe. In the nineteenth century the English aristocracy says: For us, pious phrases; for the people, Christian practice. The classical saints of Christianity castigated *their* bodies for the salvation of the souls of the masses; the modern, educated saints castigate the *body of the masses* for the salvation of their own souls.

This alliance between a dissolute, degenerate, and pleasure-seeking aristocracy and a church propped up by the filthy profit calculus of beer magnates and monopolistic wholesalers led yesterday to a mass demonstration in Hyde Park, the like of which London has not seen since the death of George IV, the "first gentleman of Europe." We were spectators from beginning to end, and we do not think we exaggerate in saying that the *English revolution began yesterday in Hyde Park.* The latest news from the Crimea acted as an effective ferment on this "unparliamentary," "extraparliamentary," and "antiparliamentary" demonstration.

Lord Robert Grosvenor, the author of the Sunday Trading Bill, when reproached on the score that it was a law against the poor and not against the rich classes, replied: "The aristocracy to a large extent refrains from using its servants and horses on Sundays."

In the last days of the past week one could read on the walls of London a Chartist poster in big letters:

New Sunday Bill prohibiting newspapers, shaving, smoking, eating and drinking and all kinds of recreation and nourishment, both corporal and spiritual, which the poor people still enjoy at the present time. An open-air meeting of artisans, workers and "the lower orders" generally of the capital will take place in Hyde Park on Sunday afternoon to see how religiously the aristocracy is observing the Sabbath and how anxious it is not to use its servants and horses on that day, as Lord Robert Grosvenor said in his speech. The meeting is called for three o'clock on the right bank of the Serpentine on the side toward Kensington Gardens. Come and bring your wives and children in order that they may profit by the example their "betters" set them!

It should be kept in mind that what Longchamps is to Parisians, the road along the Serpentine in Hyde Park is to English high society—the place where of an afternoon, particularly on Sunday, they parade their splendid carriages and horses with all their trappings, followed by swarms of lackeys. It will be realized from the above poster that the struggle against clericalism in England assumes the same character as every other serious struggle there—that of a *class struggle* of the poor against the rich, the people against the aristocracy, the "lower orders" against their "betters."

At three o'clock approximately 50,000 people had gathered at the announced spot on the right bank of the Serpentine in Hyde Park's vast meadows—and from the approaches on the other bank this swelled to at least 200,000. One could see smaller groups of milling people being shoved about from place to place. The large number of constables present were obviously trying to deprive the organizers of the meeting of what Archimedes had asked for to move the earth, namely, a place to stand on. Finally, a large crowd made a firm stand, and [James] Bligh, the Chartist, constituted himself chairman on a small eminence in the midst of the throng. He had hardly begun his harangue when Police Inspector Banks, at the head of forty truncheon-swinging constables, informed him that the park was the private property of the Crown and that no meeting was permitted to be held there.

After some *pourparlers*, with Bligh attempting to demonstrate to Banks that parks were public property and the latter answering that he had strict orders to arrest him if he persisted in his intentions, Bligh shouted amidst the immense roar of the crowds surrounding him: "Her Majesty's police declare that Hyde Park is private property of the Crown and that Her Majesty is unwilling to let her land be used by the people for their meetings. So let's move to Oxford Market."

With the ironic cry, "God save the Queen!" the throng broke up

to move to Oxford Market. But meanwhile [James] Finlen, a member
of the Chartist executive committee, rushed to a tree some distance
away, followed by a crowd which quickly formed so tight and compact
a circle around him that the police abandoned their attempt to get
through to him. "Six days a week," he said, "we are treated like slaves,
and now Parliament wants to rob us of the little bit of freedom we still
have on the seventh. These oligarchs and capitalists allied with the
sanctimonious parsons want to do penance by mortifying us instead
of themselves for the unconscionable murder of the sons of the people
in the Crimea."

We left the group to approach another, where a speaker stretched
out on the ground harangued his audience from this horizontal position.
Suddenly shouts sounded on all sides: "Let's go to the road, let's go to
the carriages!" Meanwhile, the heaping of insults on horse riders and
occupants of carriages had already begun. The constables, who constantly received reinforcements from the city, drove the promenading
pedestrians off the carriage road. They thus helped to make both sides
of the road become deeply lined with people, from Apsley House up
Rotten Row along the Serpentine as far as Kensington Gardens—a
distance of more than a quarter of an hour's walk. The spectators
consisted of about two-thirds workers and one-third members of the
middle class, all with women and children. The involuntary actors,
elegant ladies and gentlemen, "commoners and lords," in their tall
coaches-and-four with liveried lackeys fore and aft, joined by a few
mounted elderly fellows slightly flushed by port wine, this time did
not pass in review but were made to run the gantlet. A Babel of
jeering, taunting, discordant shouts, in which no language is as rich as
English, soon bore down upon them from both sides. As it was an
improvised concert, instruments were lacking. The chorus, therefore,
had only its own organs at its disposal and had to confine itself to
vocal music. And a diabolic concert it was: a cacophony of grunting,
hissing, whistling, squeaking, snarling, growling, croaking, shrieking,
groaning, rattling, howling, gnashing sounds! A music that could drive
one mad and move a stone. To this must be added outbursts of genuine
Old English humor peculiarly mixed with long-contained boiling wrath.
"Go to church!" were the only articulate sounds that could be distinguished. One lady appeasingly offered a prayer book in orthodox
binding from her carriage in her outstretched hand. "Give it to your
horses to read!" came the thundering reply, echoing a thousand voices.
When the horses started to shy, buck, and finally run away, jeopardiz-
ing the lives of their elegant burdens, the derisive cries grew louder,
more menacing, more ruthless. Noble lords and ladies, among them Lady
Granville, wife of a Minister and President of the Privy Council, were
forced to alight and make use of their own legs. When elderly gentle-

men, wearing broad-brimmed hats and otherwise so appareled as to betray their special claim to perfection in religion, rode by, the strident outbursts of fury were extinguished, as if in obedience to a command, by irrepressible laughter. One of those gentlemen lost his patience. Like Mephistopheles, he made an indecent gesture, sticking out his tongue at the enemy. "He is a windbag, a parliamentary man! He fights with his own weapons!" someone shouted on one side of the road. "He is a saint! He is singing psalms!" was the antistrophe from the opposite side. In the meantime the metropolitan telegraph had informed all police stations that a riot was about to break out in Hyde Park and the police were ordered to the theater of military operations. Soon one detachment of police after another marched at short intervals through the double file of people, from Apsley House to Kensington Gardens, each received with the popular ditty:

Where are the geese?
Ask the police!

This was a hint at a notorious theft of geese recently committed by a constable in Clerkenwell.

The spectacle lasted three hours. Only English lungs could perform such a feat. During the performance one heard among various groups such opinions as: "This is only the beginning," "That is the first step," "We hate them," etc. While rage was to be read on the faces of the workers, such smiles of blissful self-satisfaction covered the physiognomies of the middle classes as we had never seen there before. Shortly before the end, the demonstration increased in violence. Canes were raised against the carriages and through the endless dissonance one could hear the cry: "You rascals!" During the three hours zealous Chartists, men and women, plowed their way through the crowd and distributed leaflets which stated in big type:

Reorganization of Chartism!
A big public meeting will take place next Tuesday, June 26, in the Literary and Scientific Institute in Friar Street, Doctors' Commons, to elect delegates to a conference for the reorganization of Chartism in the capital. Admission free.

Most of the London papers today carry only a brief report of the events in Hyde Park. No editorials as yet, except in Lord Palmerston's *Morning Post*. "A spectacle," the editorial says, "both disgraceful and dangerous in the extreme has taken place in Hyde Park, an open violation of law and decency—an illegal interference by physical force in the free action of the legislature. The scene must not be allowed to be repeated next Sunday, as has been threatened."

At the same time, however, it declares that the "fanatical" Lord Grosvenor is solely "responsible" for this mischief, being the man who had provoked the "just indignation of the people"! As if Parliament had not adopted Lord Grosvenor's bill in three readings! Or perhaps he too brought his influence to bear "by physical force on the free action of the legislature?"

II

The anti-Sunday Bill demonstration was repeated yesterday in Hyde Park—on a larger scale, under more menacing auspices, with more serious consequences. This is attested to by the sullen excitement that prevails in London today.

The posters which called for a repetition of the meeting also contained an invitation to assemble Sunday morning, ten o'clock, in front of pious Lord Grosvenor's house to accompany him on his way to church. The pious gentleman, however, had meanwhile already left London on Saturday in a private coach in order to travel incognito. That he is more fit by nature to martyrize others than to become a martyr himself was proved by the statement he published in all the London newspapers, in which, on the one hand, he sticks to his bill and, on the other, endeavors to show that it is senseless, purposeless, and meaningless. His house was occupied all of Sunday not by psalm singers but by constables, two hundred in number. Likewise that of his brother, the Marquis of Westminster, renowned for his wealth.

Sir Richard Mayne, London's chief of police, had plastered the walls of London on Saturday with posters in which he "prohibited" the holding not only of any meeting in Hyde Park but also of any assembly there "in great numbers" or the manifestation of any sign of approval or disapproval. The result of these ukases was that even according to the account given in the police bulletin at half past two 150,000 people of every age and social estate already surged up and down the park and that gradually the throng swelled to such dimensions as were gigantic and enormous even for London. Not only was London present *en masse;* once again the crowd lined both sides of the drive along the Serpentine, only this time the lines were denser and deeper than the previous Sunday. However, high society did not put in an appearance. Altogether perhaps twenty carriages showed up, mostly small gigs and phaetons. These were allowed to pass unmolested, while their more imposing, bigger-bellied counterparts with higher box seats and more gold trimmings were greeted with the old cries, with the old Babel of shouts whose reverberations this time rent the air for a mile around. The police ukases were nullified by this mass meeting and the exercise of their lungs by the thousands of its participants. High society had given wide berth to the place of combat and by its absence had acknowledged *vox populi* to be sovereign.

It got to be four o'clock and it looked as if for lack of nutrition the demonstration was going to simmer down to harmless Sunday amusements, but the police reckoned differently. Were they going to withdraw amidst general laughter, casting melancholy farewell glances at their own big-lettered placards posted up on the portals of the park? Besides, their grand dignitaries were present: Sir Richard Mayne and Chief Superintendents Gils and Walker superbly mounted, Inspectors Banks, Derkin, and Brennan on foot. Eight hundred constables had been strategically distributed, mostly in buildings and ambuscades. Big squads were stationed in neighboring localities to serve as reinforcements. The house of the chief superintendent of the park, the powder magazine, and the buildings of the life-saving societies, all situated at one spot where the drive along the Serpentine turns into a path leading to Kensington Gardens, had been converted into improvised blockhouses held by strong police forces and equipped for the reception of prisoners and wounded. Cabs were lined up at the Vine Street, Piccadilly, Police Station, under orders to proceed to the battle scene and haul back the vanquished safely escorted. In brief, the police had drawn up a plan of campaign which was "of a far more vigorous description," according to the *Times*, "than any of which we have yet had notice in the Crimea." The police were in need of bloody heads and arrests so as not to fall from the sublime to the ridiculous without some intermediate link. Thus as soon as the rows of people thinned and the masses separated into groups spread over the vast space of the park and at some distance from the drive, their chiefs planted themselves in the middle of the drive, between the two lines of people, and with an air of importance issued orders right and left from their seats on horseback—allegedly for the protection of passing carriages and riders. But as both carriages and riders stayed away and there was therefore nothing to protect, they began to single some individuals out of the crowd and have them arrested "on false pretenses," on the pretext that they were pickpockets. When this experiment was repeated more and more often and the pretext no longer sounded plausible, the crowd raised one big cry. At once the constabulary rushed from ambush, whipped their truncheons out of their pockets, began to beat people's heads until the blood ran profusely, yanked individuals here and there out of the vast multitude (a total of 104 were thus arrested), and dragged them to the improvised blockhouses. Only a small strip of land separates the left side of the drive from the Serpentine. Here an officer of the police and his detail maneuvered the spectators to the very brink of the lake, threatening to give them a cold-water bath. To escape the clubbing one of the crowd swam across the Serpentine to the opposite shore, but a policeman followed him in a boat, caught him, and brought him back triumphantly.

How the character of the scene had changed since last Sunday! Instead of stately carriages dirty cabs, which drove off from Vine Street Police Station to the improvised prisons in Hyde Park and then returned to the station house. Instead of a lackey a constable was seated on the box beside the drink-sodden cabby. Instead of elegant ladies and gentlemen the cab inmates were people under arrest, their heads bloody, their hair disheveled, their clothes torn, their bodies exposed, under guard of suspicious fellows—Irish gutter proletarians pressed into the service of the London police. Instead of the waving of fans in the air—the swishing of constables' truncheons. Last Sunday the ruling classes showed their fashionable physiognomy; this time they showed their state physiognomy. The background of the old gents with friendly grins, of the stylish fops, the genteel superannuated widows, the beauties arrayed in cashmere, ostrich feathers, and diamonds and fragrant with garlands of flowers, was the constable with his waterproof jacket, greasy oilskin hat, and truncheon. It was the reverse side of the medal. Last Sunday the masses were confronted by the ruling class as individuals. This time it appeared as the state power, the law, the truncheon. This time resistance meant insurrection, and the Englishman must be provoked for a long time before he breaks out in insurrection. Hence the counterdemonstration was confined, in the main, to hissing, jeering, and whistling at the police wagons, to isolated and feeble attempts at liberating the arrested, but above all to passive resistance in phlegmatically standing their ground.

Characteristic was the role assumed in this spectacle by the soldiers, some of whom belonged to the Guards and others to the 66th Regiment. There was quite a contingent. Twelve of the Guards, some decorated with Crimea medals, found themselves in a group of men, women, and children on whom the police were exercising their truncheons. A blow knocked an old man to the ground. "The London stiffstaffs" (a nickname for the police) "are worse than the Russians at Inkerman," exclaimed one of the Crimea heroes. The police laid hands on him. He was immediately freed amidst the shouts of the crowd: "Three cheers for the army!" The police considered it advisable to move on. Meanwhile a number of grenadiers had come up. They formed into a squad and, surrounded by a mass of people shouting "Long live the army!" "Down with the police!" "Down with the Sunday Bill!" they proudly marched up and down the park. The police stood irresolute when a sergeant of the Guards came up and took them loudly to task for their brutality. He then calmed down the soldiers and persuaded some of them to follow him to the barracks to avoid more serious collisions. But most of the soldiers remained and right there in the midst of the crowd gave vent to their fury against the police in unrestrained measure. The antagonism between the police and the army is as old as the hills in England. The present moment, when the army is the "pet child" of the masses, is certainly not apt to weaken it.

An old man by the name of Russell is said to have died today from the wounds he received; half a dozen wounded are lying in St. George's Hospital. During the demonstration several attempts were again made to hold separate meetings in various places. At one of them, near Albert's Gate, outside the part of the park which the police had originally occupied, an anonymous speaker harangued his audience somewhat as follows:

"Men of Old England! Awake, rise from your slumbers, or be forever fallen! Oppose it every succeeding Sunday, as you have done today. . . . Don't be afraid to demand your rights and privileges, but throw off the shackles of oligarchical oppression and misrule. If you do not do as I tell you, you will be irretrievably oppressed and ruined. Is it not a pity that the inhabitants of this great metropolis—the greatest in the civilized world—should have their liberties placed in the hands of my Lord Robert Grosvenor and such men as Lord Ebrington? . . . His lordship wants to drive us to church and make us religious by Act of Parliament; but it won't do. Who are we and who are they? Look at the present war; is it not carried on at the expense and the sacrifice of blood of the producing classes? And what do the nonproducing classes do? They bungle it."

The speaker as well as the meeting were stopped, of course, by the police.

In Greenwich, near the observatory, the Londoners likewise held a meeting, attended by 10,000–15,000 people. This too was broken up by the police.

From *Grundrisse der Kritik*
der Politischen Ökonomie

The Grundrisse, *written 1857–1858, consists of detailed notes rather than a systematic outline. The text here is based on a translation by* S. W. Ryazanskaya *for the new edition,* A Contribution to the Critique of Political Economy, *Progress Publishers, Moscow, 1970.*

LUTHER AS AN ECONOMIST[*]

THUS Misselden, a London merchant, in his book, *Free Trade, or, the Meanes to Make Trade Florish.*[1] London, 1622 (p. 7). He compares the order of the exchange system of money and commodities with the fate of both sons of old Jacob, who put his right hand on the younger son and the left one on the older one. . . .

In the same way as Misselden, the oldest German national economist, Dr. Martin Luther, complains: "This it cannot be denied, that buying and selling are a necessary thing, with which one cannot dispense, and can well be of Christian use, especially in things that serve need and honor. For the Patriarchs too sold and bought: cattle, wool, grain, butter, milk, and other goods. These are God's gifts, which he gives from the earth and apportions among men. But the foreign commerce which brings goods from Calcutta and India and such, those precious silks and gold works and spices, which only serve for splendor and are of no practical use, and suck the money from country and people, ought not to be permitted. . . ."

---

[*] From Chapter 3, Appendix, Heft III.
1. Edward Misselden, *Free Trade, or, the Meanes to Make Trade Florish. Wherein, The Causes of the Decay of Trade in this Kingdome are Discouered: And the Remedies also to Remove the Same are Represented.*

THE MEDIEVAL CHURCH AND MONEY*

The imposition by the Popes of church tax estimates in practically all Catholic Christian countries contributed not a little to the development of the entire monetary system in industrial Europe and, in consequence, to the genesis of various attempts at circumventing the Church's command (against interest). The Pope made use of the Lombards for the exaction of investiture moneys and other dues from the archbishoprics. These leading usurers and pawnbrokers were under papal protection. Known as long ago as the middle of the twelfth century, they called themselves "official *usurarii*," "Roman episcopal money dealers," in England. Some bishops of Basel, among others, pawned to Jews episcopal rings, silken garments, all the Church paraphernalia, for trifling sums, on which they paid interest. But bishops, abbots, priests themselves also practiced usury with Church paraphernalia by pawning them to Tuscan money dealers from Florence, Siena, and other cities for a portion of the gain. . . .

When money is the *universal equivalent, the general power of purchasing,* everything is purchasable, everything is exchangeable for money. But a thing can be transformed into money only when it is alienated, when the possessor has divested himself of it. Everything external or of indifference to the individual is therefore alienable. The so-called *inalienable, eternal* possessions and the immovable, fixed property relationships corresponding to them thus break down before money. Furthermore, when money itself is in circulation merely to be exchanged for gratification, etc.—for values that can in the end be dissolved in purely personal gratifications—everything becomes valuable only to the extent that it exists for the individual. The independent value of things—its relativity, its exchangeability—except in so far as it exists merely for other things, is thereby dissolved. Everything is sacrificed to egoistical gratification. For just as everything is alienable for money, so everything is obtainable with money. Everything is to be had for "cash money," since, in existing externally to the individual, it is to be caught[2] by fraud, violence, etc. Hence everything is acquirable by everybody, and it is a matter of accident as to what the individual may or may not acquire, since it depends only on the money in his possession. Thereby the individual by himself is placed as the lord of everything. There are no absolute values, since value as such is relative to money. There is nothing inalienable, since everything is alienable through money. There is nothing higher, more sacred, etc., since everything is acquirable with money. The *"res sacrae"* ["holy

---

* From Heft VII.
2. Marx used the old English word "catched."

things"] and *"religiosae,"* which could be *"in nullius bonis,"* *"nec aestimationem recipere, nec obliquari alienarique posse"* [could neither have money estimation nor be put aside"], which are exempt from *"commercio hominum"* ["commercial man"], do not exist before money—as all are equal before God. Beautiful, how the Roman Church in the Middle Ages is itself the chief propagandist of money.

As the Church law against usury had long lost all meaning, Martin[3] also abolished the word itself in 1425 . . . In no country in the Middle Ages was there a general rate of interest. Only the priests were strict. Uncertainty of judicial institutions for the security of loans. Hence the higher the interest rate in individual cases. The scanty circulation of money, the necessity to pay in cash, since the exchange business is still undeveloped. Hence great variation in the consideration of interest and the notion of usury. In the times of Charlemagne, it was considered usurious only when a hundred percent was charged. In Lindau and Bodensee, 1344, native citizens charged $216\frac{2}{3}$ percent. In Zurich the city council set the legal rate of interest at $43\frac{1}{3}$ percent . . . In Italy, 40 percent occasionally had to be paid, although from the twelfth to the fourteenth centuries the usual rate did not exceed 20 percent . . . Verona ordered the legal rate at $12\frac{1}{2}$ percent . . . Frederick II in his decree . . . 10 percent, but applying only to Jews. He would not deign to speak for Christians. In Rhenish Germany in the thirteenth century 10 percent was the usual.[4]

CHRISTIANITY'S CRITICISM OF HEATHENISM*

The Christian religion was able to contribute to an objective understanding of earlier mythologies only when its self-criticism was to a certain extent prepared, as it were potentially. Similarly, only when the self-criticism of bourgeois society had begun was bourgeois political economy able to understand the feudal, ancient, and Oriental economies. Insofar as bourgeois political economy did not simply identify itself with the past in a mythological manner, its criticism of earlier economies—especially of the feudal system, against which it still had to wage a direct struggle—resembled the criticism that Christianity directed against heathenism, or Protestantism directed against Catholicism.

---

3. Pope Martin V.
4. This paragraph, in a slightly different version, is also found in *Capital*, Vol. III, Chapter 36.
* From the Introduction to Section III.

From *Capital*

The first volume of Capital, Marx's classic work, was published in
German in September, 1867. An English translation by Samuel Moore
and Edward Aveling, under Engels' supervision, did not come out until
1887. Volumes II and III were brought out by Engels in 1893 and 1894,
after Marx's death. The selections here are translated from the fourth
German edition.

THE FURIES OF PRIVATE INTEREST—CHURCHLY AND OTHER*

IN the field of political economy, free scientific inquiry meets not
merely the same enemy as in all other fields. The peculiar nature of
the material it treats brings into the field of battle against it the most
violent, the most petty, the most hateful passions of the human breast,
the furies of private interest. The High Church of England, for
example, will more readily pardon an attack on 38 of its 39 Articles
of Faith than on $\frac{1}{39}$th of its money income. Nowadays, atheism itself
is *culpa levis* [a small sin], as compared with criticism of inherited
property relationships. Still, there is an unmistakable advance. I am referring, for example, to the Blue Book published a few weeks ago,
"Correspondence with Her Majesty's Missions Abroad, Regarding
Industrial Questions and Trades Unions." The representatives of the
English Crown abroad declare here in so many blunt words that in
Germany, in France, in brief, in all the civilized states of the
European continent, a transformation in the existing relations between
capital and labor is as palpable and as inevitable as in England. At the
same time, on the other side of the Atlantic, Mr. Wade, Vice-President

---

* From the Preface to the first German edition, July 25, 1867.

of the United States of North America,[1] declared in public meetings: After the abolition of slavery, a transformation of the relations between capital and landed property is the order of the day! These are signs of the times, not to be hidden by purple mantles or black cassocks. They do not signify that tomorrow a miracle will happen. They show that within the ruling classes themselves the presentiment is dawning that the present society is not solid crystal, but is an organism capable of transformation and in constant process of transformation.

RELIGION AND THE MATERIAL CONDITIONS OF SOCIETY*

For a society of commodity producers, whose general social relationship of production consists of retaining their relation to their products as commodities, and hence as values, and thereby reducing their private labor to a form of homogeneous human labor—for such a society, Christianity with its *cultus* of abstract man, particularly in its bourgeois developments, Protestantism, Deism, etc., is the most suitable form of religion. In the modes of production of ancient Asia, of Antiquity, etc., we find that the conversion of products into commodities, and hence the existence of men as mere producers of commodities, plays a subordinate role, which, however, increases in importance as the ancient communities approach closer and closer to the stage of their decline. Trading nations proper exist in the ancient world only in its interstices, like the gods of Epicurus in Intermundia, or like the Jews in the pores of Polish society. These ancient social organisms of production are extraordinarily more simple and transparent than the bourgeois ones, but they are based either on the immaturity of the individual man, who has not yet severed the umbilical cord that unites him naturally with his own species, or on direct master-and-servant relationships. They are conditioned by a lower stage of development of the productive power of labor and the correspondingly encompassing relationships of men within their material life-generating processes, and hence to each other and to nature. This actual narrowness is reflected ideally in the ancient worship of nature and in folk religions. The religious reflex of the real world can vanish altogether only when the relationships of practical everyday life offer men daily visible and reasonable relationships to each other and to nature. The shape of the life process of society, that is, the material process of production, strips off its misty veil only when it is put forth as a

---

1. This is a slight error. Benjamin Franklin Wade, a senator from Ohio, was chosen president *pro tem* of the Senate on March 2, 1867; as such, he would have succeeded President Andrew Johnson if the latter had been removed by impeachment.

* From Vol. I, Chapter 1, Section 4.

product of freely associated men, under their conscious control according to plan. This, however, requires a material groundwork of society, or a series of material conditions of existence which, in their turn, are the natural product of a long and painful process of development.

Political economy has, to be sure, analyzed, even if incompletely, value and its magnitude, and discovered the hidden content in these forms. It has never asked the question why that content assumes that form, and why labor is represented by the value of its product and the labor time by the magnitude of that labor product. Formulas which carry on their forehead the inscription that they belong to a state of society in which the productive process has mastery over man, and man does not yet have mastery over the productive process—such formulas appear to the bourgeois consciousness as much a self-evident necessity of nature as productive labor itself. Hence prebourgeois forms of the social organism of production are treated by them in much the same way as the Church Fathers treated pre-Christian religions.

ST. JEROME*

In order, therefore, that a commodity may in practice act effectively as exchange value, it must quit its bodily shape, must transform itself from mere imaginary into real gold, although to the commodity such transubstantiation may be more difficult than to the Hegelian "concept," the transition from "necessity" to "freedom," or to a lobster the casting of his shell, or to the Church Father St. Jerome the stripping off of Old Adam.[2]

ST. PETER*

If the owner of the iron were to go to the owner of some other worldly commodity, and were to refer him to the price of the iron as proof that it was already money, the owner of the latter would reply as did St. Peter to Dante in reciting to him the creed:

Assai bene è trascorsa
d'esta moneta già la lega e'l peso,
Ma dimmi se tu l'hai nella tua borsa.[3]

---

* From Vol. 1, Chapter 3, Section 1.

2. As in his youth St. Jerome had to wrestle with the bodily flesh, as is shown by his struggle in the desert with the attractive women of his imagination, so he had to do the same in his old age with the spiritual flesh. "I thought," he says for example, "I was in spirit before the Judge of the Universe." "Who art thou?" asked a voice. "I am a Christian." "Thou liest," thundered the Judge of the Universe; "thou art only a Ciceronian."—K.M.

---

* From Vol. I, Chapter 3, Section 1.

3. Right well hath now been traversed this coin's alloy and weight; but tell me if thou hast it in thy purse.

Working on the Sabbath*

In England, for example, even now occasionally in rural districts a worker is condemned to imprisonment for desecrating the Sabbath by working in the little garden in front of his house. The same worker is punished for breach of contract if he stays away from his metal, paper, or glass works, even if it be from a religious whim. The orthodox Parliament has no ear for Sabbath desecration if it occurs in the "process of making" capital. A memorial (August, 1863) in which the London day laborers in fish and poultry shops asked for the abolition of Sunday labor states that their work in the first six days of the week runs to an average fifteen-hour day, and on Sunday eight to ten hours. One learns from this memorial that the ticklish gourmandise of the aristocratic hypocrites of Exeter Hall encourages this "Sunday labor." These "holy ones," so zealous *in cute curanda* [in the care of their physical well-being], show their Christianity by the humility with which they bear the overwork, the privations, and the hunger of other persons. *Obsequium ventris istis perniciosius est.* [Gluttony is for them (the workers) much more pernicious.]

The Material Basis of Religion*

Darwin has turned our attention to the history of the technology of nature, that is, to the formation of the organs of plants as instruments of production for the life of plants and animals. Does not the history of the formation of the productive organs of social man, the material basis of all social organization, deserve equal attention? And would it not be easier to compose, since, as Vico says, human history differs from natural history in this, that we have made the one and not the other? Technology reveals the active relationship of man to nature, the direct production process which sustains his life, and thereby it also lays bare his social life relationships and the mental conceptions flowing from them. Every history, even of religion, that is abstracted from this material basis is—uncritical. It is, in reality, much easier to discover by analysis the earthly core of misty religious concepts than, conversely, to develop from actual life relationships their heavenly forms. The latter method is the only materialistic, and hence the only scientific method.

---

* From Vol. I, Chapter 8, Section 5, footnote 104.

---

* From *Capital*, Vol. I, Chapter 13, Section 1, footnote 89.

Economic Original Sin*

This primitive accumulation plays in political economy approximately the same role as original sin in theology. Adam bit into the apple, and thereupon sin came over the human race. Its origin is explained by its being told as an anecdote of the past. In times long past there was, on the one side, a diligent, intelligent, and above all frugal elite; and, on the other, lazy rascals spending their substance, and more, in dissipation. The legend of the theological original sin tells us, to be sure, how man came to be condemned to earn his bread by the sweat of his brow; but the history of economic original sin reveals to us why there are people to whom this is by no means necessary. Never mind! So it came to pass that the former sort accumulated wealth, and the latter, in the end, had nothing to sell except their own skin. And from this original sin dates the poverty of the great mass that, despite all its labor, has nothing to sell but itself, and the wealth of the few that increases constantly, although they have long since ceased to work. Such stale childishness in defense of property is still being chewed over with statesmanlike solemnity by M. Thiers, for example, to the French who once were so intellectual. But as soon as the question of property comes into play, it becomes a sacred duty to adhere to the standpoint of the children's fable as the only one fit for all ages and states of development. In actual history, it is known, conquest, enslavement, robbery with murder, in short, violence, play the great role. In gentle political economy, the idyllic reigns from way back.

The Reformation and the Pauperization of the Masses*

The process of forcible expropriation of the people in the sixteenth century received a new and frightful impulse from the Reformation, and from the consequent colossal theft of Church property. At the time of the Reformation, the Catholic Church was the feudal proprietor of a great portion of English soil and landed property. The suppression of the monasteries, etc., hurled their inmates into the proletariat. The Church estates themselves were largely given away to rapacious royal favorites, or sold at a ridiculous price to speculating tenant farmers and citizens, who drove out, *en masse*, the old, hereditary subtenants and combined their holdings into one. The legally guaranteed property of the poorer country people in a portion of the Church's tithes was tacitly confiscated. *"Pauper ubique jacet"* ["The pauper is everywhere subdued"], cried Queen Elizabeth after a journey through England.

---

* From Vol. I, Chapter 24, Section 1.

---

* From Vol. I, Chapter 24, Section 2.

In the forty-third year of her reign it was finally necessary to recognize pauperism officially by the introduction of a poor tax.

"The authors of this law seem to have been ashamed to state the grounds of it, for [contrary to traditional usage] it has no preamble whatever."[4]

By the sixteenth [year of the reign] of Charles I . . . it was declared perpetual, and in fact only in 1834 did it take a new and harsher form. The immediate effects of the Reformation were not its most lasting ones. Church property had formed the religious bulwark of the traditional landed property relationships. With its fall, these were no longer tenable.[5]

PROTESTANT PARSONS AND THE POPULATION THEORY*

If the reader reminds me of Malthus, whose *Essay on Population* appeared in 1798, I remind him that this work in its first form is nothing more than a schoolboyish, superficial plagiary of Defoe, Sir James Stewart, Townsend, Franklin, Wallace, etc., and does not contain a single sentence thought out by himself. The great sensation this pamphlet caused was due solely to party interest. The French Revolution had found passionate defenders in the United Kingdom; the "principle of population," slowly worked out in the eighteenth century, and then in the midst of a great social crisis proclaimed with drums and trumpets as the infallible antidote to the teachings of Condorcet, etc., was greeted with jubilance by the English oligarchy as the great destroyer of all hankerings after human development. Malthus, hugely astonished at his success, gave himself to stuffing into his book materials superficially compiled, and adding to it new matter, not discovered but annexed by him. Note further: Although Malthus was a parson of the High Church of England, he had taken the monastic vow of celibacy. This was one of the conditions of a fellowship in the Protestant University at Cambridge: "We do not allow the members of the Colleges to be married; as soon as one takes a wife he ceases forthwith to be a member of the College." (*Reports of Cambridge University Commission*, p. 172.) This circumstance favorably distinguishes Malthus from the other Protestant parsons, who have by themselves shuffled off the Catholic command of priestly celibacy and have taken "Be fruitful and multiply" as their special mission, so that

---

4. William Cobbett, *A History of the Protestant Reformation, in England and Ireland* (London, 1824), par. 471.—K.M.

5. Mr. Rogers, although formerly Professor of Political Economy in the University of Oxford, the ancestral seat of Protestant orthodoxy, emphasizes in his *History of Agriculture* [Oxford, 1866] the pauperization of the masses by the Reformation.—K.M.

* From Vol. I, Chapter 25, Section 1, footnote 2.

they generally contribute everywhere to an increase of population to a really indecent degree, while at the same time they preach to the workers the "principle of population." It is characteristic that the economical burlesque of the Fall of Man, Adam's apple, the "urgent appetite," the "checks which tend to blunt the shafts of Cupid," as Parson Townsend merrily puts it—that this ticklish point was and is monopolized by the Reverends of Protestant theology, or rather of the Protestant church. With the exception of the Venetian monk Ortes, an original and clever writer, most of the population-theory teachers are Protestant parsons. For example, Bruckner, *Théorie du Système animal*, in which the whole subject of modern population theory is exhausted, and to which the passing quarrel between Quesnay and his pupil, Mirabeau *père*, furnished ideas on the same topic; then Parson Wallace, Parson Townsend, Parson Malthus and his pupil the arch-Parson Thomas Chalmers, to say nothing of the lesser Reverend scribblers in this line. Originally political economy was studied by philosophers like Hobbes, Locke Hume; by businessmen and statesmen like Thomas More, Temple, Sully, De Witt, North, Law, Vanderlint, Cantillon, Franklin; and in theory particularly, and with the greatest success, by medical men like Petty, Barbon, Mandeville, Quesnay. Even in the middle of the eighteenth century, the Reverend Mr. Tucker, an important economist of his time, apologized for occupying himself with Mammon. Later, and with this very "principle of population," the hour of the Protestant parsons struck. As if he had a presentiment of their business bungling, Petty, who treats population as the basis of wealth, and was, like Adam Smith, an outspoken enemy of the parsons, says: "That religion best flourishes when the Priests are most mortified, as was before said of the Law, which best flourisheth when lawyers have least to do." He therefore advises the Protestant parsons, if they will not once and for all follow the Apostle Paul and "mortify" themselves by celibacy, "not to breed more Churchmen than the benefices, as they are now shared out, will receive, that is to say, if there be places for about twelve thousand in England and Wales, it will not be safe to breed up twenty-four thousand ministers, for then the twelve thousand which are unprovided for will seek ways to get themselves a livelihood, which they cannot do more easily than by persuading the people that the twelve thousand incumbents do poison or starve their souls, and misguide them in their way to Heaven." (Petty, *A Treatise of Taxes and Contributions*, p. 57.) Adam Smith's position vis-à-vis the Protestant priesthood of his time is characterized by the following. In *A Letter to A. Smith, LL.D, on the Life, Death and Philosophy of his Friend, David Hume. By One of the People called Christians* (4th ed., Oxford, 1784), Dr. Horne, High Church Bishop of Norwich, reproves Adam Smith because in a published letter to Mr. Strahan he "embalmed his friend David" (Hume) because he told the public how "Hume amused himself on his deathbed with Lucian and whist," and because he even had the impudence to write of Hume: "I have always considered him both in his lifetime and since his death, as approaching as nearly to the idea of perfectly wise and virtuous man, as, perhaps, the nature of human frailty will permit." The Bishop cries out angrily: "Is it right in you, sir, to hold up to our view as 'perfectly wise and virtuous' the character and conduct of one who seems to have been possessed with an incurable antipathy to all that is called religion; and who strained every nerve to explode, suppress, and extirpate the spirit of it among men, that its very name, if he could effect it, might no more be had in remembrance?" (Loc. cit., p. 8.) "But let not the lovers of truth be discouraged. Atheism cannot be of long continuance" (p. 17). Adam Smith "had the atrocious wickedness to propagate atheism through the land . . . Upon the whole, Doctor, your meaning is good; but I think you will not succeed this time. You would persuade us, by the example of David Hume, Esq., that atheism is the only cordial for low spirits, and the proper antidote against the fear of death . . . You may smile over Babylon in ruins and congratulate the hardened Pharaoh on his overthrow in the Red Sea." (Loc. cit., pp. 21–22.) One orthodox individual among A. Smith's college visitors writes after his death: "Smith's well-placed affection for Hume . . . hindered him from being a Christian. When he met with honest men whom he liked . . . he would believe almost anything they said. Had he been a friend of the worthy ingenious Horrox he would have believed that the moon sometimes disappeared in a clear sky without the interposition of a cloud . . . He approached to republicanism in his political principles." (*The Bee*, by James Anderson, 18 vols., Edinburgh, 1791–1793, Vol. 3, pp. 166, 165.) Parson Thomas Chalmers suspects Adam Smith of having invented the category of "unproductive laborers" specifically out of malice against the Protestant parsons, in spite of their blessed work in the vineyard of the Lord.

RELIGION AND THE MONETARY SYSTEM*

The monetary system is essentially a Catholic institution, the credit system essentially Protestant. "The Scotch hate gold." In the form of paper, the monetary existence of commodities is only a social existence. It is *faith* that brings salvation. Faith in money value as the immanent spirit of commodities, faith in the mode of production and its predestined order, faith in the individual agents of production as

---

* From Vol. III, Chapter 35, Conclusion.

mere personifications of self-converting capital. But the credit system does not emancipate itself from the basis of the monetary system any more than Protestantism has emancipated itself from the foundations of Catholicism.

THE CHURCH AND THE PROHIBITION OF INTEREST*

"Taking interest was forbidden by the Church; but selling property for the purpose of finding succor in distress was not prohibited. It was not even forbidden to transfer property to the moneylender as security for a certain term, until the repayment of the loan, leaving the moneylender free to enjoy the usufruct of the property as compensation for his money . . . The Church itself, and its associated communes and *pia corpora* [pious foundations], derived great profit from this, particularly during the Crusades. This brought a very large portion of national wealth into the possession of the 'dead hand,' the more so as the Jew was barred from engaging in such usury because the possession of such fixed liens could not be concealed . . . Without the prohibition of interest, churches and cloisters could not have become so rich."

---

* From *Capital*, Vol. III, Chapter 36, concluding note. The quotation is from Johann Georg Büsch, *Theoretisch-praktische Darstellung der Handlung in ihren mannichfaltigen Geschäften* (*Theoretical-Practical Presentation of Commerce in its Various Transactions*) (3rd ed., Hamburg, 1808), Vol. II.

From *The Civil War in France*

THE "PARSON POWER" OF FRANCE*

HAVING once got rid of the standing army and the police, the physical-force elements of the old government, the Commune was anxious to break the spiritual force of repression, the "parson power," by the disestablishment and disendowment of all churches as proprietary bodies. The priests were sent back to the recesses of private life, there to feed upon the alms of the faithful in imitation of their predecessors, the Apostles. The whole of the educational institutions were opened to the people gratuitously, and at the same time cleared of all interference of church and state. Thus not only was education made accessible to all, but science itself freed from the fetters which class prejudice and government force had imposed upon it.

In the preliminary "second draft," which Marx wrote in the middle of May, 1871, this passage reads:

THE standing army and the government police, the instruments of physical oppression, were to be eliminated. Through the dissolution of the churches as proprietary bodies, and the banishment of religious instruction from all public schools (together with the introduction of free education) to the quiet of private life, there to exist on the alms of the faithful; through the emancipation of all the educational

---

* From Part III. For the complete text, see *Karl Marx on Revolution*, Vol. I of The Karl Marx Library (1971), pp. 332–372. *The Civil War in France*, a brochure published in English in June, 1871, was an eloquent defense of the Paris Commune.

institutions from the guardianship and the slavery of government, the instrument of spiritual repression was to be broken, and science not only made accessible to all, but also liberated from all fetters of governmental pressure and class prejudice.

VANDALISM*

If the acts of the Paris workingmen were vandalism, it was the vandalism of defense in despair, not the vandalism of triumph, like that which the Christians perpetrated upon the really priceless art treasures of heathen antiquity; and even that vandalism has been justified by the historian as an unavoidable and comparatively trifling concomitant to the titanic struggle between a new society arising and an old one breaking down.

---

* From Part IV.

The Old Christians' Contempt for Politics*

SOMEDAY the worker must seize political power in order to build up the new organization of labor; he must overthrow the old politics which sustain the old institutions, if he is not to lose heaven on earth, like the old Christians who neglected and despised politics.

* From a speech delivered in Amsterdam, September 8, 1872. For the complete text, see *Karl Marx on Revolution*, Vol. I of The Karl Marx Library (1971), pp. 63–65.

Freedom of Conscience*

"FREEDOM of conscience"! If one desired at this time of the *Kultur-kampf*[1] to remind liberalism of its old catchwords, it surely could have been done only in the following form: Everyone should be able to attend to his religious as well as his bodily needs without the police sticking their noses in. But the Workers' party ought at any rate in this connection to have expressed its awareness of the fact that bourgeois "freedom of conscience" is nothing but the toleration of all possible kinds of religious freedom of conscience, and that for its part it endeavors rather to liberate the conscience from the witchery of religion. But one chooses not to transgress the "bourgeois" level.

---

* From *Critique of the Gotha Program—Marginal Notes to the Program of the German Workers' Party*, May, 1875. For the complete text, see *Karl Marx on Revolution*, Vol. I of The Karl Marx Library (1971), pp. 488–506.
1. Cultural struggle; the reference is to Bismarck's struggle with the Catholic Church in Germany.

Notes on the Protestant Reformation

*These notes, often cryptic and elliptical, necessitating editorial inser-
tions, were made by Marx in the late 1870s and early 1880s, from
Friedrich Christoph Schlosser's multivolume* World History *for the
German People (1844–57). The following are selections dealing with
the Reformation and its background. The words in parentheses are by
Marx; those in brackets are by the German editor, as are the explanatory
footnotes.*

*The notes are from the manuscript in the Institute for Marxism-
Leninism, Moscow, as published in Marx-Engels,* Über Deutschland
und die deutsche Arbeiterbewegung, *Vol. I (Dietz Verlag, Berlin,
1961).*

1. THE SALE OF INDULGENCES

In 1517 Tetzel had already been a seller of indulgences in Germany
for three years (trumpeting forth indulgences as market commodities);
appointed a deputy commissioner who was even more shameless than
he. Both relied on the singular theory of accumulation: that the numerous martyrs and saints of the Church had acquired such a surplus of
merits with God that a reserve stock had accumulated [altogether like
"surplus labor" with the forefathers of the capitalists], that the head
of the visible Church, the Pope, could give away or sell to other faithful who had too little merit or even a heavy burden of sin (a minus).
Finally, Tetzel set up his booth in the vicinity of Wittenberg, in
Jüterbog and Zerbst, whither many people flocked.

On All Saints' Night, 1517, Luther flung at him his "challenge";
that is, he nailed ninety-five theses on the door of the castle church at

Wittenberg (these theses soon circulated in all of Europe), offering to defend them himself. Tetzel did not show up, but twice he announced countertheses, and disputed over the second of them, probably composed by the Frankfurt professor Wimpina.

January 20, 1518, in Frankfurt an der Oder, Tetzel had Luther's religious dogmas burned; in Wittenberg the same was done to his by Luther's friends; furious sermons by the Dominicans against the "Augustinian monk."[1] Struggle soon becomes a struggle over the papal reputation and the authority of the Scholastics (in addition to the Bible). Obscene writings against Luther appear in the *Dialogues* (dedicated to the Pope) by the Roman Court Dominican, Sylvester Prierias (*Magister Sacri Palatii*), and Johann Eck (Chancellor of the University of Ingolstadt and Canon at Eichstädt), in his *Obelisci*, which Luther answers in his *Asterisca* (Eck wrote in *favor* of the indulgence business). In the conflict with Luther [there appeared] among others also the Cologne *Oberketzermeister* [Chief Heretic Master]. Hoogstraaten (one of the "four *viri obscuri*" [dark men], known through the satires of Reuchlin, von Hutten, Crotus, etc.). Luther's opponents turn to the Pope. . . .

2. LUTHER'S CHALLENGE

End April, 1518: At a general assembly of the Augustinian hermit orders at Heidelberg, Luther held a disputation against the Scholastics and slightly against the infallibility of the Pope, in the presence of Bucer, Brennius, Schnepf, Theobald Billican—these [men] spread his doctrines in their circles [Bucer soon joins Zwingli and Bullinger, this Swiss movement arose *independently* of Luther]. Count Palatine Wolfgang, brother of Ludwig V of the Pfalz, joins Luther, and the Würzburg bishop, Lorenz von Bibra, recommends him to the Elector of Saxony, who, however, lets Luther know he for his part does not want to break with the Emperor and the Pope; thereupon follows a humble letter by Luther to his diocesan bishop and the Pope.

August, 1518: Maximilian writes to the Pope he should put an end to the religious uproar, but warns him about the indulgence scandal vexing the German princes and cities; but preceding that, Leo X had already set up an ecclesiastical court, with the Dominican, Sylvester Prierias, as treasurer, in consequence of which [on]

August, 1518, Luther received an invitation to appear before that court in Rome within sixty days. But as a result of Maximilian's letter and the request of the Elector of Saxony, Leo X ordered Cardinal Thomas de Vio (called Cajetanus, after his native place, Gaeta), who had already been sent to the Diet in Augsburg, to treat with Luther in

---

1. Luther.

October. (In the meantime, Luther delivers a vehement sermon—which he also printed—against the right of the Pope to pronounce an anathema.) Luther was ordered by his Elector to the Diet at Augsburg. In Augsburg [Luther had] three interviews with Cajetanus (who wanted from him a public recantation, or if not, his extradition); the Elector of Saxony had already left.

October 19, 1518, the matter was so delicate that Luther's friends decided to take him away secretly from Augsburg. (But Luther was on guard, a horse was provided by von Staupitz, and without trousers or boots he made eight miles in one ride.)

In January, 1519, Maximilian died. Elector Friedrich of Saxony (Luther's protector) [became] *pro hinc* the main person (as soon as the Interim [began]) in Germany. Leo X, in his own Bull—without naming Luther—pleads for the authority of the Roman See and indulgences, and damns the most recent opponents. Luther appeals [to a future] Council against the Papal Bull; shortly after Luther's absence from Wittenberg, Philipp Melanchthon arrived there. Karl von Miltitz (Saxon), a chamberlain of the Pope, was sent to Elector Friedrich to hand him [the] "consecrated gold rose" and to settle the conflict. He puts an end to the Tetzel scandal (Tetzel dies in the year 1519) and in Altenburg has a meeting with Luther, whom he persuades to write a humble letter to the Pope. He will keep silent only if silence is also imposed on his opponents.

July 19, 1519, a disputation tournament is set up in Leipzig, the residence of the fanatical Catholic Duke George, head of the ducal line of Saxony (ten points proposed by Eck, thirteen by Luther), Next to Luther, Karlstadt and Melanchthon [also participate].

1520: Eck goes to Rome; for his traffic, Leo X quite secretly hands to him the anathema Bull; it was opened, completed on June 15, 1520, in order to make it known in Germany that Eck is allied with the Leipzig professor, Jerome Emser, whom Luther had rudely attacked soon after the Leipzig disputation. [For the rest], at that time not only were most of the cities [German] but also a portion of the German princes tired of the Roman pressure. An Article in the Election Capitulation, imposed on Emperor Charles V in October, 1520, read: He obligates himself to "abolish everything that the Roman court had hitherto taken up against the concordats of the German nation and to urge its observance in all earnestness." At the time when Eck tarried in Rome, Elector Friedrich of Saxony wrote to his vassal, Valentin von Teutleben, who was then in Rome [among other things]: "*Non esse eum nunc qui olim Germaniae statum, efflorescere bonas artes et litteras et* plebejos etiam cognoscende scripturae desiderio teneri; *inde fore, si pontifex nonnisia vi ecclesiasticae potestatis agat et conditionem a Luthero propositam denegato examine doctrinae recuset, nec ex scrip-*

tura sacra testimonia et solida argumenta proferantur, ut maximi sint orituri motus, *ex quibus ad pontificem nulla sit reditura utilitas.*"[2] Luther receives news of the Bull long before it becomes known in Germany. . . .

January, 1520: Luther's letter to Charles V; he attacks Holy Communion.

June, 1520: Luther, in his *Of the Christian Nobility of the German Nation,* challenges the German imperial knighthood to throw off the papal yoke. Ulrich von Hutten [goes further, in that], in his pamphlets he simply preaches: Strike at them; but monk Luther [replies]: It is not his intention that one should fight for the Gospel with force.

August 1, 1520: Luther breaks entirely with the papacy in his book, *The Babylonian Captivity of the Church.* He had previously written to Spalatin: "I fear that practically without doubt the Pope is the Antichrist whom the whole world awaits. Everything that lives, acts, speaks ends on this point."[3]

Early October, 1520: Eck peddles his Bulls in Germany (he even informs the bishops about it, but only "for notification"; the bishops see in this an attack on their rights, and only a few announce it), he sends it to the rector of the University of Wittenberg, who takes no notice of it, as not being sent officially. (In Bull 41, selected sentences from Luther's writings are condemned as insolent, offensive, or heretical; Luther himself is there challenged to send his recantation to Rome within sixty days or to bring it personally, otherwise he will be excommunicated at the end of the due date, and everybody who protected him [would be among those who are] excommunicated and would suffer the loss of all honors and benefices.) Luther issued his sermon, "About the Mass," in print. In that, instead of the seven Sacraments of the Church, there were only three: Baptism, Penance, Holy Communion. At the urging of Miltitz, who is back in Germany, Luther once again writes to the Pope, politely, but not with the former monkish humility. He includes this letter in his *Book About Christian Freedom.* In the same month, October, 1520, Luther publishes *Against the Bulls of Antichrist;* even angrier is Ulrich von Hutten's *Der Bullentöter,*[4] etc. . . .

October 23, 1520: Charles V's coronation at Aachen; wrote im-

---

2. Today these conditions in Germany are not like when the fine arts and sciences flourished there, *even the plebeians are eager for a knowledge of the Scriptures,* when all the same, the Pope proceeds with the power of ecclesiastical authority and emphatically disavows the doctrines brought out by Luther, offering neither testimony from Holy Writ nor firm arguments, *thus great unrest will come about,* with no useful return to the papacy.

3. Luther to George Spalatin, February 24, 1520: "*Ego sic angor ut prope non dubitem Papam esse proprie Antichristum [illum], quem vulgata opinione [expectat] mundus. Adeo conveniunt omnia, quae vivit, facit, loquitur, statuit.*"

4. The Bull Killer.

mediately to the Diet at Worms. When Charles arrived at Cologne, the Papal Nuncio requested from him that—as [the] Pope had burned Luther's picture and writings in Rome [so]—the same be done in Mainz, Cologne, and Liège.

December 10, 1520, 9 o'clock in the morning: After he invited everybody in Wittenberg by a placard, Luther (in Wittenberg), accompanied by doctors, magisters, and students, enters the city through the Elstertor, has one of the magisters build a funeral pyre; into it are thrown the canon law, and the writings of Eck and von Emser; at the end, Luther himself throws in the Papal Bull against him and says: "As thou hast cast down the holy one of the Lord" (does he mean by this "himself," the holy *Ketzermeister* Martinus Luther?), "so I cast thee down, and may the eternal flame consume thee!"

The Pope had sent Cardinals Aleander and Caraccioli to Germany on account of Luther. Charles V does not dare—at this time he needs the friendship of the Elector of Saxony as well as that of the Pope—to forbid Luther in all of Germany, as Aleander demanded of him; he secured against the incendiary fire only in Belgium and the Rhenish ecclesiastical foundations.

Throughout the entire month of November, 1520, Charles V was in Cologne; negotiations between him and Elector Friedrich; the Nuncio Aleander and Doctor Eck as plenipotentiaries of the Pope [demanded from the Elector that he] should leave the interrogation of Luther's doctrine to them; despite this, the Elector thumbs his nose at it and travels back home, ditto Charles up the Rhine, and Luther, emboldened by the position taken by his *Landesherr* [ruling lord], dared the scene that took place on December 10, 1520.

January 3, 1521: Leo X issues a new excommunication Bull not only against Luther but against all who would protect him, hence also against the German princes friendly to reform; the latter are now officially declared to be heretics, since they had not recanted within the date set by the first Bull. [In his writing against the excommunication Bull] Luther, vehement, says, among other things: "All the articles by Jan Hus, condemned at Constance, are entirely Christian and I confess that here the Pope and his people acted as a *real Antichrist*, condemned the Holy Gospels together with Jan Hus, and replaced them with the doctrine of hellish dragons."

[In the writing] against Ambrosius Katharinus, later Bishop of Cosenza, who continued the struggle for the papacy begun by Prierias, Luther (the thickheaded fanatical monk) proves that the Kingdom of Antichrist described in the Bible literally means the papacy. Charles V, who had already demanded it before, now insists that Luther appear before the Diet of Worms.

From May, 1520, to April, 1531, all these increasingly reckless attacks on the papacy by Luther are treated in the Diet of Worms. Aleander and Johannes von Eck (Chancellor and Vicar of the Archbishop of Trier, not to be confused with the Eck of the disputation) are chosen to examine Luther about the right faith.

[At the time] the Lutheran doctrine has been joyfully greeted in northeastern Germany up to Livonia, Estonia, and Prussia, as a means of secularization of the properties in the lifelong possession of Grand Masters and Commanders. Elector Friedrich of Saxony, Luther's protector, and his drunken successor revered the Augustinian monk as a messiah; Ludwig V of the Palatinate and Philip, Landgraf of Hesse, were on the verge of declaring for him. Charles V wanted no deterioration [of relations] either with these imperial princes or with the Pope. It was even very useful for him [Charles V] to frighten him with Germany, since the Pope was still oscillating between him and Francis I (in regard to the Italian matters). As later the princes and aristocrats disseminated Lutheranism in Germany, as did the democracy in Bohemia with Hussiteism, Charles V, for political reasons, became as vehement a persecutor of Lutheranism as the Pope.

March 6, 1521: Luther "politely" invited through the imperial herald, Kaspar Storm, to appear in Worms within three weeks. [At the same time] the Pope placed Luther and all his well-wishers in the annually read Bull, "*In coena domini*,"[5] for which Luther gave him a rough thrashing in a printed work in the following year.[6]

April 16, 1521, Luther entered Worms in a peasant wagon covered with cloth.

April 17: the Hereditary Imperial Marshal Utzen or Ulrich von Pappenheim led him into the Imperial Assembly; Luther appears there in his "papal" monk's uniform (before that, 101 grievances against the Pope were submitted by a committee of Charles V's Diet). Luther's speech before the Diet ended: "Here I stand, I can do no other, God help me, amen!" (Even Duke Georg of Saxony declared church reform to be necessary, ditto his brother Heinrich, resident in Freiberg, who, however, dared to reform only in 1523.)

April 26, 1521, Luther leaves Worms; on the road, after a meeting with Elector Friedrich, [he is] brought by masked mercenaries on

May 4, 1521, through little-known roads, to the Wartburg at Eisenach, where his stay remains secret; there he translates the Bible into German. ...

May 26, 1521, at the Diet of Worms the declaration of ostracism

---

5. The "*Bulla in coena domini*" ("Holy Communion Bull"), read every Maundy Thursday, was begun by Urban V in 1364; it damned heretics and all who aided them.

6. Luther, *Bulla coena domini, das ist die bulla vom Abentfressen des allerheyligsten hern, des Bapsts . . . (Bulla coena domini, This Is the Bull of the Night Feeding of the All-Holy Lord, the Pope . . .).*

against Luther and all his followers [is passed]. (Charles has the ostracism dated May 8, so that it appeared as passed with the consent of all the Imperial Estates); same [ostracism] was stylized and elucidated by Aleander, former secretary of Cesare Borgia! Among other things, it states: *"Illum unum* [namely Luther] *non ut hominem* sed ut diabolum ipsum *sub hominis specie ad perniciem generis* [*humanis*] *assumta monachi cuculla,* [*quam*] *plurimorum haereticorum damnatissimas haereses jam diu sepultas in unam sentinam congesisse, aliquas etiam de suo excogitasse,"* etc.[7] At the Diet of Worms the Luther affair was of secondary importance; the main subject [was] the discussion from

January 3 to May, 1521, [of the question] of the Imperial regime and the Imperial Supreme Court. . . .

1520, marriage of Melanchthon (who was never a monk), nor received ordination.

1521: As various priests married, [it was] Luther who still warned [against it], although he was in love with the nun Katharina de Bore. While he was absent in the Wartburg at Wittenberg, Karlstadt (his name was really Bodenstein) (and the monks of the Augustinian monastery) transformed the whole religious system. Melanchthon follows passively. Hence conflict between the vehement and the moderate; [it often came to violent] scenes; hence in

November, 1521, Luther [arrived] incognito at Wittenberg for a few days.

End 1521: [The] Augustinians of Thuringia and Meissen decide, at the Synod in Wittenberg, on the abolition of all ordered masses; they declare that vows and the rules of the orders [are] incompatible with [the] Gospel. At the turmoils by students and citizens in Wittenberg, [the] main role [was] played by the leaders Karlstadt and the Augustinian monk Gabriel Didymus. Karlstadt, at the head of students and citizens, suddenly stops all ceremonies of the Roman worship, reads the mass in German, [gives] Holy Communion without confession under both forms; no longer [is the] raising of the host [cultivated]; [then follows] the ejection of images from the churches, [the] destruction of the altars, etc. This occurred tumultuously. "All restless" heads streamed into Wittenberg; hence

May 7, 1522, Luther returned to Wittenberg, there to preach reaction and [to deliver] "paternal reprimands." At the same time Thomas Münzer [acts] in Zwickau; alongside of him [are the other] chiefs of [the] visionaries, tradesmen there, among them [is] Nicolaus Storch,

---

7. This one [Luther], not a man *but a wicked devil* in the guise of a man, [had], in the assumed monk's cowl, assembled many heretics and highly condemned heresies, which had been concealed for a long time, in a stinking puddle and thought out some new ones, etc.

[who has] more influence than Münzer; some of them want a communist kingdom. [The] authorities of Zwickau put a damper on, some who flee from there [go] to Wittenberg, precisely at the time when the "reactionary" of the Wartburg [Luther] returns. The "restless" must leave Wittenberg. Karlstadt [betakes] himself to Basel, scourges there the gross "monk" Luther. Thomas Münzer is received in Allstedt as prophet, but must flee on account of two pamphlets against the "rotten meat in Wittenberg" and his doctrines; he [was also] driven out of Nuremberg. . . .

July, 1523: In Magdeburg, without consulting Archbishop Albrecht, the Council arms, to show their teeth, armed, to the Imperial Court and the Imperial regime, should they seriously proceed with the declaration of ostracism against the Council.

June 23, 1523, the Magdeburg citizenry assembled in the Augustinian monastery [and] demanded from the Council a new ecclesiastical arrangement [which thereupon took place].

[On] Laetere Sunday,[8] 1523, a parson [heretical to the Reformation] was driven by the people from the church at Frankfurt am Main [and the] Reformation was inaugurated by the Council.

In the same year, Luther [issued] the work, *Of the Arrangement of the Divine Service in the Community;* at the same time he himself now demands the changes that he had hitherto opposed. He handed over the Augustinian monastery, where until then only the Prior and he had held out, to the Elector [and] put away the monk's garb.

October 9, 1524, he did not preach in the cowl, but [in] the "clerical coat" (for which the Elector [had] given him the cloth). What mainly favored the progress of the Reformation [was the] secularization of the Church properties for the benefit of the families of the knighthood and the princes; in addition, [it was] the "marriage" of the converted "clergy."

3. THE SPREAD OF THE REFORM MOVEMENT

a. Sebastian Franke

1524: Peasants [are] set into motion (serfs and retainers; hundreds of pamphlets; numerous unfrocked monks preach wildly; the great Sebastian Franke (his *Chronicles* [are] reproduced in numerous reprints). Sebastian Franke is [a] mystical pantheist [who] constantly [published his writings] to the great anger of the thickheaded Luther. *Paradoxa or 280 Wondrous Speeches from Holy Writ* (1533). *Sebastian Franke's Writings* (born at Donauwörth in 1500) appeared particularly

---

8. The last Sunday before Lent.

in the period of 1528–1545; alternately he [was] driven out of Nuremberg, Ulm, Strasbourg; [to him] Christ is merely a human hero reformer; *Collection of German Proverbs,* read by citizens and peasants as much as the Bible (German); in addition, *Chronica, Record and Biblical History from the Beginning to the Year 1531,* and *Germania, i.e. Chronicle of All of Germany and Origin of all German Peoples, etc.* [He] treats all religions and sects as equal, speaks of the Christ in us, etc. Thus his work serves later as antidote to "Concordance formulae" and Luther's faith in the Word; later enlarged by continuations; this work was [printed] in Ulm in 1551 in three folios. Theoretically—of course, indirectly in the twelve Articles drawn up by the German peasants—the followers of the Swiss republican Reformers, who from the very first are much bolder than the dumb-fanatical, devil-believing Luther (philistine), influence the Peasant War. . . .

b. Prussia and the Hohenzollerns

1524. [Sensation] stirring [was the] example [given] by the Grand Master of the Order of the German Knights in Prussia; [it was] soon imitated by the "brothers-of-the-sword," for whom there were secularizing estates and commanderies in Livonia, Estonia, and Courland.

After [the] death of the Brandenburg "Achilles," the House of Hohenzollern split into two lines, of which the one ruled in Brandenburg and the other in Ansbach and Bayreuth. In Brandenburg, Johann Cicero (son of Albrecht Achilles) is succeeded by Elector Joachim I, and [he was] an implacable enemy of Luther, who had evilly jumped around his brother Albrecht, Bishop of Mainz and Magdeburg, the main beneficiary of Tetzel's indulgence business; this louse Joachim was succeeded,

in 1535, by his son Joachim II, and this noble, who was entirely Lutheran, had an eye to business,[9] i.e., on Prussia, which his cousin, the Grand Master of the German Knights, Albrecht von Ansbach and Bayreuth, had acquired for himself.

1526: the "Brandenburger" Albrecht von Ansbach and Bayreuth, on his return from the Nuremberg Diet, converses with Luther and Melanchthon in Wittenberg; they advise him to secularize the Order of the Knights Prussia [where Albrecht was then Grand Master], as was the case, "upon their" instruction, with the monasteries and foundations in Germany. Herr Albrecht then brought this property of the order into his family, in that he transferred Prussia from Germany to Poland; i.e., [he did not do it before] he made an accord with the Polish King Sigismund I, then

---

9. These four words were written in English.

in 1525, he "publicly" declared himself in favor of the Evangelical doctrine, made Prussia into a duchy, [the] estates of the order into secular benefices; by an agreement with Sigismund, a part of Prussia remained with Poland, while the portion belonging to the Knights, on

April 8, 1525, was given to the Brandenburg Grand Master "Albrecht" as "Duke" (as a Polish fief). Thus Albrecht rid himself of the Emperor and Empire, and [thus he] delivered Prussia over to Poland, which had hitherto been in conflict with the Knights over it. Albrecht's brother Georg, Duke of Jägerndorf, [had] previously [become] Lutheran and had "encouraged!" "Albrecht" (in his doings)....

c. Thomas Münzer

1522: Thomas Münzer is driven from Allstedt and then [from] all of Saxony and Nuremberg; [he] is active in the Peasants' Revolt in Upper Swabia, 1523, and (as the disturbances spread from Swabia to Thuringia) appears again in Thuringia, as well as in the territory of Fulda, where he is arrested.

End 1524: [Münzer is active] in the Imperial City Mühlhausen [and in the neighboring Harz]; Mühlhausen [was] then entirely independent, [had] some 10,000 inhabitants [and a] territory of twenty villages and country spots. Thomas Münzer had been there before. [The] way is paved for him by Pfeifer (also called "Schwertfeger"[10]) [a Premonstratensian monk], together with a number of zealous pupils. [The] magistrates cannot prevent the masses of the people from electing Münzer chief pastor and making Mühlhausen the seat of his prophetism. The envious Luther, who [is] pope only in his circle, writes: *"Münzer Mulhusii rex et imperator est, non solum doctor."*[11] [The] people hope from the "communalization of property," [the introduction] of the Bible as the sole code of law in Christian courts, as [the] Koran is with the Mohammedans; from all over people pour into Mühlhausen, the Council there was [forced] to "give up," i.e., it was [newly] elected [on]

March 17, 1525, under [the] name of "The Eternal Council"; Münzer [had the] chairmanship; [the] Council itself consists of his most zealous followers. All calumnies against Münzer—that he drove the Knights of St. John from the city and confiscated their properties *pour le bien publicum* [for the public good]—are the inventions of the louse Melanchthon; [they] entered into all German history books, only after 1848 [were] Melanchthon's lies refuted with historical documents.

---

10. Sword-cutler, or smith.

11. Luther to Nicolaus von Amsdorf, April 11, 1525: "Münzer is king and emperor of Mülhausen, not merely a teacher."

[In] May, 1525, the exodus from Mühlhausen [began], in order to propagate the Biblical kingdom. The princes' servant [Luther] scolds Münzer as "murder prophet." [The] counties Hohenstein, Stolberg, Mansfeld, Beichlingen, and the Erfurt country [were] in full movement; [the] tidings penetrated into the Schwarzburg, Altenburg, Meissen, Koburg, Eichsfeld, and Brunswick regions.

April, 1525, vainly the princes' servant Luther travels about, preaching "obedience to authority," making a stink even in his own birthplace, Eisleben. Even then Münzer had already established a formal alliance against authority and the existing order; the records of the alliance were in charge of Pfeifer, [who] demanded the extermination of the godless. From the Rhone to the Harz the twelve peasant Articles become basic law; all lesser lords [are] compelled to enter the Evangelical brotherhood; Fulda (city) [is] captured, [the] city of Hersfeld [is] forced by 5,000 peasants to enter the brotherhood. Fortunate progress of all peasant undertakings from [the] Saale to the Weser and Elbe; Pfeifer's annihilating campaign into Eichsfeld, plundering of Erfurt by thousands of peasants, etc. Now Luther calls the princes to murder, etc.; [he is a] true Simon de Montfort minus the "personal bravery," he acts as a raving, thundering "pope" in his outpourings. He wrote in [a] letter to Dr. Rühel: "As for compassion which is asked for the peasants, God will certainly save and protect the few innocent who are among them, as he did for Lot" (a fine example!) "and Jeremiah. If He does not do it, they are surely not innocent, but have at least kept silence and approved . . . The wise man sayeth: *Cibus, onus et virga asino,* in a peasant ([writes] this peasant transformed into a monk) it should be oat straw. They do not listen to the word [the papal dictates of Martin] and are senseless, and so they must listen to the *virgam,* the muskets, and it serves them right. Let us pray for them that they should obey; if not, then not much compassion applies to them. Just let the muskets roar among them, otherwise it would be a thousand times worse."[12] After the victory of the murdering and torturing knighthood, this same scoundrel wrote of the Thuringian scenes: He would, of course, be sorry about the victory of the lords(!) as much as he would be about that of the peasants. If the latter had been victorious, the devil would have become an abbot; but if the tyrannical lords had won, the devil's mother would have become an abbess. ([But] before he was "sorry" for the peasants, there was victory—the victory of God, which is here this time identical with "the devil's mother.") Luther's flood of shameful speeches founder on the Elector Friedrich the Wise, but soon [after his death in]

---

12. Luther to Johann Rühel, May 30, 1525.

early May, 1525, [he] is followed by his brother, Johann the Steadfast, the drunkard who believes Luther's word as the [word of the] Bible, [and who] joins the armies of Landgrave Philipp von Hesse, Duke Georg of Saxony, Count Albrecht von Mansfeld, and Duke Heinrich von Brunswick.

Thomas Münzer, after he ordered artillery guns to be cast in the last months, moves out of Mühlhausen bivouacs with some 8,000 untrained and unarmed peasants near Frankenhausen (in Schwarzburg-Sondershausen).

March, 1525, Philipp von Hesse [was] on the verge of turning against the peasants, with Trier and Pfalz, whence many abbots, prelates, [the] Elector of Trier, [the] bishops of Würzburg and Bamberg had taken refuge in Heidelberg, when he discovered that everything was in revolt between the Saale, Werra, and Elbe rivers; now with his army, the horsemen of the knighthood, and with artillery from the Tauber, [he] drives out the peasants and all those who had joined them, occupies Fulda and Hersfeld, [is] merciless with the peasants; and then, summoned by his father-in-law, Duke Georg of Saxony, to Thuringia, meets with him at Buttelstädt; Heinrich of Brunswick unites with him—altogether they are 3,500 foot soldiers strong (apart from the knights and mounted mercenaries), [march thence] to Frankenhausen. The speech delivered by the Landgrave Philipp to his army before Frankenhausen is highly confused (as reported by Melanchthon). [He said] among other things: "We do not mention our worries and efforts, compared to which your taxes and burdens are slight."[13] Horrible bloodthirstiness by the princely and knightly lance cannibals on [the] battlefield; Münzer [is] cannibalized, in Mülhausen [they leave behind them a] blood mark after the capture of same by the "order" *canaille*. Like Münzer, Pfeifer [is also] tortured; [the peasants suffer as] martyrs under the avenging lords who [had] suffered from the peasants and to whom the prisoners [had been] handed over. Philipp camps at Fulda, later in Thuringia, together with Georg of Saxony, Heinrich of Brunswick, and Count von Mansfeld, [behaving] like Tamerlane (what a caricature of Tamerlane!). Bishop Konrad of Würzburg moves around the country with executioners. Casimir of Brandenburg-Bayreuth orders the eyes of sixty–eighty peasants to be gouged! Even his brother Georg, Duke of Jägerndorf, "furious" about this, asks him in a letter "who would feed them if he slew all the peasants"! ...

All calumnies against Münzer—who drove the monks and the Knights of St. John from the city and (to his own enrichment) sold [but actually] confiscated their property for *le bien publicum*—are

---

13. This speech, a forgery by Melanchthon, is in his pamphlet, *Histori Thome Müntzers* ... (Hagenau, 1526).

fabrications by the louse Melanchthon; [they] got into all German history books, but only since 1848 have Melanchthon's lies been refuted with historical documentation. ...

d. Brunswick

1538–1542: duel of insults, supported by the respectable princely private theologians (above all, also the lout Luther), waged between Duke Heinrich of Brunswick, Landgrave Philipp of Hesse, and Elector Johann Friedrich of Saxony (the drunkard).

Heinrich of Brunswick perpetrates acts of brutality against the city of Brunswick (as a consequence of the gradually bought privileges from the emperors, as did many other small towns in the sixteenth century, Brunswick is practically a republic); [Brunswick], after being admitted to the Schmalkaldic League, asserts its defiance against its sovereign, Heinrich; similarly Goslar, which makes a thorough break with Heinrich over the Rammelsberg and its mines. The Imperial Supreme Court (hostile to the Protestants) pronounces in favor of the duke, imposes an imperial ostracism on Goslar; Charles V and Ferdinand I, to be sure, order a temporary delay of its execution (at the petition of the Protestants), but Heinrich (of Brunswick) attacks Goslar. (Luther, in an obscene polemic against Heinrich, favoring his own hereditary ruler, reached "the highest peak of the fish market." The book is called *Against Hans Worst*, it is the coarsest and most ill-mannered book of the sixteenth century.) This ignominious princely literature appears in 1540–1542.

e. Ulrich Zwingli

Since 1519 the cantons of Zurich, Bern, Basel, and Schaffhausen, [which had] separated late from the German Empire and were still until then under the German Electors in ecclesiastical matters, begin to separate from the Church.

1519, Leo X sent to Switzerland the Guardian of a Milan (city) barefoot [Franciscan] monastery, Bernhardin Samson, as a seller of indulgences; [acting] even more shamelessly than Tetzel, he sells the remission of sins, past and future. (This papal commissioner-general extolled himself as a real "Samson": "At eighteen he had captured 1,800,000 ducats [from the Swiss] for three popes.") In the small cantons and in Bern he reaps [a rich] harvest; in Lenzburg he ran into resistance; in Bremgarten the deacon blocks his entry (both places are in the Aargau). This deacon was Bullinger; Samson excommunicates him. He goes to Zurich, where the Diet [was] then [in session]. [The] indulgences merchant [was] driven from there; [the]

Bishop of Constance, to whose diocese Zurich belonged, opposed the Roman carryings-on, and his vicar general [had in the year]

1518 summoned the benevolent Zwingli to Zurich; the latter immediately ready [to fight] with word, pen, and gun butts. [He] had participated in [the] campaign in Italy[14] and there experienced the deceit of Matthew Schinner and the bestialization of the Swiss by foreign military service; before that, as a student in Vienna, he had also tested the Roman stupidity, [was] engaged in Glarus [for ten years as] preacher, preached the Bible in Einsiedeln (pilgrimage place in the Schwyz canton), whither he [was] called for precisely this purpose.

September, 1519, [he was] engaged as a *Leut* priest in the great munster in Zurich; [he] was *not* a student of Luther's [in fact, emerged before him].

In 1520 the Great Council of Zurich had already [issued] the decree that only the Gospel should be preached; the Small Council —here the doctrines of the old found their followers. At the instigation of Clement VII the Diet in Switzerland, as also the majority of the Diet in Germany, seeks to prevent [the] introduction of [a] new official religion ([this was] just the trouble, that it was an "official religion"). . . .

4. THE JESUITS

[They became] the nerve center of the Catholic Church only after the Religious Peace of Augsburg (1555) and the Council of Trent (1545–1563). At the time of the founding of the Jesuit Order, there was also founded the Order of the dirty "Capucines" for the *infima plebs*.[15]

1521: At the defense of Pamplona (against the French), its commander, Ignatius of Loyola, [was] so gravely wounded in both feet that he had to give up his military career. During his long convalescence he occupied himself in his paternal castle with legends and lives of the saints, as did Don Quixote with knightly romances. [He] had "visions," drew on spiritual adventures; [made a] pilgrimage to Rome and Jerusalem (in the latter he attempted a conversion of the Turks), then roamed around Spain as a preacher of repentance and begged for money in the Netherlands to be able to study in Paris; there, in 1534, he became magister (he lived in Paris

---

14. The war between the Holy League (Ferdinand I, the Venetians, and the Pope) and France, 1511–1515, for which Venice and the Pope recruited Swiss. It ended in a victory for France.
15. Lower classes.

for nine years). According to his biographer Ribadeneira, in Paris he already denounced to the Inquisition the Lutheran heretics among the university teachers. (Burning of heretics was [the] fashion under Francis I and Henry II.) He wins over Francis Xavier (Spaniard from Navarre), whose philosophy lectures he attended in the Paris Collegium Beauvais, as well as those of the Savoyard savant, Peter Faber; later Jacob Laynez, Alphonse Salmeron, Nicolas Bobadilla, and Simon Rodriguez joined them.

1534, Loyola reads to them [a] solemn mass in the underground chapel of a convent in Montmartre, receives their vow to go together to Jerusalem or Rome, there to throw themselves at the feet of the Pope, to offer him [as traveling knights] [their] lives and services for the defense of the Holy See. Then Ignatius [betakes himself] to Spain; [he] lives there, not in the castle of his brother, but in the hospital; [he] begs, preaches repentance, torments [himself], performs miracles. He wanders across Spain [and sets out] then by ship for Venice. Thither come his comrades, augmented by other Spanish students from Paris; the Jerusalem plan is given up; Ignatius, Faber, and Laynez [travel] to Rome, the others separate to recruit [for the order] in Italian universities.

1538 and 1539, the plan of the Rules of the Order is worked out as the constant service of the Pope [not just the Church], and even before he has expressed his opinion [of the new order], [in]

April, 1539, the vows of poverty and chastity [were] added to the blind military obedience to the future chiefs of the order; the order is destined, not for [the] monastery, but for the outside world. After negotiations with the procrastinating Pope, who in the meantime recognizes the Capucin Order, [on]

May, 1539, a fourth vow is added: the "obligation of a very special obedience to the Papal See" and the vow "to let themselves be used freely in all matters at the pleasure of the Popes."

At the request of the Portuguese Government, Loyola sends missionaries, particularly Simon Rodriguez and Francis Xavier, overseas for the conversion [of the natives] for [the benefit of] the Portuguese proprietors in the East Indies. Francis Xavier as missionary in Japan, as martyr and saint, gave the order the same luster that St. Dominic and Francis of Assisi [once] did their orders. [Thus Loyola becomes the founder of the Portuguese missions in the East.]

Autumn, 1540: Paul III confirms the Order by the Bull *"Consueverunt."*[16] Ignatius Loyola becomes first General of the Order. After the approval of the order, Simon Rodriguez, supported by the

---

16. The actual title of the Bull was *"Regimini ecclesiae militantis."*

favor of John III in Portugal, rages against Jews and Marranos, against which the people and the nobility vainly complain. In Scotland the Jesuits Salmeron and Brouet, sent there by the Pope, estrange the Scots from Catholicism; in Germany the emissaries Faber, Bobadilla, and Le Jay, who were sent there, frustrate the religious negotiations in Worms and Regensburg. Le Jay is appointed professor in Ingolstadt by the Duke of Bavaria, and thence Jesuitism [then] spreads through [all of] Germany. Bobadilla set up his center in Vienna. Faber [went] first to Mainz, to frustrate there, with the help of the Pope, the Archbishop's attempted Reformation; then to Cologne, where he wins over to the order the Dutchman Peter Canisius, who was studying there and who as a learned theologian became a new cornerstone of the order.

[In] 1543, Paul III eliminated the postscript to his founding Bull, according to which the number of [the order's] members was to be limited to sixty; soon all Catholic countries, particularly Spain, Portugal, the Netherlands, teemed with them. [The] universities, schools, and confessionals of the courts [are] soon in the power of the Jesuits; these [have] a different attraction from the German Reformers who were then losing themselves in dry dogmatics. Beginning with the middle of the sixteenth century, the order is active everywhere; [the Jesuits] also take the exact sciences into their hands.

[The] best work on the arrangements of the Jesuit Order [is] the one by Melchior Inchhofer, *Monarchia Solipsorum* (Monarch of Arch-Egoists). Inchhofer occupied important posts in the order in the first half of the seventeenth century, [he] lived in Rome, was [the] friend of Pope Innocent X; the latter forced the Jesuits, who had forcibly abducted him [Inchhofer] under his [the Pope's] eyes, to return him to Rome, although Melchior's [authorship], which had been anonymous, was discovered and he had brought out his book, without naming the Jesuits, in the form of an allegory. [On] the Jesuit side, [the work was issued] as *Imago primi seculi societatis Jesu*, in which everything was naturally idealized. [A] dirty lying counterwork against Inchhofer [was written] by [the] Jesuit Gottlieb Raynaud, whose works [were] published in twenty volumes. [Loyola's] village and monastery of Guipuzcoa, twenty miles southeast of San Sebastian, is Ignatius' birthplace; [he was] born in 1491, of a noble Spanish family, [at] the Château de Loyola in Biscay; he died in 1556, was made a communicant by Pope Gregory XV; his festival [is] celebrated [on] July 3; his *Constitutions of the Jesuits* was translated from Spanish into Latin in Rome, 1588, and his *Exercitia spiritualia* [into] Spanish, and into Latin, Rome, 1548. Père Dominique Bouhours published *La Vie de St. Ignace* in 1679, and his [Loyola's] *Maxims* in 1683. . . .

5. The Peace of Augsburg

1555: the Diet at Augsburg (Ferdinand I had already arrived there at the end of December, 1554). The instruction to the imperial ambassadors [is] entirely in the Spanish-Roman spirit; but Ferdinand's [proposal] that peace be secured for the whole Empire without a discussion of the religious conflict, was adopted.

In the first months of 1555 the so-called Augsburg Religious Peace [was] essentially completed (as Charles V had in mind to lay down the crown); in the peace [document] there is actually mention only of the Lutherans; but they did not dare directly to exclude the Calvinists. [The document] says: No *Reichsstad* [imperial estate] should molest any other on account of the Augsburg Confession or doctrine and faith altogether; not only the princes and independent lords, but also the free and imperial cities and the knights depending on Catholic lords, and the cities and communities, should have the same religious rights as the independent ones. Should some government tolerate only one religion, the adherents of the other [are] permitted to transfer, without money fees or any kind of infringement; Protestants and Catholics are to sit in the Imperial Supreme Court. Through the stupidity of the Protestants [the] general secularization is indeed prevented. Spiritual and secular princes were not differentiated [in the treaty]. The Protestant asses made this (which had been silently decided upon) an object of contention only when they wanted to be accorded the same right regarding change of religion as the secular and spiritual estates; whereupon [there began] a vehement squabble with the now shrewd Catholics. Hence: after April, 1555, many months of wrangling [could be devoted] to this point.

September 13, 1555: On this day of signing of the Augsburg Religious Peace, at the behest of Ferdinand I and the Catholic estates there was interpolated [the] *"Reservatum ecclesiasticum"* ["Ecclesiastical Reservation"] [which stated] that, when an archbishop, bishop, prelate, or another spiritual estate wished to transfer from the old religion, he must leave behind and lose his archbishopric, bishopric, or other benefice, and with it all usufructs and income! (A truly delicious irony!) [This is the] source of the Thirty Years' War. . . .

6. The Treaty of Westphalia

[On] August 6, 1648, at Osnabrück, the Peace of Westphalia was concluded between Sweden, [the] Emperor, and the Protestant imperial estates; [on]
September 17, 1648, at Münster, [it was concluded] with the French.

October 29, 1648, at the Town Hall in Münster, all the participants in the [Thirty Years'] War signed both treaties. . . .

[In regard to religion]:

1. [The] Reformed [have] the same rights as [the] Lutherans.

2. The normal year [that is, the year which should regulate the conditions in connection with possession of ecclesiastical properties] of their restoration [is] 1619, for the Pfalz and its allies, and for the other princes the year 1624.

3. Protestants and Catholics who change their religion lose their ecclesiastical incomes.

4. No government has to tolerate citizens who do not belong to its religion; but it must give them three years' time to emigrate.

5. In the future, the Imperial Supreme Court is to consist of twenty-four Protestant and twenty-six Catholic members. On a subject of religious interest, the Imperial Assembly should never decide by a majority of the votes.

Judaism and Jews

On the Jewish Question*

I

THE German Jews desire emancipation. What kind of emancipation do they desire? *Civil, political* emancipation.

Bruno Bauer answers them: Nobody in Germany is politically emancipated. We [Christians] are also unfree. How shall we liberate you? You Jews are egoists when you demand a special emancipation for yourselves as Jews. As Germans, you should work for the political emancipation of Germany; as men, for the emancipation of mankind; and you should feel the particular form of your oppression and your shame not as an exception to the rule but rather as its confirmation.

Or do Jews desire to be put on an equal footing with the Christian subjects? If so, they recognize the Christian state as legitimate, as the regime of general subjection. Why should they be displeased with their special yoke when they are pleased with the general yoke? Why should the German interest himself in the emancipation of the Jew when the Jew does not interest himself in the emancipation of the German?

The Christian state recognizes only *privileges.* In it the Jew has the privilege of being a Jew. As a Jew he has rights that Christians do not have. Why does he desire rights that he does not have and that Christians enjoy?

* "On the Jewish Question" was written fall, 1843, and published in *Deutsch-Französische Jahrbücher,* 1844. This article is a review of two books by Bruno Bauer, *Die Judenfrage (The Jewish Question)* (Brunswick, 1843) and *Die Faehigkeit der heutigen Juden und Christen, frei zu werden (The Capacity of Today's Jews and Christians to become Free)* (Zurich and Winterthur, 1843).

When the Jew wants to be emancipated from the Christian state, he asks that the Christian state abandon its religious prejudice. Does he, the Jew, abandon *his* religious prejudice? Has he, then, the right to demand of another this abdication of religion?

By its very nature the Christian state cannot emancipate the Jew; but, Bauer adds, the Jew by his very nature cannot be emancipated. So long as the state remains Christian and the Jew Jewish, both are equally incapable of giving or receiving emancipation.

The Christian state can behave toward the Jew only in the manner of the Christian state, that is, in a privileged way, in that it permits the separation of the Jew from the rest of the subjects and makes him feel the pressure of other separated spheres all the more heavily, since the Jew stands in religious opposition to the dominant religion. But the Jew, too, can behave toward the state only in a Jewish manner, that is, as an alien, in that he contraposes his chimerical nationality to actual nationality, his illusory law to actual law, imagining himself justified in his separation from humanity, abstaining on principle from participation in historical movement, looking to a future that has nothing in common with the general future of mankind, regarding himself as a member of the Jewish people and the Jewish people as a chosen people.

On what basis, then, do you Jews desire emancipation? Because of your religion? It is the mortal enemy of the religion of the state. As citizens? There are no citizens in Germany. As men? You are not men, any more than those to whom you appeal.

After giving a critique of former positions and solutions, Bauer formulates the question of Jewish emancipation in a new way. What, he asks, is the nature of the Jew who is to be emancipated, and the Christian state which is to emancipate him? He answers with a critique of the Jewish religion, analyzes the religious antagonism between Judaism and Christianity, and explains the essence of the Christian state, all this with dash, acuteness, wit, and thoroughness, in a style as precise as it is meaty and energetic.

How, then, does Bauer solve the Jewish question? What is the result? The formulation of a question is its solution. The critique of the Jewish question is the answer to the Jewish question. The résumé is as follows:

The most persistent form of antagonism between the Jew and the Christian is *religious* antagonism. How does one solve an antagonism? By making it impossible. And how is a religious antagonism made impossible? By *abolishing religion*. As soon as Jew and Christian recognize their respective religions as nothing more than *different stages of evolution of the human spirit*, as different snakeskins shed by history, and recognize *man* as the snake who wore them, they will no longer find themselves in religious antagonism but only in a critical, scientific, and human relationship. *Science* constitutes their unity. Contradictions in science, however, are resolved by science itself.

The German Jew is particularly affected by the lack of political emancipation in general and by the pronounced Christianity of the state. In Bauer's view, however, the Jewish question has a universal significance, independent of specific German conditions. It is the question of the relation of religion to the state, of the *contradiction between religious bias and political emancipation*. The emancipation from religion is presented as a condition both for the Jew who wants to be politically emancipated and for the state which is to emancipate him and is to be emancipated itself as well. . . .[1]

Bauer thus demands, on the one hand, that the Jew give up Judaism and man in general give up religion, to be emancipated *as a citizen*. On the other hand, he holds that the consequence of the *political* abolition of religion is simply the abolition of religion altogether. The state that makes religion a presupposition is not yet a true or real state.

"The religious view, to be sure, gives the state guarantees. But what state? What kind of state?"

At this point Bauer's one-sided conception of the Jewish question becomes apparent.

It by no means suffices to inquire: Who should emancipate? Who should be emancipated? Criticism has to concern itself with a third question. It must ask: *What kind of emancipation* is involved? What are the underlying conditions of the desired emancipation? Criticism of *political emancipation* itself was at first the final critique of the Jewish question and its true resolution in the "universal question of the age."

Since Bauer does not raise the question to this level, he falls into contradictions. He presents conditions that are not rooted in the essence of political emancipation. He raises questions that are not relevant to his problem, and he solves problems that leave his questions unanswered. When Bauer says of the opponents of Jewish emancipation that "their mistake simply lay in their assuming the Christian state to be the only true state and not subjecting it to the same criticism they applied to Judaism," we find his error to be that he subjects *only* the "Christian state," and not the state in general, to criticism, that he fails to examine the *relation between political emancipation and human emancipation,* and hence he posits conditions that are explainable only by his uncritical confusion of political emancipation with universal human emancipation. While Bauer asks

---

1. Several quotations from Bauer are omitted.

the Jews whether from their standpoint they have the right to demand political emancipation, we on the contrary ask: Has the standpoint of political emancipation the right to demand from the Jews the abolition of Judaism and from men in general the abolition of religion altogether?

The Jewish question has a different aspect, varying according to the state in which the Jew finds himself. In Germany, where there is no political state and no state as such exists, the Jewish question is a purely *theological* question. The Jew finds himself in *religious* opposition to a state that acknowledges Christianity as its foundation. This state is theology *ex professo* [by profession]. Criticism is here criticism of theology, a double-edged criticism—critique of Christian and critique of Jewish theology. But however *critical* we may be, we are still moving in the realm of theology.

In France, a constitutional state, the Jewish question is a question of constitutionalism, a question of the incompleteness of political emancipation. As the semblance of a state religion is preserved there— even if only by the meaningless and contradictory formula of a *religion of the majority*—the relation of the Jews to the state also retains the semblance of a religious, theological antithesis.

Only in the free states of North America—at least in one part of them—does the Jewish question lose its theological significance and become a truly *secular* question. Only where the political state exists in its full development can the relation to the political state by the Jew, or the religious man in general, appear in its proper and pure form—that is, the relation of religion to the state. Criticism of this relation ceases to be theological criticism the moment the state abandons a *theological* posture toward religion and relates itself to religion as a state, that is, *politically*. Criticism then becomes *criticism of the political state*. At this point, where the question ceases to be *theological*, Bauer's criticism ceases to be critical.

"In the United States there exists neither a state religion nor a religion declared to be that of the majority, nor a preeminence of one faith over another. The state is foreign to all cults." (Gustave-Auguste de Beaumont, *Marie ou l'esclavage aux États-Unis* [Brussels, 1835].) There are even some North American states where "the constitution does not impose religious beliefs or sectarian practice as a condition of political rights" (op. cit., p. 225). Yet "no one in the United States believes that a man without religion can be an honest man" (op. cit., p. 224).

Nevertheless, North America is preeminently the land of religiosity, as Beaumont, De Tocqueville, and the Englishman Hamilton[2] assure

---

2. Thomas Hamilton, author of *Men and Manners in America* (1833).

us unanimously. The North American states, however, serve us only as an example. The question is: What is the relation of complete political emancipation to religion? If we find even in a country with complete political emancipation that religion not only exists but is fresh and vital, we have proof that the existence of religion is not incompatible with the full consummation of the state. Since, however, the existence of religion implies a deficiency, the source of this deficiency can be sought only in the nature of the state itself. We no longer take religion to be the *foundation* but only the *manifestation* of secular narrowness. We therefore explain religious prejudice in free citizens as coming from their secular prejudice. We do not claim that they must do away with their religious prejudice to elevate their secular limitations. We do claim that they will eliminate their religious prejudice as soon as they have elevated their secular limitations. We do not convert secular questions into theological ones. We convert theological questions into secular ones. After history has been, for much too long, resolved into superstition, we now resolve superstition into history. The question of the *relation of political emancipation to religion* becomes for us a question of the *relation of political emancipation to human emancipation*. We criticize the religious weakness of the political state by criticizing the political state, apart from its religious weakness, in its secular construction. The contradiction between the state and a particular religion, such as Judaism, we humanly resolve in the contradiction between the state and particular secular elements, and the contradiction between the state and religion in general into the contradiction between the state and its presuppositions in general.

The political emancipation of the Jew, the Christian, the religious man in general, is the *emancipation of the state* from Judaism, from Christianity, from *religion* in general. In a form and manner corresponding to its own nature, the state as such emancipates itself from religion when it emancipates itself from the state religion, that is, when the state as a state recognizes no religion but rather recognizes itself simply as the state. The political emancipation from religion is not the completed and consistent emancipation from religion because political emancipation is not the completed and consistent form of *human* emancipation.

The limits of political emancipation are seen at once in the fact that the state can liberate itself from a limitation without man really being free from it, without the state becoming a free state and man becoming a free man. Bauer himself tacitly admits this when he sets this stipulation for political emancipation:

"Every religious privilege in general, including also the monopoly of a privileged church, must be abolished, and if a few or many or

even the overwhelming majority still feel obliged to fulfill their religious obligations, such a practice must be left to them as a purely
private matter."

The *state* can thus emancipate itself from religion, even if the
overwhelming majority is still religious. And the overwhelming
majority does not cease to be religious by being religious *in private*.

But the attitude of the state, particularly the free state, to religion
is still only the attitude of the *human beings* who make up the state.
Hence it follows that man frees himself from a limitation *politically*,
through the state, when, in contradiction with himself, he overcomes
the limitation in an *abstract, limited*, and partial manner. It follows,
furthermore, that when man frees himself *politically*, he does so indirectly, through an *intermediary*, even if the intermediary is necessary. Finally, it follows that man, even when he proclaims himself
an atheist through the medium of the state, that is, when he proclaims the state to be atheistic, is still captive to religion because he
recognizes his atheism indirectly, through an intermediary. Religion
is merely the indirect recognition of man, through a *mediator*. The
state is the mediator between man and the freedom of man. As
Christ is the mediator on whom man unburdens all his own divinity
and his whole *religious burden*, so also the state is the mediator on
which man places all his unholiness and his whole *human burden*.

The political elevation of man above religion shares all the defects
and all the advantages of political elevation in general. If the state
as state, for example, abolishes private property, man proclaims private
property is abolished politically as soon as he does away with property
qualifications for active and passive voting eligibility, as has been
done in many North American states. Hamilton interprets this fact
quite correctly from a political point of view: "The great majority
of the people have won a victory over property owners and financial
wealth." Is not private property abolished in idea when the have-
nots come to legislate for the haves? Property qualification is the last
political form for recognizing private property.

Nevertheless, the political annulment of private property not only
does not abolish private property but even presupposes it. The state
abolishes distinctions of *birth, rank, education*, and *occupation* in its
own fashion when it declares them to be *nonpolitical*, when it proclaims that every member of the community participates *equally* in
popular sovereignty without regard for these distinctions, and when
it treats all elements of the actual life of the nation from the standpoint of the state. Nonetheless, the state permits private property,
education, and occupation to operate and manifest their particular
nature as private property, education, and occupation in their *own*
ways. Far from removing the *factual* distinctions, the state does rather

exist only by presupposing them, is aware of itself as a *political state* and makes its universality effective only in opposition to these elements. Hegel therefore correctly defines the relation of the *political state* to religion when he says:

"If the state is to be realized as a self-aware ethical actuality of the spirit, it must be distinct from the form of authority and faith; this distinction, however, emerges only insofar as the ecclesiastical sphere comes to a division within itself; only thus has the state attained universality of thought, the principle of its form, transcending particular churches and bringing it into existence." (Hegel's *Philosophy of Law*, 1st ed., p. 346.)

Exactly! Only thus, by being *above* the *particular* elements, does the state constitute itself as a universality.

In its nature the perfected political state is man's *species life* in contrast to his material life. In civil society all the presuppositions of this egoistic life remain outside the sphere of the state, but as qualities of civil society. Where the political state has reached full development, man leads a double life, a heavenly and an earthly life, not only in thought and consciousness but also in reality, as a *communal being* in the life of the *political community* and as a *private person* in the life of *civil society*, treating other men as means, reducing himself to a means, and becoming the plaything of alien powers. The political state is related spiritually to civil society as heaven is to earth. It stands in the same opposition to civil society and transcends it in the same way religion transcends the limitation of the profane world; that is, by recognizing, restoring, and letting itself be dominated by it. In his innermost essence, in civil society man is a profane being. Here, where he counts as an actual individual to himself and others, he is a fictitious phenomenon. On the other hand, in the state, where man counts as a species being, he is an imaginary member of an imagined sovereignty, stripped of his actual individual life and filled with an unreal universality.

The conflict in which man, as a believer in a particular religion, finds himself with his own citizenship, a member of the community along with other men, reduces itself to a secular split between the political state and the civil society. For man as bourgeois, "life in the state is only a semblance or a momentary exception to the real nature of things and to the general rule." The bourgeois, to be sure, like the Jew, participates in the life of the state only sophistically in the same way the *citoyen* remains only sophistically a Jew or bourgeois; but this sophistry is not personal. It is the sophistry of the political state itself. The difference between the religious person and the citizen is the difference between the shopkeeper and the citizen, between the day laborer and the citizen, between the landowner and the citizen, between the *living individual* and the *citizen*. The contradiction between the religious person and the political person is the same as that between the bourgeois and the *citoyen*, between the member of civil society and his political lion skin.

This secular conflict, to which the Jewish question ultimately reduces itself—the relation between the political state and its presuppositions, whether the latter be material elements, such as private property, etc., or spiritual elements, such as education and religion, the conflict between the *general* interest and the *private* interest, the split between the *political state* and the *civil society*—these secular contradictions are untouched by Bauer, while he polemicizes against their *religious* expression.

"It is precisely its basis, its necessity, that assures the maintenance of civil society and guarantees its necessity, that exposes its maintenance to constant dangers, sustains in it an element of uncertainty, and produces in civil society a constantly alternating mixture of poverty and riches, misery and prosperity, and change in general" (p. 8).

Consider his entire section, "Civil Society" (pp. 8-9), which is constructed along the main lines of Hegel's philosophy of law. Civil society in its opposition to the political state is recognized as necessary because the political state is recognized as necessary.

Political emancipation is indeed a great step forward; it is not, to be sure, the final form of human emancipation in general, but it is the final form of human emancipation *within* the prevailing world order. It goes without saying that we are here speaking of actual, practical emancipation.

Man emancipates himself politically from religion in that he banishes it from the sphere of public law into private right. It is no longer the spirit of the state, where man—even if in a limited fashion, in a particular form and in a particular sphere—associates as a species being in community with other men; it has become the spirit of civil society, the sphere of egoism, the *bellum omnia contra omnes* [war of all against all]. It is no longer the essence of *community* but the essence of *division*. It has become an expression of *separation* of man from his *community*, from himself and other men—as it was originally. It is now only the abstract acknowledgment of particular perversity, of private whim, of caprice. The endless splits of religion in North America, for example, already give it the external form of a purely individual matter. It has been thrown among numerous private interests and exiled from the commonwealth as a community. But one must not be deceived about the scope of political emancipation. The division of man into *public* and *private* persons, the displacement of religion from the state into civil society, is not merely a step in political emancipation but its *fulfillment,* which abolishes man's actual religiosity as little as it seeks to abolish it.

The breaking up of human beings into Jew and citizen, into Protestant and citizen, into religious man and citizen—this splintering is not a lie *against* citizenship or a circumvention of political emancipation; it is *political emancipation itself,* the political mode of emancipation from religion. To be sure, in periods when the political state as such is forcibly born from civil society, when men strive to liberate themselves under the form of political self-liberation, the state can and must go so far as to *abolish* religion to the point of *destroying* it, but only in the way it abolishes private property by setting a maximum, by confiscation, by progressive taxation, or only in the way it abolishes life by the guillotine. In moments of special concern for itself, political life seeks to repress its presuppositions, civil society and its elements, and to constitute itself as the actual, consistent life species of man. But it can do that only in violent contradiction to its own life conditions by declaring the revolution to be *permanent,* and thus the political drama is bound to end with the restoration of religion, private property, and all elements of civil society, just as war ends with peace.

Indeed, the perfected Christian state is not the so-called Christian state professing Christianity as its foundation, as its state religion that excludes all others; it is, rather, the *atheistic* state, the *democratic* state, the state that classifies religion as among the other elements of civil society. The state that is still theological and still officially prescribes belief in Christianity has not yet dared to proclaim itself *as a state* and has not yet succeeded in expressing in secular and human form, in its *actuality* as a state, the *human* foundation whose supreme expression is Christianity. The so-called Christian state is simply only a *nonstate,* for it is not Christianity as a religion but only the *human background* of the Christian religion that can realize itself in actual human creations.

The so-called Christian state is the Christian denial of the state, but in no way the political actualization of Christianity. The state that still professes Christianity in the form of religion does not profess it in political form because it still behaves religiously toward religion, that is, it is not the *actual expression* of the human basis of religion because it still provokes the unreality and the imaginary form of this human core. The so-called Christian state is an *imperfect* state, and the Christian religion serves as supplement and as sanctification of its imperfection. Religion, therefore, becomes necessarily its means to an end, and the state is a hypocrite. There is a great difference between a perfected state that counts religion as one of its prerequisites because of a lack in the general nature of the state, and an imperfect state which, in its particular existence and deficiency, proclaims religion as its foundation. In the latter case, religion becomes *imperfect politics*. In the former case, the imperfection of even perfected politics is revealed in religion. The so-called Christian state needs the Christian religion to complete itself *as a state*. The democratic state, the real state, needs no religion for its political fulfillment. It can, rather, divorce itself from religion because in it is fulfilled the human basis of religion in a secular way. The so-called Christian state, on the other hand, behaves politically toward religion and religiously toward politics. As it reduces political forms to mere appearance, so also does it reduce religion to a mere appearance.

To elucidate this contradiction, let us consider Bauer's construct of the Christian state, a construct that derives from his view of the Christian-Germanic state. . . .[3]

Bauer goes on to show how the people of a Christian state constitute a non-nation; they have no will of their own, but have, rather, their true existence in their ruler, to whom they are subject but who, however, is alien to them by origin and nature, that is, given to them by God without their own consent; furthermore, the laws of this people are not their own doing but are positive revelations. Bauer shows how the supreme ruler requires privileged mediators with his own people, the masses; how the masses themselves split into a multitude of distinct spheres formed and determined by chance, and differentiated from each other by their interests, particular passions and prejudices, but given the privilege of isolating themselves from each other (p. 56).

But Bauer himself says: "Politics, if it is to be nothing more than religion, cannot be politics any more than cleaning cooking pans, if it is to be treated religiously, can be regarded as an economic matter" (p. 108).

In the Christian-Germanic state, however, religion is an "economic matter," just as an "economic matter" is religion. In the Christian-Germanic state the dominance of religion is the religion of domination.

The separation of the "spirit of the Gospel" from the "letter of the Gospel" is an *irreligious* act. The state that permits the Gospel to speak in the words of politics or in any other words than those of the Holy Spirit commits a sacrilege, if not in the eyes of men at least in the eyes of its own religion. The state that acknowledges Christianity as its highest rule and the Bible as its charter must be confronted with the words of Holy Writ, for the Writ is holy in every word. This state, as well as the human rubbish on which it is based, falls into a painful and, from the standpoint of religious consciousness, insoluble contradiction, in the light of the teaching of the Gospel, which "it not only

---

3. A quotation from Bauer is omitted.

does not follow, but also cannot do so unless it wants to dissolve itself completely as a state." And why does it not want to dissolve itself completely? It cannot answer this question either for itself or for others. In its own consciousness, the official Christian state is an *ought* whose realization is unattainable, which knows how to legitimize the actuality of its existence only by lying, and hence always remains a subject of doubt, unreliable and problematic. Criticism is thus completely right in forcing the state based on the Bible into a mental derangement in which it no longer knows itself whether it is illusion or reality, in which the infamy of its secular purposes, for which religion serves as its cloak, irreconcilably conflicts with the integrity of its religious consciousness, to which religion appears as the purpose of the world. Such a state can free itself from its inner torment only by becoming the myrmidon of the Catholic Church. In the face of that church, which claims secular power as its servant, the state, the secular power claiming domination over the religious spirit, is impotent.

In the so-called Christian church, what counts, indeed, is *alienation*, but not *man*. The only man who does count, the *king*, is a being who is specifically differentiated from other men, who is personally religious and directly connected with heaven, with God. The relations prevailing here are still *religious* relations. The religious spirit is still not yet secularized.

But the religious spirit cannot actually be secularized, for what is it, in fact, but the *unsecular* form of a stage in the evolution of the human spirit? The religious spirit can be actualized only if the stage of evolution of the human spirit, whose religious expression it is, emerges into and assumes its *secular* form. This is what occurs in the democratic state. The basis of the democratic state is not Christianity but the human basis of Christianity. Religion remains the ideal, unsecular consciousness of its members, because it is the ideal form of the stage of human development fulfilled in the democratic state.

The members of the political state are religious because of the dualism between individual life and the life of the species, between the life of civil society and political life; they are religious inasmuch as man regards his true life as the political life remote from his actual individuality; they are religious inasmuch as religion is here the spirit of civil society, the expression of separation and alienation of man from man. Political democracy is Christian in that it regards man—not merely one man but every man—as *sovereign*, as the highest being; but this means man in his uncivilized and unsocial aspect, in his fortuitous existence, and just as he is, corrupted by the entire organization of our society, lost to himself, alienated, oppressed by the domination of inhuman relations and elements—in a word, man who is not yet an *actual* species being. The sovereignty of man, although an alien being distinct from actual men, which is the chimera, the dream, and the postulate of Christianity, is a tangible and present reality, a secular maxim, in democracy.

In the perfected democracy, the religious and theological consciousness appears to itself all the more religious and theological for being seemingly without political significance or earthly purposes, secluded from the world—an expression of reason's limitation, a product of caprice and fantasy, an actual life in the beyond. Christianity here achieves the *practical* expression of its universal religious significance in that the most varied views are grouped together as a form of Christianity, the more so since the state does not require anyone to profess Christianity, or any other religion in general. (See Beaumont, op. cit.) [In a democracy] the religious consciousness revels in the wealth of religious contradictions and multiplicity.

We have thus shown: Political emancipation from religion permits religion, although not a privileged religion, to continue. The contradiction in which the adherent of a particular religion finds himself in relation to his citizenship is only *one aspect* of the universal *secular contradiction between the political state and civil society*. The fulfillment of the Christian state is a state that acknowledges itself as a state and ignores the religion of its members. The emancipation of the state from religion is not the emancipation of actual man from religion.

We thus do not say with Bauer to the Jews: You cannot be politically emancipated without radically emancipating yourselves from Judaism. Rather we tell them: Because you can be politically emancipated without completely and consistently renouncing Judaism, *political emancipation* itself is not thereby *human* emancipation. If you Jews want to be politically emancipated without emancipating yourselves humanly, the incompleteness and contradiction lies not only in you but in the *essence* and *category* of political emancipation. If you are encompassed in this category, you share a general bias. Just as the state *evangelizes* when, in spite of being a state, it behaves toward the Jew in a Christian way, so the Jew *politicizes* when, in spite of being a Jew, he demands civil rights.

But if man, even if he is a Jew, wants to be politically emancipated and acquire civil rights, can he claim and acquire the so-called rights of man? Bauer denies it. . . .[4]

According to Bauer, man must sacrifice the "privilege of faith" to be able to acquire the universal rights of man. Let us for a moment consider these so-called rights of man, and particularly those rights in

---

4. A quotation from Bauer is omitted.

their most authentic form, the form they have among their discoverers, the North Americans and the French. In part, those rights are *political* that can be exercised only in community with others. Participation in the community, and particularly in the *political* community, the *state*, constitutes their substance. They belong in the category of political freedom, of civil rights, which, as we have seen, by no means presupposes the consistent and positive abolition of religion, including Judaism. There remains now for consideration the other part, the rights of man insofar as they are distinct from the rights of the citizen.

Among these one finds freedom of conscience, the right to practice one's chosen religion. The *privilege of faith* is expressly recognized either as a right of man or as a consequence of a right of man, freedom. . . .[5]

The incompatibility of religion with the rights of man is so little implied in the concept of the rights of man that the right to be religious according to one's liking, and to practice one's own particular religion, is explicitly included among the rights of man. The privilege of religion is a universal human right.

The rights of man as such are distinguished from the rights of the citizen, from civil rights. Who is this *man* distinguished from the *citizen?* None other than the *member of civil society*. Why is the member of civil society called "man," simply man, and why are his rights called the rights of man? How can we explain this fact? By the relation of the political state to civil society and by the nature of political emancipation.

First of all, let us note that the so-called rights of man as distinguished from the rights of the citizen are only the rights of a member of civil society, that is, of egoistic man, man separated from other men and from the community. The most radical constitution, the [French] Constitution of 1793, may be quoted:

Declaration of the Rights of Man and of the Citizen. Article 2. "These rights, etc." (the natural and imprescriptible rights) "are: equality, liberty, security, property."

What is this *liberty?*

Article 6. "Liberty is the power belonging to each man to do anything which does not impair the rights of others," or, according to the *Declaration of the Rights of Man* of 1791: "Liberty consists of the power to do anything which does not harm others."

Liberty is thus the right to do and perform anything that does not harm others. The limit within which each can act without harming

---

5. Quotations from the French *Declaration of the Rights of Man* and from some American state constitutions are omitted.

others is determined by law just as the boundary between two fields is marked by a stake. What is involved here is the liberty of man as an isolated monad, withdrawn into himself. Why, according to Bauer, is the Jew not capable of acquiring human rights? "So long as he remains a Jew, the limited nature which makes him a Jew must triumph over the human nature which should link him as a man with other men and must separate him from non-Jews."

But liberty as a right of man is not based on the association of man with man, but rather on the separation of man from man. It is the *right* of this separation, the *right* of the *limited* individual, limited to himself.

The practical application of the right of liberty is the right of *private property*.

Of what does the right of private property consist? Article 16 (Constitution of 1793): "The right of property is that belonging to every citizen to enjoy and dispose of his goods, his revenues, the fruit of his labor and of his industry, as he wills."

The right of private property is thus the right to enjoy and dispose of one's possessions as one wills, without regard for other men and independently of society. Individual freedom, as well as its application, constitutes the foundation of civil society. It lets every man find in other men not the *realization* but rather the *limitation* of his own freedom. It proclaims above all the right of man "to enjoy and dispose of his goods, his revenues, the fruit of his labor and of his industry, *as he wills*."

There still remain the other rights of man, equality and security.

Equality, here used in its nonpolitical sense, is nothing but the equality of the above-mentioned liberty, namely: that every man is equally viewed as a self-sufficient monad. The Constitution of 1795 defines the concept of equality, according to its significance, as follows:

Article 3: "Equality consists in the fact that the law is the same for all, whether it protects or whether it punishes."

And security?

Article 8 (Constitution of 1793): "Security consists in the protection accorded by society to each of its members for the preservation of his person, his rights and his property."

Security is the supreme social concept of civil society, the concept of the police, the concept that the whole society exists only to guarantee to each of its members the preservation of his person, his rights, and his property. In this sense, Hegel calls civil society "the state of necessity and rationality."

Civil society does not raise itself above its own egoism through the concept of security. Rather, security is the *guarantee* of egoism.

Thus none of the so-called rights of man goes beyond egoistic man, man withdrawn into himself, his private interest and his private choice, and separated from the community as a member of civil society. Far from viewing man here in his species being, his species being itself, society, appears rather to be an external framework for the individual, as a limitation of its original independence. The only bond that unites men is natural necessity, need, and private interest, the maintenance of their property and their egoistic persons.

It is quite curious that a nation just beginning to liberate itself, to tear down all barriers among the various members, and to build a political community, should solemnly proclaim (Declaration of 1791) the justification of the egoistic man, separated from his fellow men and from the community, and should even repeat this proclamation at a moment when only the most heroic sacrifice, which is urgently required, can save the nation, when the sacrifice of all the interests of civil society is made the order of the day and egoism has to be punished as a crime (*Declaration of the Rights of Man* of 1793). This becomes even more curious when we observe how the political liberators reduce citizenship, the *political community*, to a mere *means* for the preservation of these so-called rights of man and that the citizen is thus declared to be the servant of the egoistic man, the sphere in which man acts as a member of the community is degraded below that in which he acts as a fractional being, and finally man as bourgeois rather than man as citizen is considered to be the *proper* and *authentic* man.

"The goal of all political association is the preservation of the natural and imprescriptible rights of man" (*Declaration of the Rights of Man*, 1791, Article 2). "Government is instituted to guarantee man's enjoyment of his natural and imprescriptible rights" (*Declaration*, etc., of 1793, Article 1).

Thus even at the moment of its youthful enthusiasm, fired by the urgency of circumstances, political life is proclaimed to be a mere *means* whose goal is life in civil society. Revolutionary practice, to be sure, stands in flagrant contradiction to its theory. While security, for example, is proclaimed to be one of the rights of man, the violation of the privacy of the mails is publicly established as the order of the day. While the "*unlimited* freedom of the press" (Constitution of 1793, Article 122) as a consequence of the rights of man and individual freedom is guaranteed, freedom of the press is completely destroyed because "freedom of the press should not be permitted if it compromises public liberty" (Robespierre *jeune*, in *Parliamentary History of the French Revolution*, by Buchez and Roux, Vol. 28, p. 159). This means, therefore, that the human right of liberty ceases to be a right when it comes into conflict with political life, while theoretically political life is only the guarantee of the rights of man, the rights of individual men, and should be abandoned once it contradicts its *goal*, which is the rights of man. But the practice is only the exception, and the theory is the rule. Even if we choose to regard revolutionary practice as the correct expression of this relationship, the puzzle is still to be solved as to why, in the consciousness of the political emancipators, the relationship is turned upside down and the end appears as the means, and the means as the end. This optical illusion of their consciousness would always remain the same puzzle, even though a psychological and theoretical puzzle.

The enigma is easily solved.

Political emancipation is at the same time the *dissolution* of the old society on which rests the sovereign power, the state as alienated from the people. The political revolution is the revolution of civil society. What was the character of the old society? One word characterizes it: *Feudalism.* The old civil society had a *directly political* character—that is, the elements of civil life, such as property, for example, the family, or the mode and manner of work, were raised into elements of political life in the form of landlordism, estates, and corporations. In this form they determined the relationship of the particular individual to the *state as a whole*, that is, his political relationship, his separation and exclusion from other parts of society. For the feudal organization of national life had not raised ownership and labor to the level of social elements, but rather completed their separation from the state as a whole and established them as separate societies within society. Thus the life functions and life conditions of civil society always remained political, even if political in the feudal sense, that is, they excluded the individual from the state as a whole and transformed the special relationship between his corporation and the state into his own general relationship to national life, just as they transformed his specific civil activity and situation into a general activity and situation. As a consequence of this organization, there necessarily appears the unity of the state, as well as its consciousness, will, and activity—the general political power—likewise as the special business of the ruler and his servants, separated from the people.

The political revolution, which overthrew this domination and raised political affairs into people's affairs, and made the political state *everybody's* business—that is, an actual state—necessarily destroyed all estates, corporations, guilds, and privileges which had been the various expressions of the separation of the people from their community. The political revolution thereby abolished the political character of civil society. It shattered civil society into its constituent parts, on the one hand *individuals* and on the other the *material* and *spiritual elements* which constituted the vital content and civil situation of these individuals. It released the political spirit, which had been broken, fragmented, and lost, as it were, in various cul-de-sacs of feudal society; it gathered up this scattered spirit, liberated it from its entanglements with civil life, and turned it into the sphere of the community, the general concern of the people ideally independent of these particular elements of civil life. A definite activity and situation in life now sank to a merely individual significance. These no longer partook of the general relationship of the individual to the state as a whole. Public affairs as such became, rather, the general affairs of every individual and the political function became his general function.

But the fulfillment of the idealism of the state was at the same time the fulfillment of the materialism of civil society. The casting off of the political yoke was at the same time the casting off of the bond that had kept the egoistic spirit of civil society in fetters. Political emancipation was at the same time the emancipation of civil society from politics, from the very *semblance* of a political content.

Feudal society was dissolved into its foundation, into *man*. But into man as he actually was as its foundation, into *egoistical* man.

This man, the member of civil society, is now the basis and presupposition of the political state. He is recognized by it as such in the rights of man.

But the freedom of egoistic man and the recognition of this freedom is rather the recognition of the unbridled movement of the spiritual and material elements which form his life's content.

Thus man was not freed from religion; he received religious freedom. He was not freed by property. He received freedom of property. He was not freed by the egoism of occupation, but received freedom of occupation.

The constitution of the political state and the dissolution of civil society into independent individuals—whose relations are law just as the relations of estates and guilds were privilege—is accomplished in *one and the same act*. As a member of civil society, man is nonpolitical man but necessarily appears to be natural man. The rights of man appear as natural rights because self-conscious activity is concentrated in the political act. Egoistic man is the passive and preexisting result of the dissolved society, an object of immediate certainty, hence a *natural* object. The political revolution dissolves civil life into its constituent elements without revolutionizing those elements or subjecting them to criticism. It regards civil society—the world of needs, labor, private interests, private rights—as the basis of its existence, as a presupposition that needs no further ground, and hence as its *natural basis*. Finally, man, as a member of civil society, is regarded as *authentic man, man* as distinct from *citizen*, because he is man in his sensuous, individual, and most intimate existence, while political man is only the abstract and artificial man, man as an allegorical, moral person. Actual man is recognized only in the form of an egoistic individual; authentic man only in the form of abstract citizen.

The abstraction of the political man is correctly depicted by Rousseau: "Whoever dares to undertake the construction of a nation must feel himself capable of changing, so to speak, human nature and transforming each individual, who is himself a complete but isolated whole, into a part greater than himself from which he somehow derives his life existence, substituting a partial and moral existence for physical and independent existence. It is necessary to deprive man of his own powers and to give him alien powers which he cannot use without the aid of others." (*Social Contract*, Book II, London, 1782, p. 67.)

All emancipation is *restoration* of the human world and of the relationships of *men themselves*.

Political emancipation is the reduction of man to a member of civil society, to an egoistic, independent individual on the one hand, and to a citizen, a moral person, on the other.

Only when the actual, individual man has taken back into himself the abstract citizen and in his everyday life, his individual work, and his individual relationships has become a *species being*—only when he has recognized and organized his own powers as *social* powers so that social force is no longer separated from him in the form of *political* power, only then is human emancipation complete.

II

Here Bauer deals with the relation between the Jewish and Christian religions and their relation to criticism. Their relation to criticism is their relation to "the capacity to become free."

Thus: "The Christian has only one stage to surmount, namely, his religion, in order to abandon religion in general" and thus become free; "the Jew, on the other hand, has to break not only with his Jewish nature but also with the development of the completion of his religion, a development that has remained alien to him" (p. 71).

Thus Bauer transforms the question of Jewish emancipation into a purely religious one. The theological scruple as to whether Jew or Christian has the better prospect of salvation is here reproduced in the enlightened form: Which of the two is *more capable of emancipation?* Thus the question is no longer: Does Judaism or Christianity emancipate? But, on the contrary: What makes more free, the negation of Judaism or the negation of Christianity?

"If they want to be free, the Jews should not embrace Christianity but Christianity in dissolution and religion generally in dissolution, that is, enlightenment, criticism [of religion] and its results, free humanity" (p. 70).

For the Jew, what is still involved here is *professing a faith*, not Christianity, but rather Christianity in dissolution.

Bauer demands that the Jew break with the essence of the Christian religion, a demand which, as he says himself, does not follow from the development of the Jewish essence.

When Bauer, at the end of his *Jewish Question*, interpreted Judaism merely as a crude religious criticism of Christianity and hence gave it "only" a religious significance, it was to be expected that he would also transform the emancipation of the Jews into a philosophical-theological act.

Bauer conceives the *ideal* abstract essence of the Jew, his *religion*, as his *whole* nature. Hence he correctly concludes: "The Jew contributes nothing to mankind if he disregards his narrow law," if he eliminates all his Judaism (p. 65).

The relation of Jews and Christians thus becomes the following: The sole interest of the Christian in the emancipation of the Jew is a general human interest, a *theoretical* interest. Judaism is an offensive fact to the religious eye of the Christian. As soon as the Christian's eye ceases to be religious, this fact ceases to be offensive. In and for itself, the emancipation of the Jew is not the business of the Christian.

The Jew, on the other hand, in order to emancipate himself, not only has to do his own work but also at the same time to go through the work of the Christian—the *Critique of the Synoptics* [by Bruno Bauer] and the *Life of Jesus* [by David Friedrich Strauss]. "They can look after themselves: they will determine their own destiny; but history does not allow itself to be mocked" (p. 71).

We will try to break the theological formulation of the question. The question concerning the Jew's capacity for emancipation becomes for us the question: What particular *social* element is to be overcome in order to abolish Judaism? For the modern Jew's capacity for emancipation is the relation of Judaism to the emancipation of the modern world. This relation follows necessarily from the particular position of Judaism in today's enslaved world.

Let us consider the actual, secular Jew; not the *Sabbath Jew*, as Bauer does, but the *everyday Jew*.

Let us not look for the secret of the Jew in his religion, but let us look for the secret of religion in the actual Jew.

What is the secular basis of Judaism? Practical need, self-interest.

What is the worldly cult of the Jew? Haggling. What is his worldly god? Money.

Very well! Emancipation from haggling and money, and thus from practical and real Judaism, would be the self-emancipation of our age.

An organization of society which would abolish the preconditions of haggling and thus its opportunity for existence would render the

Jew impossible. His religious consciousness would dissolve like stale smoke in the actual life-giving air of society. On the other hand, when the Jew recognizes this practical nature of his as invalid and strives to eliminate it, he simply works away from his previous development toward general *human emancipation* and turns against the highest practical expression of human self-alienation.

Thus we perceive in Judaism a general contemporary antisocial element, which has been carried to its present apex by a historical development to which the Jews have zealously contributed—an apex at which it must necessarily dissolve itself.

The emancipation of the Jews, in the final analysis, is the emancipation of mankind from *Judaism*.

The Jew has already emancipated himself in a Jewish way. "The Jew who is only tolerated in Vienna, for example, determines the fate of the whole empire through his financial power. The Jew, who may be without rights in the smallest German state, decides the destiny of Europe. While corporations and guilds exclude the Jew or are unfavorable to him, audacity in industry mocks the obstinacy of these medieval institutions." (B. Bauer, *The Jewish Question*, p. 114.)

This is no isolated fact. The Jew has emancipated himself in a Jewish way not only by acquiring financial power but also because, with and without him, *money* has become a world power, and the practical Jewish spirit has become the practical spirit of Christian nations. The Jews have emancipated themselves insofar as the Christians have become Jews.

"The pious and politically free inhabitant of New England," Colonel Hamilton, for example, reports, "is a kind of Laocoön who does not even make the slightest effort to free himself from the serpents which strangle him. Mammon is his idol to whom he prays not only with his lips but with all the power of his body and soul. In his eyes, the world is nothing but a stock exchange, and he is convinced that here below he has no other destiny than to become richer than his neighbors. Haggling dominates his every thought, exchange of things constitutes his only recreation. When he travels, he carries, so to speak, his shop or office on his back and talks of nothing but interest and profit. If he loses sight of his own business for a moment, it is only in order to sniff out that of others."

Yes, the practical domination of Judaism over the Christian world in North America has achieved such clear and common expression that the very *preaching of the Gospel*, the Christian ministry, has become an article of commerce and the bankrupt merchant takes to the Gospel while the minister who has become rich goes into business.

"That man whom you see at the head of a respectable congregation began as a merchant; his business having failed, he became a minister; the other one started with the ministry, but as soon as he had acquired a sum of money, he left the pulpit for business. In the eyes of many, the religious ministry is a true commercial career" (Beaumont, op. cit., pp. 185, 186).

According to Bauer, it is "a hypocritical situation when the Jew is deprived of political rights in theory while he wields enormous power in practice and exercises his political influence wholesale which is denied to him in retail" (*The Jewish Question*, p. 114).

The contradiction existing between the practical political power of the Jew and his political rights is the contradiction between politics and financial power in general. While the former is ideally superior to the latter, in actual fact it has become its serf.

Judaism has persisted alongside Christianity not only as the religious critique of Christianity, not only as the incorporated doubt about the religious origin of Christianity, but equally because the practical Jewish spirit, Judaism, has perpetuated itself in Christian society and even attained its highest development there. The Jew, who exists as a special member of civil society, is only the special manifestation of civil society's Judaism.

Judaism has survived not in spite of history but by means of history.

Out of its own entrails, civil society constantly produces the Jew.

What, actually was the foundation, in and of itself, of the Jewish religion? Practical need, egoism.

Hence the Jew's monotheism is in reality the polytheism of many needs, a polytheism that makes even the toilet an object of divine law. *Practical need, egoism* is the principle of *civil society* and appears purely as such as soon as civil society has fully delivered itself of the political state. The god of *practical need and self-interest* is *Money*.

Money is the jealous god of Israel before whom no other god may exist. Money degrades all the gods of mankind—and converts them into commodities. Money is the universal, self-sufficient *value* of all things. Hence it has robbed the whole world, the human world as well as nature, of its proper worth. Money is the alienated essence of man's labor and life, and this alien essence dominates him as he worships it.

The god of the Jews has been secularized and has become the god of the world. The bill of exchange is the actual god of the Jew. His god is only an illusory bill of exchange.

The view of nature achieved under the rule of private property and money is an actual contempt for and practical degradation of nature, which, to be sure, does exist in the Jewish religion but only in imagination.

In this sense, Thomas Münzer declared it to be intolerable "that every creature should be turned into property, the fish in the water, the birds in the air, the plants on the earth—the creature must also become free."[6]

What is contained abstractly in the Jewish religion—contempt for theory, for art, for history, for man as an end in himself—is the *actual conscious* standpoint and virtue of the money-man. The species relation itself, the relation between man and woman, etc., becomes an object of commerce! The woman is haggled away.

The chimerical nationality of the Jew is the nationality of the merchant, of the money-man in general.

The Jew's unfathomable and unbounded law is only the religious caricature of baseless and bottomless morality and law in general, the caricature of merely *formal* rites with which the world of self-interest surrounds itself.

Here, too, the highest relation of man is the *legal* relation, the relation to laws which apply to him not because they are laws of his will and nature, but because they are in force and because defection from them will be avenged.

Jewish Jesuitism, the same practical Jesuitism that Bauer finds in the Talmud, is the relationship of the world of self-interest to the laws governing it, whose cunning is the chief art of that world.

Yes, the movement of that world within its laws is necessarily an abrogation of the law.

Judaism could not develop further as religion, could not develop further theoretically, because the perspective of practical need is limited by its very nature and is soon exhausted.

By its very nature, the religion of practical need could not find fulfillment in theory but only in practice, precisely because practice is its truth.

Judaism could create no new world; it could only draw world creations and world conditions into the compass of its own activity because practical need, whose rationale is self-interest, remains passive and does not extend itself willingly but only finds itself extended by the continuous development of social conditions.

Judaism reaches its apex with the perfection of civil society; but civil society achieves perfection only in the Christian world. Only

---

6. Quoted from Thomas Münzer's anti-Luther pamphlet, *Hoch verursachte Schutzrede und Antwort wider das geistlose, sanftlebende Fleisch zu Wittenberg, welches mit verkehrter Weise durch den Diebstahl der heiligen Schrift die erbaermliche Christenheit also ganz jaemmerlich besudelt hat (Highly Motivated Defense Speech and Reply Against the Insipid, Soft-living Flesh at Wittenberg, Which in a Topsy-Turvy Way, Through the Theft of Holy Scriptures, Has Quite Miserably Befouled Wretched Christianity)* (1524).

under the reign of Christianity, which makes all national, natural, moral, and theoretical relationships *external* to man, could civil society separate itself completely from political life, sever all man's species ties, substitute egoism and selfish need for those ties, and dissolve the human world into a world of atomistic individuals confronting each other in mutual hostility.

Christianity arose out of Judaism. It has again dissolved itself into Judaism.

From the beginning, the Christian was the theorizing Jew; the Jew is, therefore, the practical Christian, and the practical Christian has again become a Jew.

Christianity overcame real Judaism only in appearance. It was too *noble*, too spiritual, to eliminate the crudeness of practical need except by elevating it into the heavens.

Christianity is the sublime thought of Judaism, and Judaism is the common practical application of Christianity; but this application could become universal only after Christianity as the completed religion had *theoretically* completed the alienation of man from himself and from nature.

Only then could Judaism attain universal dominion and convert divested man and divested nature into *alienable* and salable objects subservient to egoistic need, dependent on haggling.

Selling is the practice of alienation [of property]. As long as man is religiously captivated, knows his nature only as objectified, and thus makes it into an alien, illusory being, so under the dominion of egoistic need he can only act practically, only produce objects practically, by subordinating his products, as well as his activity, to the domination of an alien being, bestowing upon it the significance of an alien being—Money.

The Christian salvation-egoism in its practical fulfillment necessarily becomes the material egoism of the Jew, heavenly need is converted into earthly need, subjectivism into self-interest. We do not explain the Jew's tenacity from his religion but rather from the human basis of his religion, from practical need, from egoism.

Since the Jew's real nature has been generally actualized and secularized in civil society, civil society could not convince the Jew of the unreality of his religious nature, which is precisely the ideal perception of practical need. Hence not only in the Pentateuch or the Talmud but also in present society do we find the nature of the contemporary Jew, not as an abstract being but as a highly empirical one, not only as the Jew's own narrowness but also as the Jewish narrowness of society.

As soon as society succeeds in abolishing the empirical essence of Judaism—haggling and its presuppositions—the Jew becomes impossible, because his consciousness no longer has an object, because the subjective basis of Judaism—practical need—is humanized, because the conflict between individual-sensuous existence and man's species existence is abolished.

The *social* emancipation of the Jew is the *emancipation of society from Judaism.*

Questions of Judaism from *The Holy Family**

THE JEWISH QUESTION, No. 1—SETTING OF THE QUESTION

THE "SPIRIT," contrary to the mass, immediately behaves in a *critical* way by considering its own limited work, Bruno Bauer's *Die Judenfrage*, as absolute, and only the opponents of that work as sinners. In Reply No. 1 to attacks on that treatise, he does not show any inkling of its defects; on the contrary, he declares he has developed the "true," "general" (!) significance of the Jewish question. In later replies we shall see him obliged to admit his "oversights."

"The reception my book has had is the beginning of the proof that the very ones who so far have advocated freedom and still do advocate it must rise against the spirit more than any others; the defense I am now going to provide it with will supply further proof of how thoughtless the spokesmen of the mass are; they have God knows what a great opinion of themselves for supporting emancipation and the dogma of the 'rights of man.'"

On the occasion of a treatise by Absolute Criticism the "mass" must necessarily have begun to prove its opposition to the spirit; for it is its opposition to Absolute Criticism that determines and proves its existence.

The polemic of a few liberal and rationalist Jews against Herr Bruno's *Die Judenfrage* has naturally quite a different critical meaning than the massy polemic of the liberals against philosophy and of the

---

* *The Holy Family* was published by Marx and Engels in 1845. The text used here is based on that of the Foreign Languages Publishing House, Moscow, 1956, by R. Dixon.

rationalists against Strauss. Incidentally, the originality of the above quoted remark can be judged by the following passage from Hegel:

"We can here note the particular form of evil conscience manifest in the kind of eloquence with which that shallowness" (of the liberals) "plumes itself, and first of all in the fact that it speaks most of spirit where it has the least, and uses the word life where it is most dead and withered," etc.

As for the "rights of man," it has been proved to Herr Bruno ("*Die Judenfrage*," *Deutsch-Französische Jahrbücher*) that it is "he himself," not the spokesmen of the mass, who has misunderstood and dogmatically mishandled the essence of those rights. Compared to his discovery that the rights of man are not "innate"—a discovery which has been made innumerable times in England during the past forty years—Fourier's assertion that the right to fish, to hunt, etc., are innate rights of men is one of genius.

We give but a few examples of Herr Bruno's fight against Philippson, Hirsch and others. Even such poor opponents as these are not disposed of by Absolute Criticism. It is by no means preposterous of Mr. Philippson, as Absolute Criticism maintains, to say: "Bauer imagines a peculiar kind of state . . . a philosophical ideal of a state."

Herr Bruno, who confuses the state with humanity, the rights of man with man, and political emancipation with human emancipation, was bound, if not to conceive, at least to imagine a peculiar kind of state, a philosophical ideal of a state.

"Instead of writing his boring statement the rhetorician" (Herr Hirsch) "would have done better to refute my proof that the Christian state, having as its vital principle a definite religion, cannot allow adherents of another religion . . . complete equality with its own estates."

Had the rhetorician Hirsch really refuted Herr Bruno's proof and shown, as is done in the *Deutsch-Französische Jahrbücher*, that the state of estates and exclusive Christianity is not only an incomplete state but an incomplete *Christian* state, Herr Bruno would have answered as he does to that refutation: "Objections in this instance are meaningless."

Herr Hirsch is quite correct when in answer to Herr Bruno's statement, "By pressure on the mainsprings of history the Jews provoked counterpressure," he recalls: "Then they must have been something in the making of history, and if Bauer himself asserts this, he has no right to assert, on the other hand, that they did not contribute to the making of modern times."

Herr Bruno answers: "An eyesore is something too—does that mean it contributes to develop my eyesight?"

Something which has been an eyesore to me since my birth, as the

Jews have been to the Christian world, which grows and develops with me, is not an ordinary sore, but a wonderful one, one that really belongs to my eye and must even contribute to a highly original development of my eyesight. The critical "eyesore" does not therefore hurt the rhetorician Hirsch. However, the criticism quoted above revealed to Herr Bruno the significance of Jewry in "the making of modern times."

The theological mind of Absolute Criticism feels so offended by a Rhine Landtag deputy's statement that "the Jews are queer in their own Jewish way, not in our so-called Christian way," that it is still "calling him to order for using such an argument."

When another deputy maintained "civil equality can be given to Jews only where Jewry no longer exists," Herr Bruno observed: "Correct! Correct, to be precise, when the critical point made by me in my treatise" (that point being that Christianity must lso have ceased to exist) "is taken into account."

We see that in its Reply No. 1 to the attacks upon the *Judenfrage* Absolute Criticism still considers the abolition of religion, atheism, to be the condition for civil equality. In its first stage it has therefore not yet acquired any deeper insight into the essence of the state than into the "oversight" of its "work."

Absolute Criticism feels offended when one of its *intended* "latest" scientific discoveries is betrayed as an already generally accepted view. A Rhineland deputy remarked: "Nobody has yet maintained that France and Belgium were remarkable for particular clarity in recognizing principles in the organization of political relations."

Absolute Criticism could have objected that that assertion transported the present back into the past by representing as traditional the now trivial view that the principles of French policy are inadequate. Such a relevant objection would not have suited Absolute Criticism. On the contrary, it must give the old-fashioned view as that of the present and proclaim the now prevailing view a critical mystery which *its* investigation still has to reveal to the mass. Hence it must say:

"It" (the antiquated prejudice) "has been asserted by very many" (the mass); "but a thorough investigation of history will provide the proof that even after the great work done by France to comprehend the principles, much still remains to be achieved."

A thorough investigation of history itself will therefore not achieve the comprehension of the principles. It will only prove in its thoroughness that "much still remains to be achieved." A great achievement, especially after the works of the socialists! Nevertheless Herr Bruno already achieves much for the comprehension of the present social situation by his remark: "The certainty prevailing at present is uncertainty."

Hegel says that the prevailing Chinese certainty is "Being"; the prevailing Indian certainty is "Nothingness," etc. Absolute Criticism joins him in the "pure" way when it resolves the character of the present time in the logical category "Uncertainty," and all the purer as "Uncertainty," like "Being" and "Nothingness," belongs to the first chapter of speculative logic, to the chapter on "Quality."

We cannot leave No. 1 of *Die Judenfrage* without a general remark.

One of the chief pursuits of Absolute Criticism consists in first bringing all questions of the day into the right setting. For it does not answer the real questions—it substitutes quite different ones. As it makes everything, it must also first make the "questions of the day," make them its own questions, the questions of Critical Criticism. If it were a question of the Napoleonic Code, it would prove that it is properly a question of the Pentateuch. Its setting of "questions of the day" is critical distortion and misplacement of them. It thus distorted the Jewish question in such a way that it did not need to investigate political emancipation, which that question deals with, but could be satisfied with a criticism of the Jewish religion and a description of the Christian-Germanic state.

This method, like all Absolute Criticism's originalities, is the repetition of a *speculative* witticism. *Speculative* philosophy, to be exact, Hegel's philosophy, must transpose all questions from the form of human common sense to the form of speculative reason and change the real question into a speculative one to be able to answer it. Having distorted my question on my lips and put its own question on my lips like the catechism, it could naturally have a ready answer to all my questions, also like the catechism.

THE JEWISH QUESTION, NO. 2—CRITICAL DISCOVERIES IN
SOCIALISM, JURISPRUDENCE, AND POLITICS (NATIONALITY)

To the mass of material Jews is being preached the Christian doctrine of freedom of the spirit, freedom in theory, that spiritualist freedom which imagines itself to be free even in chains, whose soul is satisfied with "the idea" and embarrassed by any kind of mass existence.

"The Jews are emancipated to the extent of their progress in theory, they are free to the extent that they wish to be free."

From that proposition one can immediately measure the critical gap which separates massy, profane communism and socialism from *Absolute* socialism. The first proposition of profane socialism rejects emancipation *in mere theory* as an illusion and for *real* freedom it demands besides the idealistic "will" quite palpable material conditions.

How low "the mass" is in comparison with holy Criticism, the mass which considers material, practical upheavals necessary to win the time and means required even to deal with "theory"!

Let us leave purely spiritual socialism an instant for politics!

Herr Riesser argues against Bruno Bauer that *his* state (i.e., the Critical state) must exclude "Jews" and "Christians." Herr Riesser is right. Since Herr Bauer confuses *human* emancipation with *political* emancipation, since the state can react to adverse elements—and Christianity and Judaism are considered treasonable elements in the *Judenfrage*—only by forcible expulsion of the *persons* representing them (the Terror, for instance, wished to do away with corn hoarding by guillotining the hoarders), Herr Bauer must have both Jews and Christians hanged in his "Critical state." Having confused political emancipation with human emancipation, he had to be consistent and confuse the *political means* of emancipation with the *human means*. But as soon as Absolute Criticism hears the definite meaning of its deductions formulated, it gives the answer Schelling once gave to his opponents who substituted real thoughts for his phrases:

"Criticism's opponents are its opponents because they not only measure it with their dogmatic yardstick but consider it dogmatic itself: they oppose criticism because it will not recognize their dogmatic distinctions, definitions, and evasions."

It is, indeed, adopting a dogmatic attitude to Absolute Criticism, as to Herr Schelling, to attribute to it definite, real significance, thought and views. In order to be accommodating and to prove to Herr Riesser its humanity "Criticism," however, decides to resort to dogmatic distinctions, definitions, and, to be precise, to evasions.

Thus we read: "Had I in that work" (*Die Judenfrage*) "had the will or the right to go beyond criticism, I ought" (!) "to have spoken" (!) "not of the state, but of society, which excludes nobody but from which only those exclude themselves who do not wish to take part in its development."

Here Absolute Criticism makes a *dogmatic distinction* between what it ought to have done if it had not done the contrary and what it actually did. It explains the narrowness of its *Die Judenfrage* by the "dogmatic evasions" of having the will and having the right which prohibited it from "going beyond criticism." What? "Criticism" should go beyond "criticism." This quite massy notion occurs to Absolute Criticism because of the dogmatic necessity for, on the one hand, asserting its conception of the Jewish question as absolute, as Criticism, and, on the other hand, admitting a more comprehensive conception.

The mystery of its not having the will and not having the right will later be revealed as the Critical dogma according to which all apparent limitations of "Criticism" are nothing but necessary adaptations to the powers of comprehension of the mass.

It had not the *will!* It had not the *right* to go beyond its narrow conception of the Jewish question! But what would it have done had it the will or the right? It would have given a *dogmatic definition.* It would have spoken of "society" instead of the "state," in other words it would not have studied the real relation of Jewry to civil society today! It would have given a dogmatic definition of the "society" as distinct from the "state" in the sense that whereas the state expels those who do not wish to take part in its development, such people exclude themselves from society!

Society behaves just as exclusively as the state, only in a more polite form: it does not throw you out, but it makes it so uncomfortable for you that you go out of your own will.

In substance the state does not behave otherwise, for it does not expel anybody who is satisfied with *its* demands and orders and *its* development. In its perfection it even closes its eyes and declares *real* contradictions to be *nonpolitical* contradictions which do not disturb it. Besides, Absolute Criticism itself has argued that the state excludes Jews only because and insofar as the Jews exclude the state and hence exclude *themselves* from the state. If these relations have a more courteous, a more hypocritical, and a more crafty form in Critical "society" that on.y proves that "Critical society" is more hypocritical and less developed in its structure.

Let us follow Absolute Criticism deeper in its "dogmatic distinctions" and "definitions," to be precise, in its "evasions."

Herr Riesser, for example, demands of the critic "that he distinguish what belongs to the domain of law" from "what is beyond it."

The Critic is indignant at the impertinence of this juridical demand.

"So far," he retorts, "both feeling and conscience have, however, interfered in law, supplemented it, and, because of the quality based on its *dogmatic form*" (not, therefore, on its *dogmatic essence?*) "have always had to supplement it."

The Critic forgets that *law*, on the other hand, distinguishes itself quite explicitly from "feeling and conscience," that this distinction is based on the one-sided *essence* of *law* as well as on its dogmatic form, that it is even one of the *main dogmas* of law; that, finally, the practical implementation of that distinction is just as much the peak of the *development of law* as the separation of religion from all profane content makes it abstract, absolute religion. The fact that "feeling and conscience" interfere in law is sufficient reason for the Critic to speak of feeling and conscience when it is a matter of law and of theological dogmatics when it is a matter of juridical dogmatics.

The "definitions and distinctions" of Absolute Criticism have prepared us sufficiently to hear its latest "discoveries" about "society" and "law."

"The world form that Criticism is preparing and the thought of which it is even first preparing is no merely legal form but" (collect yourself, Reader) "a form of society about which at least this much" (this little?) "can be said: whoever has not made his contribution to its formation and does not live with his feeling and conscience in it, does not feel at home in it and cannot take part in its history."

The world form that "Criticism" is preparing is defined as *not merely* legal, but social. This definition can be interpreted in two ways. The sentence quoted may be taken as *"not legal but social"* or "not merely legal, but *also* social." Let us consider its content according to both readings, beginning with the first. Earlier, Absolute Criticism defined the new "world form" distinct from the "state" as "society." Now it defines the noun "society" by the adjective "social." If Herr Hinrichs was three times given the word "social" in contrast to his "political," Herr Riesser is now given "social society" in contrast to his "legal." If the Critical explanations for Herr Hinrichs came to the formula "social" + "social" + "social" $= 3$ a, Absolute Criticism passes in its second campaign from addition to multiplication and Herr Riesser is referred to society multiplied by itself, society to the *second* power, social society $= a^2$. In order to complete its deductions on society all Absolute Criticism now has to do is to go on to fractions, to extract the square root of society, and so forth.

If on the other hand we take the second reading: the "not merely legal but also social" world form, this hybrid world form is nothing but the world form existing today, the world form of society today. It is a great, a venerable Critical miracle that "Criticism" in its pre-world thinking is only just preparing the future existence of the world form which already exists today. But however it be with "not merely legal but also social society" Criticism can for the time being say no more about it than *"fabula docet"* ["the fable teaches"] the moral application. Those who do not believe in that society with their feeling and their conscience will "not feel at home" in it. In the end, nobody will live in that society except "pure feeling" and "pure conscience," that is, "the spirit," "Criticism" and its supporters. The mass will be excluded from it one way or another so that "massy society" will dwell outside "social society."

In a word, this society is nothing but the *Critical heaven* from which the real world is excluded as being the *un-Critical hell*. In its pure thinking Absolute Criticism is preparing this transfigured world form of the antithesis between "Mass" and "Spirit."

From the same Critical depths as these explanations on "society" come the explanations Herr Riesser is given on the destiny of nations.

The Jews' desire for emancipation and the desire of Christian states to "classify" the Jews in "their government scheme"—as though the Jews had not long ago been classified in the Christian government schemes!—leads Absolute Criticism to prophecies on the "decay of nationalities." See by what a complicated detour Absolute Criticism arrives at the present historical movement—by the *detour of theology*. The following illuminating words of the oracle show us what great results Criticism achieves in this way:

"The future of all nationalities—is—very—gloomy!"

But let the future of nationalities be as gloomy as it may, for Criticism's sake. The one essential thing is clear: the *future* is the *work of Criticism*.

"Destiny," it exclaims, "may decide as it will: we now know that it is our work."

As God leaves *his* creation, man, his own will, so *Criticism* gives destiny, which is *its creation*, its *own will*. Criticism, which makes destiny, is, like God, almighty. Even the "resistance" which it "finds outside itself" is its work. "Criticism makes its adversary." "Massy indignation" against it is therefore "dangerous" only for "the mass" itself

But if Criticism, like God, is almighty, it is also all-wise like him and is capable of combining its almightiness with the *freedom*, the *will* and the *natural attributes* of human individuals.

"It would not be the epoch-making force if it did not have the effect of making each one what he wills to be and showing each one irrevocably the standpoint corresponding to his nature and his will."

Leibniz could not have given a happier presentation of the pre-established harmony between the almightiness of God and human freedom and the natural attributes of man.

If "Criticism" seems to clash with psychology by not distinguishing between the *will* to be something and the *ability* to be something, it must be borne in mind that it has decisive grounds to declare such a "distinction" "dogmatic."

Let us steel ourselves for the third campaign! Let us recall once more that "Criticism *makes* its adversary!" But how could it make its adversary the "phrase" if it were not a phrasemonger?

THE JEWISH QUESTION, No. 3

"Absolute Criticism" does not remain where it is when it has proved by its autobiography its own singular omnipotence which "first creates the old, properly speaking, just as much as the new." It does not remain where it is when it has written in person the apology of its past. It now sets a third party, the rest of the profane world, the Absolute "task," the "task which is now the main one," the apology of Bauer's deeds and "works."

Deutsch-Französische Jahrbücher published a criticism of Herr Bauer's *Die Judenfrage*. His basic error, the confusion of "political" with "human" emancipation, was revealed. Granted, the old Jewish question was not at first given its "correct setting"; the Jewish question was dealt with and resolved in the setting which new developments have given to old questions and as a result of which the latter have become "questions" of the present instead of "questions" of the past.

Absolute Criticism's third campaign, it seems, is to reply to *Deutsch-Französische Jahrbücher*. At first Absolute Criticism admits: "In *Die Judenfrage* the same 'oversight' was made—the human and the political were identified."

Criticism notes: "it would be too late to reproach Criticism for the stand which it still adopted partially two years ago." "The question is rather to give the explanation why Criticism . . . had to engage even in politics."

"Two years ago"? We must reckon according to the Absolute chronology, from the birth of the Critical Redeemer, Bauer's *Literatur-Zeitung!* The Critical Redeemer was born in 1843. In the same year the second enlarged edition of *Die Judenfrage* was published. The "Critical" treatise on the Jewish question in *Einundzwanzig Bogen aus der Schweiz* appeared later in the same year, 1843, old style. After the downfall of *Deutsche Jahrbücher* and *Rheinische Zeitung*, in the same momentous year 1843, old style, or *anno* 1 of the Critical era, appeared Herr Bauer's fantastic-political work *Staat, Religion und Partei*, which exactly repeated his old errors on "the essence of politics." The apologist is forced to falsify chronology.

The "explanation" why Herr Bauer "had to" engage "even" in "politics" remains of general interest only under certain conditions. The fact is that if the infallibility, purity, and absoluteness of Critical Criticism are assumed as the *basic dogma*, the facts contradicting that dogma are turned into riddles which are just as difficult, profound, and mysterious as the apparently ungodly deeds of God are for theologians.

If, on the other hand, "the Critic" is considered as a finite individual, if he is not separated from the limitations of his time, one can dispense with the answer to the question why he must develop even within the world, because the question itself no longer exists.

If, notwithstanding, Absolute Criticism insists on its demand, one can offer to provide a nice little scholastic treatise dealing with the following "questions of the times": "Why had the Virgin Mary's con-

ception by the Holy Ghost to be proved by no other than Herr Bruno
Bauer?" "Why had Herr Bauer to prove that the angel that appeared
to Abraham was a *real* emanation of God, an emanation which, nevertheless, lacked the consistency necessary to *digest food?*" "Why had
Herr Bauer to provide an apology of the Prussian royal house and to
raise the Prussian state to the rank of *absolute* state?" "Why had Herr
Bauer, in his *Kritik der Synoptiker,* to substitute '*infinite self-consciousness*' for *man?*" "Why had Herr Bauer in his *Das entdeckte Christen-
thum* to repeat the Christian theory of creation in a Hegelian form?"
"Why had Herr Bauer to demand of himself and others the 'explanation' for the wonder that he must have been mistaken?"

While waiting for proofs of these necessities which are just as
"Critical" as they are "Absolute" let us listen once more to "Criticism's
apologetic evasions."

"The Jewish question . . . had . . . first to be brought into its correct
setting, as a religious, theological, and political question." "As the treatment and solution of both these questions, Criticism is neither religious
nor political."

The point is that *Deutsch-Französische Jahrbücher* declares Bauer's
treatment of the Jewish question to be really theological and fantastic-
political.

To begin with, "Criticism" answers the "reproach" of theological
limitation: "The Jewish question is a religious question. The Enlightenment claimed to solve it by describing the religious contradiction as
insignificant or by denying it altogether. Criticism, on the contrary,
had to present it in its purity."

When we get to the *political* part of the Jewish question we shall
see also that in politics Herr Bauer the theologian does not deal with
politics but with theology.

But when *Deutsch-Französische Jahrbücher* attacked his treatment
of the Jewish question as "purely religious" it was concerned mainly
with his article in *Einundzwanzig Bogen aus der Schweiz,* the title of
which was "The Capacity of the Christians and Jews of Today to
Obtain Freedom."

This article has nothing to do with the old "Enlightenment." It
contains Herr Bauer's *positive* view on the ability of the Jews of today
to be emancipated, that is, on the possibility of their emancipation.

"Criticism" says: "The Jewish question is a *religious* question."

The question is; "What is a religious question, and in particular
what is a religious question today?

The *theologian* will judge by *appearances* and see a *religious*
question in a *religious* question. But "Criticism" must remember the
explanation it gave against Professor Hinrichs that the *political* interests

of the present have *social* significance, that it is "no longer a question" of political interests.

Deutsch-Französische Jahrbücher was just as right when it said to "Criticism": *Religious* questions of the day have at the present a *social* significance. It is no longer a question of religious interests as such. Only the theologian can believe it is a question of religion as religion. Granted, *Deutsch-Französische Jahrbücher* committed the error of not stopping at the word "social." It characterized the *real* position of the Jews in civil society today. Once Jewry was laid bare of the religious shell in which it was disguised and released in its empirical, worldly, practical nucleus, the practical, *really social* way in which that nucleus is to be abolished could be indicated. Herr Bauer was content with a "religious question" being a "religious question."

It was by no means denied, as Herr Bauer pretends, that the Jewish question is also a religious question. It was said, on the contrary: Herr Bauer grasps *only the religious essence* of Jewry and not the *worldly, real basis* of that religious essence. He opposes *religious consciousness* as if it were an independent being. Herr Bauer therefore explains the *real* Jews by the *Jewish religion*, instead of explaining the mystery of the Jewish religion by the *real Jews*. Herr Bauer therefore understands the Jew only insofar as he is an immediate object of theology, or a theologian.

But Herr Bauer has not an inkling that real, worldly Jewry and hence religious Judaism too, is being continually produced by the *present civil life* and finds its final development in the *money system*. He could have no inkling of this because he did not know Jewry as a link in the real world but only as a link in his world, theology; because he, as a pious godly man, considers not the *everyday Jew* but the *Jew of the Sabbath* to be the *real Jew*. For Herr Bauer, the theologian of the Christian faith, the historic significance of Jewry must cease the moment Christianity is born. Hence he must repeat the old orthodox view that it has maintained itself *in spite of* history; he must serve up again in a Critical-theological form the old theological superstition that Jewry exists only as a confirmation of the divine curse, as palpable proof of the Christian revelation; that it exists and has existed only as a vulgar religious doubt of the supernatural origin of Christianity, that is, as a palpable proof against Christian revelation.

In *Deutsch-Französische Jahrbücher* it is proved, on the contrary, that Jewry has maintained itself and developed *through* history, *in* and *with* history, and that that development is to be perceived not by the eye of the theologian, but by the eye of the man of the world, because it is to be found, not in *religious theory*, but only in *commercial* and *industrial practice*. It is explained why practical Jewry reaches perfection only in the perfection of the Christian world; why, indeed, it is the perfect *practice* of the *Christian world itself*. The existence of the present-day Jew is not explained by his religion, as though the latter were some independent being existing apart, but the survival of the Jewish religion is explained by practical factors of civil society which are *fantastically* reflected in that religion. The emancipation of the Jews to make human beings of them, or the human emancipation of Jewry, is therefore not conceived, as by Herr Bauer, as the special task of the Jews, but as the general practical task of the whole world today, which is *Jewish* to the core. It was proved that the task of abolishing the essence of Jewry is in truth the task of abolishing *Jewry in civil society*, abolishing the inhumanity of today's practice of life, the summit of which is the *money system*.

Herr Bauer, a genuine though Critical theologian or theological critic, could not get beyond the religious contradiction. In the attitude of the Jews to the Christian world he could see only the attitude of the Jewish religion to the Christian religion. He even had to restore the religious opposition *critically* in the *antithesis* between the attitudes of the Jew and the Christian to *critical* religion—atheism, the last stage of theism, the *negative* recognition of God. Finally, in his theological fanaticism he had to *limit* the capacity of "Jews and Christians of today," i.e., of the world of today, "to obtain freedom," to their capacity to grasp "the criticism" of theology and apply it themselves. For the orthodox theologian the world is dissolved in "religion and theology." (He could just as well dissolve it in politics, political economy, etc., and call theology heavenly political economy, for example, as it is the teaching of the production, distribution, exchange, and consumption of "spiritual wealth" and of the treasures of heaven!) Similarly for the radical, critical theologian, the capacity of the world to obtain freedom is dissolved in the single abstract capacity to criticize "religion and theology" as "religion and theology." The only struggle he knows is the struggle against the *religious* limitations of self-consciousness, whose critical "purity" and "infinity" is just as much a theological limitation.

Herr Bauer, therefore, dealt with religious and theological questions in the religious and theological way, if only because he saw in the "religious" question of the time a "purely religious" question. His "correct setting of the question" sets the question "correctly" only in respect of his "own capacity"—to answer!

Let us now go on to the political part of *Die Judenfrage*.

The Jews (like the Christians) are fully *politically emancipated* in various states. Both Jews and Christians are far from being *humanly* emancipated. Hence there must be a difference between *political* and *human* emancipation. The essence of political emancipation, i.e., of the developed, modern state, must therefore be studied. On the other hand, states which cannot yet politically emancipate the Jews must be rated by comparison with accomplished political states and must be considered as underdeveloped.

That was the point of view from which the "political emancipation" of the Jews should have been dealt with and is dealt with in *Deutsch-Französische Jahrbücher.*

Herr Bauer offers the following defense of "Criticism's" *Die Judenfrage:* "The Jews were shown that they labored under an illusion as to the system of which they demanded to be freed."

Herr Bauer did show that the illusion of the *German* Jews was to demand the right to take part in general political life in a land where there was no general political life and to demand political *rights* where only political privileges existed. On the other hand, Herr Bauer was shown that he himself labored under no less "illusions" as to the "German political system" than the Jews. His illusion was that he explained the position of the Jews in the German states by the alleged inability of "the Christian state" to emancipate the Jews politically. He argued in the teeth of facts and construed the state of privilege, the Christian-Germanic state, as the Absolute Christian state. It was proved to him, on the contrary, that the politically perfect, modern state that knows no religious privileges is also the perfect *Christian* state, and that hence the perfect Christian state, not only *can* emancipate the Jews but has emancipated them and by its very nature must emancipate them.

"The Jews are shown . . . that they had the greatest illusions concerning themselves when they wanted to demand freedom and the recognition of free humanity, whereas for them it was only, and could only be, a question of a special privilege."

Freedom! Recognition of free humanity! Special privilege! Edifying words by which certain questions can be apologetically by-passed!

Freedom? It was a matter of *political* freedom. Herr Bauer was shown that if the Jew demands freedom and nevertheless will not renounce his religion, he "is indulging in politics" and sets no condition contrary to *political* freedom. Herr Bauer was shown that it is by no means contrary to political emancipation to divide man into the nonreligious *citizen* and the religious *private individual.* He was shown that as the state emancipates itself from religion by emancipating itself from *state religion* and leaving religion to itself within civil society, so the individual emancipates himself *politically* from religion when his attitude to it is no longer as to a *public* but as to a *private matter.* Finally, it was shown that the *terroristic* attitude of the French Revolution to religion, far from refuting this conception, bears it out.

Instead of studying the real attitude of the modern state to religion, Herr Bauer thought it necessary to imagine a *Critical* state,
a state which is nothing else but the *critic of theology inflated to the
size of a state* in Herr Bauer's imagination. Whenever Herr Bauer is in
a fix in politics he makes politics a prisoner of his faith, *Critical* faith.
Insofar as he deals with the state he always makes out of it an
argument against "the adversary," un-Critical religion and theology.
The state acts as executor of the Critical-theological desires.

When Herr Bauer had first freed himself from orthodox, un-
Critical theology, political authority took for him the place of re-
ligious authority. His faith in Jehovah changed into faith in the
Prussian state. In Bruno Bauer's treatise *Die evangelische Landeskirche
Preußens und die Wissenschaft* not only the Prussian state but, quite
consistently, the Prussian royal house too, was construed as *absolute*.
In reality Herr Bauer had no *political* interest in that state; its merit,
in the eyes of "Criticism," was that it abolished dogmas by means of the
Unified Church and suppressed the dissenting sects with the help of
the police.

The political movement that started in the year 1840 saved Herr
Bauer from his conservative politics and raised him for a moment to
liberal politics. But here again politics was in reality only a pretext
for theology. In his work *Die gute Sache der Freiheit und meine
eigene Angelegenheit* the free state is the critic of the Bonn Theological Faculty and an argument against religion. In *Die Judenfrage*
the antagonism between state and church is the main interest, so that
the criticism of political emancipation changes into a criticism of
the Jewish religion. In his last political work, *Staat, Religion und
Partei*, the most secret wish of the critic inflated to the size of a
state is expressed. Religion is *sacrificed* to the state, or, more correctly,
the state is only the *means* by which the opponent of Criticism, un-
Critical religion and theology, is done to death. Finally, after Criticism
has been saved, if only apparently, from all politics by the socialist
ideas which were spread in Germany from 1843 onward in the same
way as it was saved from its conservative politics by the political
movement after 1840, it is finally able to proclaim its treatises against
un-Critical theology social and to indulge unhindered in its own
Critical theology, the contrasting of spirit and mass, as the annunciation of Critical Savior and the Redeemer of the world.

Let us return to our subject!

Recognition of free humanity? "Free humanity," which the Jews
did not just mean to aim at but really did aim at, is the same "free
humanity" which found classic recognition in what are called the
universal rights of man. Herr Bauer himself dealt with the Jews'

desire for the recognition of their free humanity explicitly as the desire to obtain the universal rights of man.

In *Deutsch-Französische Jahrbücher* it was expounded to Herr Bauer that this "free humanity" and the "recognition" of it are nothing but the recognition of the *selfish civil individual* and of the *uncurbed* movement of the spiritual and material elements which are the content of his life situation, the content of civil life today; that the rights of man do not, therefore, free man from religion but give him *freedom of religion;* that they do not free him from property, but procure for him *freedom of property;* that they do not free him from the filth of gain but give him *freedom of choice of a livelihood.*

He was shown that the recognition of the rights of man by the modern state means nothing more than did the recognition of slavery by the state of old. In the same way, in other words, as the state of old had slavery as its natural basis, the modern state has civil society, and the man of civil society, i.e., the independent man depending on other men only by private interest and *unconscious* natural necessity, the slave of earning his living and of his own as well as other men's *selfish* need. The modern state has recognized this as its natural basis in the universal rights of man. It did not create it. As it was the product of civil society driven beyond its bounds by its own development, it now recognizes the womb it was born of and its basis by the declaration of the rights of man. Hence the political emancipation of the Jews and the granting to them of the "rights of man" is an act the two sides of which are mutually interdependent. Herr Riesser correctly expressed the meaning of the Jews' desire for recognition of their free humanity when he demanded, among other things, the freedom of movement, sojourn, travel, earning one's living, etc. These manifestations of "free humanity" are explicitly recognized as such in the French *Declaration of the Rights of Man*. The Jew has all the more right to the recognition of his "free humanity" as "free civil society" is thoroughly commercial and Jewish and the Jew is a necessary link in it. *Deutsch-Französische Jahrbücher* further expounds why the member of civil society is called "Man" *par excellence* and why the rights of man are called "inborn rights."

The only critical thing Criticism could say about the rights of man was that they are *not* inborn but arose in the course of history; that much Hegel had already told us. Finally, to its assertion that both Jews and Christians, in order to give or receive the universal rights of man, *must sacrifice the privilege of faith*—the Critical theologian supposes his one fixed idea at the basis of all things—was specially opposed to the fact contained in all un-Critical declarations of the rights of man that the right to believe what one wishes, the right to practice any religion, is explicitly recognized as a *universal right of man*. Besides, "Criticism" should have known that Hébert's party was defeated mainly on the grounds that it attacked the rights of man in attacking freedom of religion; similarly, the rights of man were invoked later when freedom of worship was restored.

"As far as political essence is concerned, Criticism follows its contradictions to the point to which the contradiction between theory and practice had been most thoroughly elaborated for the past fifty years, to the French representative system, in which the freedom of theory was disavowed by practice and the freedom of practical life sought in vain its expression in theory.

"When the basic illusion had been done away with, the contradiction disclosed in the debates of the French Chamber, the contradiction between free theory and the practical import of privileges, between the legal import of privileges and a public system in which the egoism of the pure individual tries to dominate the exclusivity of the privileged, should have been conceived as a general contradiction in this sphere."

The contradiction that Criticism disclosed in the debates of the French Chamber was nothing but a contradiction of *constitutionalism*. Had Criticism conceived this as a general contradiction it would have conceived the general contradiction of constitutionalism. Had it gone still further than in its opinion it "should have" gone—had it, to be precise, gone as far as the *abolition* of this general contradiction—it would have proceeded correctly from constitutional *monarchy* to the *democratic representative state*, the perfect modern state. Far from having criticized the essence of political emancipation and proved its definite relation to the essence of man, it would have arrived only at the *fact* of political emancipation, the developed modern state; that is to say, only to the point where the existence of the modern state conforms to its essence and in which, therefore, not only the relative, but the absolute vices, those which constitute its very essence, could have been observed and described.

The above quoted "critical" passage is all the more valuable as it succeeds more in proving beyond any doubt that while Criticism sees the "political essence" far below itself, it is actually far below politics; it still needs to find in politics the solution of *its own* contradictions and still persists in not giving a thought to the *modern principle of statehood*.

To "free theory" Criticism opposes the "practical import of privileges"; to the "legal import of privileges" it opposes the "public system."

In order not to misinterpret the opinion of Criticism, let us recall the contradiction it disclosed in the debates in the French Chamber, the very contradiction which "should have been conceived" as a *general* one. One of the questions dealt with was the fixing of a day in the week on which children would not have to go to school. Sunday was suggested. One deputy moved that it was unconstitutional to allow Sunday to be mentioned in a law. The Minister Martin (*du Nord*) saw in that motion an attempt to assert that Christianity had ceased to exist. Monsieur Crémieux declared on behalf of the French Jews that the Jews, out of respect for the religion of the majority of Frenchmen, did not object to Sunday being mentioned. Now according to free theory Jews and Christians are equal, but according to this practice Christians have a privilege over Jews; for otherwise how could the Sunday of the Christians have a place in a law made for all Frenchmen? Should not the Jewish Sabbath have the same right, etc.? Or else the Jew is not really oppressed by Christian privileges in the practical life of the French too, but the law does not dare to express this practical equality. All the contradictions in the political essence expounded by Herr Bauer in *Die Judenfrage* are of this kind —contradictions of *constitutionalism*, that is, on the whole, the contradiction between the modern representative state and the old state of privileges.

Herr Bauer makes a very serious oversight when he thinks he is rising from the *political* to the *human* essence by conceiving and criticizing this contradiction as a "general" one. He would thus rise only from half political emancipation to full political emancipation, from the constitutional to the democratic representative state.

Herr Bauer thinks that by the abolition of *privileges* the *object* of privilege will also be abolished. Concerning the statement of Monsieur Martin (*du Nord*) he says: "There is no more religion when there is no more privileged religion. Take away from religion its exclusive force and it no longer exists."

As industrial activity is not abolished by the abolition of the privileges of the trades, guilds, and corporations, but, on the contrary, real industry begins only after the abolition of these privileges; as ownership of the land is not abolished when privileges of land ownership are abolished, but, on the contrary, begins its universal movement with the abolition of privileges and the free division and free alienation of land; as trade is not abolished by the abolition of trade privileges but finds its true materialization in free trade; so religion develops in its *practical* universality only where there is no *privileged* religion (cf. the North American states).

The modern "public system," the developed modern state, is not based, as Criticism thinks, on a society of privileges, but on a society in which *privileges are abolished* and *dissolved;* on developed *civil society* based on the vital elements which were still politically fettered in the privilege system and have been set free. Here "no privileged exclusivity" stands opposed either to any other exclusivity or to the public system. Free industry and free trade abolish privileged exclusivity and thereby the struggle between the privileged exclusivities. In its place they set man free from privilege—which isolates from the social whole but at the same time joins in a narrower exclusivity— man, no longer bound to other men even by the semblance of common ties. Thus they produce the universal struggle of man against man, individual against individual. In the same way civil society as a whole is this war among themselves of all those individuals no longer isolated from the others by anything else but their *individuality*, and the universal uncurbed movement of the elementary forces of life freed from the fetters of privilege. The contradiction between the democratic representative state and civil society is the perfection of the classic contradiction between public commonwealth and slavedom. In the modern world each one is at the same time a member of slavedom and of the public commonwealth. Precisely the slavery of civil society is in appearance the greatest freedom because it is in appearance the perfect *independence* of the individual. Indeed, the individual considers as his own freedom the movement, no longer curbed or fettered by a common tie or by man, the movement of his alienated life elements, like property, industry, religion, etc.; in reality, this is the perfection of his slavery and his inhumanity. *Right* has here taken the place of *privilege*.

It is therefore only here, where we find no contradiction between free theory and the practical import of privilege, but, on the contrary, the practical abolition of privilege, *free* industry, *free* trade, etc., conforming to "free theory," where the public system is *not* faced with any privileged exclusivity, where the contradiction expounded by Criticism is *abolished;* here only do we find *the accomplished modern state*.

Here reigns the reverse of the law which Herr Bauer, in connection with the debates in the French Chamber, formulated in perfect agreement with Monsieur Martin (*du Nord*): "As Monsieur Martin (*du Nord*) saw in the motion not to mention Sunday in the law a motion declaring that Christianity had ceased to exist, with the same right, and a completely warranted right, the declaration that the law of the Sabbath is no longer binding on the Jews would be the declaration of the dissolution of Judaism."

It is just the opposite in the developed modern state. The state declares that religion, like the other elements of civil life, begins to exist in its full scope only when the state declares it to be *nonpolitical* and thus leaves it to itself. To the dissolution of the political existence of these elements—for example, the dissolution of property by the abolition of the property qualification for electors, the dissolution of religion by the abolition of the state church—to this very proclamation of their civil death corresponds their most vigorous life, which henceforth obeys its own laws undisturbed and develops to its full scope.

Anarchy is the law of civil society emancipated from disjointing privileges, and the *anarchy of civil society* is the basis of the modern public system, just as the public system is in turn the guarantee of that anarchy. To the same extent as the two are opposed to each other they also determine each other.

It is clear how capable Criticism is of assimilating the "new." But if we remain within the bounds of "pure Criticism" the question arises: Why did Criticism not conceive as a *universal* contradiction the contradiction that it disclosed in connection with the debates in the French Chamber, although in its own opinion that is what "should have been" done?

"That step was, however, then impossible—not only because . . . not only because . . . but also because without that last remnant of interior involvement with its opposite criticism was impossible and could not have come to the point from which it had only one step to make."

It was impossible . . . because . . . it was impossible! Criticism affirms, moreover, that the fateful "one step" necessary to "come to the point from which it had only one step to make" was impossible. Who will dispute that? In order to come to a point from which there is only "one step" to make, it is absolutely impossible to make still that "one step" that leads beyond the point beyond which there is still "one step."

All's well that ends well! At the end of the encounter with the mass, who is hostile to Criticism's *Die Judenfrage*, "Criticism" admits that *its* conception of "the rights of man," *its* "appraisal of religion in the French Revolution," the "free political essence it pointed to occasionally in concluding its considerations," in a word, that the "whole time of the French Revolution was no more nor no less for Criticism than a symbol—that is to say, not the time of the revolutionary actions of the French in the exact and prosaic sense, but a symbol, only a fantastic expression of the figures which it saw at the end." We shall not deprive Criticism of the consolation that when it erred politically it did so only at the "conclusion" and at the "end" of its work. A well-known drunkard used to console himself with the thought that he was never drunk before midnight.

On the Jewish question Criticism has indisputably continually won ground from the enemy. In No. 1 of *Die Judenfrage* the treatise of "Criticism" defended by Herr Bauer was still absolute and revealed the "true" and "general" significance of the Jewish question. In No. 2

Criticism had neither the "will" nor the "right" to go beyond Criticism. In No. 3 it had still to make "one step" but that step was "impossible"—because it was "impossible." It was not its "will or right" but its involvement in its "opposite" that prevented it from making that "one step." It would have liked to clear the last obstacle, but unfortunately there was a *last remnant of mass* on its Critical seven-league boots.

Bourgeois and Jew[*]

THE bourgeois' relation to the institutions of his regime is like that of the Jew to the law; he evades them so long as it is feasible to do so in each individual case, but he wants everybody else to observe them . . . But marriage, property, the family remain unattacked, in theory . . . because in their bourgeois form they are the conditions that make the bourgeois a bourgeois, just as the constantly evaded law makes the religious Jew a religious Jew.

---

[*] From Marx and Engels, *The German Ideology* (1845–46), p. 192.

Prussian Anti-Semitism*

Cologne, November 28

In its issue of November 17 the *Neue Rheinische Zeitung* wrote:

"And now even the Jews, whose eminent representatives, at least since the emancipation of their sect, have spearheaded the counter-revolution everywhere—what awaits them? The government has not even waited for victory to hurl them back into the ghettos."

We then cited the government decree in Bromberg. Today we have to report an even more striking fact. The great Freemason Lodge of the Three Crowns in Berlin—it is well known that the Prince of Prussia is the chief leader of Prussian Freemasonry, just as Frederick William IV is the chief leader of the Prussian religion—has declared the Cologne Lodge Minerva inactive. Why? *Because it accepted Jews. A warning to the Jews!*

---

* From "News," published in the *Neue Rheinische Zeitung*, November 29, 1848.

Rothschild—"A Jewish Usurer"*

THE only points belonging properly to the present ministry are the proposed educational reform which Lord John [Russell] assures us will be of no larger size than himself, and the removal of Baronet Lionel Rothschild's disabilities. It may be questioned whether the English people will be very contented with this extension of the suffrage to a Jewish usurer who was notoriously one of the accomplices of the Bonapartist *coup d'état*.

---

* From "The Italian Insurrection—British Politics," published in the *New-York Daily Tribune*, February 25, 1853.

Removal of Jewish Disabilities—
"A Miserable Reform Farce"*

IN the session of last night Lord John Russell brought before the House of Commons his motion for the "removal of some disabilities of Her Majesty's Jewish subjects." The motion was carried by a majority of twenty-nine. Thus the question is again settled in the House of Commons, but there is no doubt that it will once more be unsettled in the House of Lords.

The exclusion of Jews from the House of Commons, after the spirit of usury has so long presided in the British Parliament, is unquestionably an absurd anomaly, the more so as they have already become eligible to all the civil offices of the community. But it remains no less characteristic for the man and for his times that, instead of a Reform Bill which was promised to remove the disabilities of the mass of the English people, a bill is brought in by Finality John[1] for the exclusive removal of the disabilities of Baron Lionel de Rothschild. How utterly insignificant an interest is taken in this affair by the public at large may be inferred from the fact that from not a single place in Great Britain has a petition in favor of the admission of Jews been forwarded to Parliament. The whole secret of this miserable reform farce was betrayed by the speech of the present Sir Robert Peel.

"After all, the House were only considering the noble Lord's private affairs." (Loud cheers.) "The noble Lord represented London with a Jew" (cheers) "and had made the pledge to bring forward annually a motion in favor of the Jews." (Hear!) "No doubt Baron

---

* From "Parliamentary Debates . . ." published in the *New-York Daily Tribune*, March 15, 1853.
1. Lord John Russell's nickname.

Rothschild was a very wealthy man, but this did not entitle him to any consideration, especially considering how his wealth had been amassed." (Loud cries of "Hear! Hear!" and "Oh! Oh!" from the ministerial benches.) "Only yesterday he had read in the papers that the House of Rothschild had consented to grant a loan to Greece, on considerable guaranties, at 9 percent." (Hear!) "No wonder, at this rate, that the House of Rothschild were wealthy." (Hear!) "The President of the Board of Trade had been talking of gagging the press. Why, no one had done so much to depress freedom in Europe as the House of Rothschild" (Hear! Hear!) "by the loans with which they assisted the despotic powers. But even supposing the Baron to be as worthy a man as he was certainly rich, it was to have been expected that the noble Lord who represented in that House a government consisting of the leaders of all the political factions who had opposed the late Administration would have proposed some measure of more importance than the present."

Jews in Jerusalem[*]

. . . the sedentary population of Jerusalem numbers about 15,500 souls, of whom 4,000 are Mussulmans and 8,000 Jews. The Mussulmans, forming about a fourth part of the whole, and consisting of Turks, Arabs, and Moors, are, of course, the masters in every respect, as they are in no way affected by the weakness of their government at Constantinople. Nothing equals the misery and the sufferings of the Jews at Jerusalem, inhabiting the most filthy quarter of the town, called *hareth-el-yahoud*, in the quarter of dirt, between the Zion and the Moriah, where their synagogues are situated—the constant objects of Mussulman oppression and intolerance, insulted by the Greeks, persecuted by the Latins, and living only upon the scanty alms transmitted by their European brethren. The Jews, however, are not natives, but from different and distant countries, and are only attracted to Jerusalem by the desire of inhabiting the Valley of Jehoshaphat; and to die on the very place where the redemption is to be expected. "Attending their death," says a French author, "they suffer and pray. Their regards turned to that mountain of Moriah where once rose the temple of Lebanon, and which they dare not approach, they shed tears on the misfortunes of Zion, and their dispersion over the world."

To make these Jews more miserable, England and Prussia appointed, in 1840, an Anglican bishop at Jerusalem, whose avowed object is their conversion. He was dreadfully thrashed in 1845, and sneered at alike by Jews, Christians, and Turks. He may, in fact, be stated to have been the first and only cause of a union between all the religions at Jerusalem.

---

[*] From ". . . Moslems, Christians, and Jews in the Ottoman Empire," published in the *New-York Daily Tribune*, April 15, 1854.

The Jewish Bankers of Europe*

TAKE Austria, for instance—a country which suffers from a chronic scarcity of cash. What is she doing at this moment? She proposes to raise money by negotiating the mortgage bonds of the landowners of the Austrian dominions. But how is such an operation possible? Through the Jewish houses, who, shut out from all more honorable branches of business, have acquired in this an inevitable degree of aptitude. There are in Vienna the Rothschilds, and Arnsteins, and Eskeles, and the Jew-Greek house of Seria, for whom the management of a loan of $100,000,000 is a matter of most easy accomplishment. The way they start at the loan is to get all their correspondents to canvass their business constituencies, and with the allurements of a particular commission, their correspondents of course do their best to ensnare their customers.

The broad facts we have pointed out have naturally produced all over Europe, especially in its northern, western, and central portions, where the indolence which prevails in the southern part (as Italy, Spain, and Portugal) is modified by climate, all manner and kinds of capitalists, speculators, and jobbers, who have no other business beyond that of dealing in money. Now there are posted in every point of Europe Jewish agents, who represent this business, and who are the correspondents of other leading Jews. It must here be borne in mind that for one big fish, like Rothschild, there are thousands of minnows. These make play and find food chiefly in Amsterdam, London, Frankfurt, Vienna, Berlin, Hamburg, Paris, and Brussels, and, as a general thing, loans are distributed among them in the following proportion:

---

* From "The Loanmongers of Europe," published in the *New-York Daily Tribune*, November 22, 1855.

Amsterdam, say	$25,000,000
London	$25,000,000
Frankfurt	$15,000,000
Vienna	$10,000,000
Berlin	$10,000,000
Hamburg	$ 5,000,000
Paris	$ 5,000,000
Brussels	$ 5,000,000
Total	$100,000,000

Beside the regular agents every one of these places swarms with Jews who aid in placing the stock. All over Germany and Holland, in Hanover, Brunswick, Cassel, Carlsruhe, Mannheim, Cologne, Rotterdam, The Hague, Antwerp, and again in Poland and the adjoining countries, in Breslau, Cracow, Warsaw, and so almost throughout Europe, there are to be found in almost every town a handful of Jews who deem it an honor to take a little of the new stock on speculation if the Rothschilds or any other of the great Jewish houses are connected with the negotiation. It is this business Free Masonry among the Jewish bankers which has brought the barter trade in government securities to its present height.

It remains to be seen, and the time is not distant, how the chief houses connected with this barter trade will stand when distrust makes their customers disgorge the securities which have been forced down their throats and the markets become overglutted with unsalable bonds. Bearing in mind the havoc which the first Napoleon's wars created among these loanmongers, we have heretofore pointed out the smash, which from a knowledge of their financial position and connections we have no hesitation in predicting as sure to happen as a consequence of the present war to the representatives of this particular race.

That very compact machinery which is their greatest power of success in times of prosperity is their greatest cause of danger in time of adversity. Let the confidence in the Rothschilds be only once slightly shaken, and the confidence in the Foulds, the Bischoffsheims, the Stieglitzes, the Arnsteins and Eskeles is gone. The results of despotism and monopolism are precisely similar. Let Louis Napoleon be chopped off, as he may be any moment by some clever Pianori, and France is in confusion. Let Lionel Rothschild of London, James of Paris stagger under any clever combination of disasters, and the whole loanmongering fabric of Europe will perish.

The Russian Loan*

THE issue of a new Russian loan affords a practical illustration of the system of loanmongering in Europe, to which we have heretofore called the attention of our readers.

This loan is brought out under the auspices of the house of Stieglitz at St. Petersburg. Stieglitz is to Alexander what Rothschild is to Francis Joseph, what Fould is to Louis Napoleon. The late Czar Nicholas made Stieglitz a Russian baron, as the late Kaiser Franz made old Rothschild an Austrian baron, while Louis Napoleon has made a Cabinet Minister of Fould, with a free ticket to the Tuileries for the females of his family. Thus we find every tyrant backed by a Jew, as is every pope by a Jesuit. In truth, the cravings of oppressors would be hopeless, and the practicability of war out of the question, if there were not an army of Jesuits to smother thought and a handful of Jews to ransack pockets.

The loan is for fifty millions of rubles, to be issued in 5-percent bonds, with dividends payable at Amsterdam, Berlin, and Hamburg, at the exceedingly moderate price of 86 rubles—that is to say, in consideration of paying 86 rubles, in several installments, the payer is entitled to 5 rubles dividend per year, which amounts to nearly 6 percent, and to a bond of 100 rubles endorsed by the Russian Government, as security for his capital, which is redeemable at some remote period between this and doomsday. It is worthy of notice that Russia does not appeal, as Austria has recently done, to the moneyed enthusiasm of her own subjects, stirred up by the stimulus of bayonets and prisons; but this shows only the greater confidence which she has

* Published in the *New-York Daily Tribune*, January 4, 1856.

in her credit abroad, and the greater sagacity which she possesses in raising money without embarrassing and therefore without disappointing the people at home. Baron Stieglitz does not propose to retain one single kopeck of the fifty millions for the Greek, Sicilian, American, Polish, Livonian, Tartarian, Siberian, and Crimean sympathizers with Russia, but distributes seventeen millions of the loan to Hope & Co. of Amsterdam, the same share to Mendelssohn & Co. of Berlin, and sixteen millions to Paul Mendelssohn-Bartholdy of Hamburg. And although British and French houses do not, for obvious reasons, court a direct participation in the loan, we shall presently show that indirectly they contribute largely to furnishing their antagonists with the sinews of war.

With the exception of a small amount of 5- and 6-percent Russian bonds negotiated at London and Hamburg, and of the last Russian loan—which was taken up by the Barings—Stieglitz of St. Petersburg, in connection with Hope & Co. of Amsterdam, have been the principal agencies for Russian credit with the capitalists of Western and Central Europe. The 4-percent Hope certificates, under the special auspices of Hope, and the 4-percent Stieglitz inscriptions, under the special auspices of Stieglitz, are extensively held in Holland, Switzerland, Prussia, and to some extent even in England. The Hopes of Amsterdam, who enjoy great prestige in Europe from their connection with the Dutch Government and their reputation for great integrity and immense wealth, have well deserved of the Czar for the efforts they have made to popularize his bonds in Holland. Stieglitz, who is a German Jew intimately connected with all his coreligionists in the loanmongering trade, has done the rest. Hope commanding the respect of the most eminent merchants of the age, and Stieglitz being one of the Free Masonry of Jews, which has existed in all ages—these two powers, combined to influence at once the highest merchants and the lowest jobbing circles, have been turned by Russia to most profitable account. Owing to these two influences, and to the ignorance which prevails about her interior resources, Russia, of all the European continental governments, stands highest in the estimation of 'Change, whatever may be thought of her in other quarters.

But the Hopes lend only the prestige of their name; the real work is done by the Jews, and can only be done by them, as they monopolize the machinery of the loanmongering mysteries by concentrating their energies upon the barter trade in securities, and the changing of money and negotiating of bills in a great measure arising therefrom. Take Amsterdam, for instance, a city harboring many of the worst descendants of the Jews whom Ferdinand and Isabella drove out of Spain, and who, after lingering awhile in Portugal, were driven thence also, and eventually found a safe place of retreat in Holland. In Amsterdam alone they number not less than 35,000, many of whom are engaged in this gambling and jobbing of securities. These men have their agents at Rotterdam, The Hague, Leyden, Haarlem, Nymegen, Delft, Groningen, Antwerp, Ghent, Brussels, and various other places in the Netherlands and surrounding German and French territories. Their business is to watch the moneys available for investment and keenly observe where they lie. Here and there and everywhere that a little capital courts investment, there is ever one of these little Jews ready to make a little suggestion or place a little bit of a loan. The smartest highwayman in the Abruzzi is not better posted up about the locale of the hard cash in a traveler's valise or pocket than those Jews about any loose capital in the hands of a trader.

These small Jewish agents draw their supplies from the big Jewish houses, such as that of Hollander and Lehren, Königswarter, Raphael, Stern, Sichel, Bischoffsheim of Amsterdam, Ezekiels of Rotterdam. Hollander and Lehren are of the Portuguese sect of Jews, and practice a great ostensible devotion to the religion of their race. Lehren, like the great London Jew, Sir Moses Montefiore, has made many sacrifices for those that still linger in Jerusalem. His office, near the Amstel, in Amsterdam, is one of the most picturesque imaginable. Crowds of these Jewish agents assemble there every day, together with numerous Jewish theologians, and around its doors are congregated all sorts and manners of Armenian, Jerusalem, Barbaresque, and Polish beggars, in long robes and Oriental turbans. The language spoken smells strongly of Babel, and the perfume which otherwise pervades the place is by no means of a choice kind.

The next Jewish loanmongering concern is that of Königswarter, who came from a Jewish colony in Furth in Bavaria, opposite Nuremberg, whose 10,000 inhabitants are all Jews with some few Roman Catholic exceptions. The Königswarters have houses at Frankfurt, Paris, Vienna, and Amsterdam, and all these various establishments will place a certain amount of the loan. Then we have the Raphaels, who also have houses in London and Paris, who belong, like Königswarter, to the lowest class of loanmongering Jews. The Sterns come from Frankfurt, and have houses at Paris, Berlin, London, and Amsterdam. One of the London Sterns, David, was for some time established at Madrid, but so disgusted the chivalrous Spaniards that he was compelled to quit. They have married the daughters of one of the rich London Goldsmids, and do an immense business in stock. The only man of ability in the family is the Paris Stern.

The Bischoffsheims are, next to the Rothschilds and Hopes, the most influential house in Belgium and Holland. The Belgian Bischoffsheim is a man of great accomplishments and one of the most respected bank directors and railway magnates. They came from

Mayence, and owing to the genius of this Belgian Bischoffsheim, have attained to their present eminence. They have houses at London, Amsterdam, Paris, Brussels, Antwerp, Frankfurt, Cologne, and Vienna, and have recently sent a clerk or agent to New York. They have intermarried with a Frankfurt Jew of the name of Goldschmidt, who, however, is not distinguished either for wealth or genius, although pretending to both. One of these Goldschmidts—and the most insignificant of the firm—presides over the London concern, while one of the Bischoffsheims rules over that of Amsterdam, and the other over those of Brussels and of Paris.

As far as the seventeen million rubles assigned to Holland are concerned, although brought out under the name of Hope, they will at once go into the hands of these Jews, who will, through their various branch houses, find a market abroad, while the small Jew agents and brokers create a demand for them at home. Thus do these loans, which are a curse to the people, a ruin to the holders, and a danger to the governments, become a blessing to the houses of the children of Judah. This Jew organization of loanmongers is as dangerous to the people as the aristocratic organization of landowners. It principally sprang up in Europe since Rothschild was made a baron by Austria, enriched by the money earned by the Hessians in fighting the American Revolution. The fortunes amassed by these loanmongers are immense, but the wrongs and sufferings thus entailed on the people and the encouragement thus afforded to their oppressors still remain to be told.

We have sufficiently shown how the Amsterdam Jews, through their machinery at home and abroad, will absorb in a very little time the seventeen millions of rubles put at the disposal of Hope. The arrangements attendant on the placing of the amount in Berlin and Hamburg are of a similar nature. The Mendelssohns of Berlin are descended from the good and learned Moses Mendelssohn, and count among the more modern members of the family the distinguished musical composer. In their case, as in that of the Lessings and a few other Frankfurt, Berlin, and Hamburg families, owing to some peculiar literary tradition or some peculiar influence of refinement, their houses are far superior in character to those of the general clique of loanmongers. Their representative in Hamburg too, Mr. Beschutz, is a man of high character, and there is little doubt that under their auspices the thirty-three millions put by Stieglitz at their disposal will soon be taken. But, as in the case of Hope of Amsterdam, the part taken by the Mendelssohns will only be nominal, and to lend the prestige of their name. Rothschilds' special agent at Berlin, Simon Bleichröder, and their occasional agents, the Veits, will very likely take a portion on speculation, and sell it with a profit to the small Jew fry of Berlin, Hanover, Magdeburg, Brunswick, and Cassel, while the Frankfurt

Jews will supply the small fry of Darmstadt, Mannheim, Carlsruhe, Stuttgart, Ulm, Augsburg, and Munich. This small fry again distribute the stock among still smaller fry, until eventually some honest farmer of Swabia, some substantial manufacturer of Crefeld, or some dowager Countess of Isenburg has the honor of becoming the permanent creditor of the Czar by locking the stock up as a permanent investment. The Jew jobbers of Breslau, Ratisbon, Cracow, and Posen, the Frankels of Warsaw, Benedick of Stockholm, Hambro of Copenhagen, Magnus of Berlin, with his extensive Polish constituency, Jacobson of the same city, and Ries and Heine of Hamburg—both houses of great influence in Jew financial circles, especially Heine—will each and all disseminate a goodly amount among their multitudinous customers and bring the stock within the reach of all the northern section of Europe. In this wise any amount, however large, is soon absorbed. It must be borne in mind that besides the local and provincial speculations, there is the immense stock-jobbing machinery between the various European gathering points of the loanmongering confederation now all connected by telegraph communication, which, of course, vastly facilitates all such operations. Moreover, almost all the Jew loanmongers in Europe are connected by family ties. At Cologne, for instance, we find the principal branch house of the Paris Foulds, one of whom married a Miss Oppenheim, whose brothers are the chief railway speculators of Rhenish Prussia and, next to Heistedt and Stein, the principal bankers of Cologne. Like the Rothschilds and the Greeks, the loanmongering Jews derive much of their strength from these family relations, as these, in addition to their lucre affinities, give a compactness and unity to their operations which insure their success.

This eastern war is destined at all events to throw some light upon this system of loanmongers as well as other systems. Meantime the Czar will get his fifty millions and, let the English journals say what they please, if he wants five fifties more, the Jews will dig them up. Let us not be thought too severe upon these loanmongering gentry. The fact that 1855 years ago Christ drove the Jewish moneychangers out of the temple, and that the moneychangers of our age enlisted on the side of tyranny happen again chiefly to be Jews, is perhaps no more than a historical coincidence. The loanmongering Jews of Europe do only on a larger and more obnoxious scale what many others do on one smaller and less significant. But it is only because the Jews are so strong that it is timely and expedient to expose and stigmatize their organization.

From *Herr Vogt*

Herr Vogt *was a book-length brochure, a polemic against Karl Vogt, a German scientist and politician who, Marx felt, had maligned him. It was published in a German-language edition in London, in 1860.*

MONSIEUR SIMON*

Now back to MONSIEUR EDOUARD SIMON, originally a Jew from Rhenish Prussia named Eduard Simon, who nevertheless cuts the most comical grimaces to appear as a real Frenchman, except that every moment his style betrays the Rhenish Prussian Jew translated into French.

SEWER JOURNALISM*

ALL London's toilets discharge their physical ordure into the Thames through an ingenious system of underground sewer pipes. In the same way, through a system of goose quills, the world metropolis daily spits all its social ordure into a big paper-made-central-sewer—the *Daily Telegraph*. Liebig justly criticizes that senseless squandering which robs the water of the Thames of its purity and the land of England of its fertilizer. But Levy, the owner of the paper-made-central-sewer, comprehends not only chemistry but also alchemy. After he has transformed the social ordure into newspaper articles, he transforms the newspaper articles into copper, and finally copper into gold. On the gate leading into the paper-made-central-sewer are inscribed the

---

* From Chapter IX of *Herr Vogt*.

---

* From Chapter X.

words, *di colore oscuro* [in dark color]: *"hic . . . quisquam faxit oletum"* ["here a stink is made"], or, as Byron has translated into fine poetry: "Wanderer, stop and—piss!"

Levy, like Habakkuk, *est capable de tout* [is capable of anything]. He is capable of printing three long editorial columns on a single case of rape. . . .

Politicians call the *Daily Telegraph* "Palmerston's mob paper," but Levy's excrement takes on a cargo of politics mainly as ballast. Hence the *Saturday Review* has accurately characterized his penny paper as "cheap and nasty." . . .

Nevertheless, Levy also has his own prudishness. Thus, for example, he carps at the theater for its immorality and, like another Cato the Censor, persecutes ballet dancers for their costumes that start too late and stop too soon. Through such fits of virtue Levy gets from the frying pan into the fire. O consistency, *The Players*, a London theater journal, exclaims, O consistency, where is thy blush? How the rogue must have laughed in his beard! . . . The *Telegraph* a preacher of decency for female stage costumes! Holy Jupiter, what will happen next? Earthquakes and fiery comets are the least things that are now to be expected. Decency! "I thank thee, Jew, for teaching me that word."[1] *The Players* advises Levy, as Hamlet did Ophelia, to be gone to a monastery, and particularly a nunnery. "Get thee to a nunnery, Levy!" Levy in a nunnery! Perhaps *nunnery* is a misprint for *nonaria*,[2] so that it should read, "get thee to a *nonaria*, Levy," and in this case everybody would [be] *"multum gaudere paratus,/Si Cynico"* (the Cynic Levy) *"Barbam petulans Nonaria vellat."*[3]

The *Weekly Mail* maintains that although Levy gives the public no *x* for a *u*, he does give it a *y* for an *i*, and, in truth, among the 22,000 Levis whom Moses counted in his march through the wilderness, there was not a single Levi who spelled it with a *y*. Just as Edouard Simon wants to be counted at all costs as a member of the Romance race, so Levy wants to be an Anglo-Saxon. Hence at least once a month he attacks the un-British policies of Disraeli, for Disraeli, "the Asiatic mystery," unlike the *Telegraph*, is not a descendant of the Anglo-Saxon race. But of what use is it for Levy to attack Mr. Disraeli and to make a *y* for an *i*, so long as Mother Nature has inscribed, with the wildest black letters, his family tree in the middle of his face? The nose of the mysterious stranger of Slawkenbergius (see *Tristram Shandy*), who fetched himself the finest nose from the promontory of noses, was merely a week's talk in Strasbourg, whereas Levy's nose

---

1. Shakespeare, *The Merchant of Venice*, Act IV, Scene 1.
2. *Nonaria* is the Latin word for whore.
3. Ready to enjoy himself to his heart's content, when the *nonaria* wantonly plucks the Cynic's beard"; from Aulus Persius Flaccus, *Satirarum Liber* (Satire I).

constitutes a year's talk in the City of London. A Greek epigrammatist describes the nose of a certain Castor that had served him for all purposes, as shovel, trumpet, sickle, anchor, etc. He concludes the description with these words:

Οὕτως εὐχρήστου σχεύους Κάστωρ τετύχηχε,
'Ρῖνα φέρων πάσης ἄρμενον ἐργασίας[4]

but Castor does not advise us what Levy needs his nose for. The English poet comes closer to it with these lines:

And 'tis a miracle we may suppose,
No nastiness offends his skillful nose.

The great art of Levy's nose in reality consists of cozying up to foul odor, to smell it out hundreds of miles away and to bring it forth. Thus Levy's nose serves the *Daily Telegraph* as an elephant snout, insect palp, lighthouse, and telegraph. One can therefore say without exaggeration that Levy writes his newspaper with his nose.

---

4. "And so Castor possesses a multifarious armament, / Bearing his nose, suitable for every occasion."

Personal Letters

Dear Friend:

Novices are the most pious, as Saxony demonstrates *ad oculos* [visibly].

[Bruno] Bauer once had a scene with Eichhorn similar to yours with the Minister of Interior. The oratorical figures of these gentlemen are as alike as two eggs. By contrast, it is exceptional that philosophy should speak intelligibly to the political wisdom of these highly sworn scoundrels, and even a little fanaticism does not hurt. To these worldly providential types, nothing is more difficult to make believable than the belief in truth and spiritual sentiment. They are such political dandies, such experienced fops, that they no longer believe in true, disinterested love. How can one reach these roués except by means of what high up there is called fanaticism? A lieutenant of the guard considers a lover with honorable intentions a fanatic. Should one therefore no longer marry? It is remarkable how the belief in the brutalization of man has become a government article of faith and a political principle. But this is no contradiction of religiosity, for the animal religion is the most consistent manifestation of religion, and perhaps it will soon be necessary to speak of religious zoology instead of religious anthropology.

This much I knew when I was still young and good, that the eggs that are laid in Berlin are not swan's eggs but goose eggs. Somewhat later came the insight that they are alligator eggs—for example, the newest egg, whereby, presumably at the request of the Rhenish estates, the unlawful restrictions of French legislation regarding high treason, burueaucratic offenses, etc., would be suspended. This time, however, because it involved objective legal decisions, the hocus-pocus was so stupid that the dumbest Rhenish jurists saw through it immediately. . . .

Now to the matter at hand: I found that the article "Concerning Christian Art," which is now changed to "Concerning Religion and Art, with Special Reference to Christian Art,"[1] has to be totally corrected, in that I had righteously taken a trumpet tone—"Thy word is a lamp unto my feet, and a light unto my path" [Psalms 119:105]. "Thou through thy commandments hast made me wiser than mine enemies: for they are ever with me" [Psalms 119:98]. "The Lord will roar from Zion" [Amos 1:2]. This trumpet tone, along with the burdensome imprisonment in Hegel's portrayal, now has to be changed to a more free and therefore a more basic treatment. In a few days I must go to Cologne, where I shall set up my new domicile,[2] because the proximity of the Bonn professors is insupportable to me. Who wants to converse forever with intellectual skunks, with people who only learn how to find new planks in all the corners of the world!

Hence under present circumstances I cannot send you the critique of the Hegelian philosophy of law for the next issue of *Anecdota* (because it was also written for "trumpets"), but I promise you that article on religious art by the middle of April, if you want to wait that long. I would prefer this, since I am treating the matter from a new point of view and presenting it also as an addition to an epilogue on the romantics. In the meantime I will work on the subject most energetically, to use a Goethean expression, and await your decision. Would you please write me at Cologne, where I will be as of the beginning of next month. Since I do not as yet have a definite domicile there, please write me at [Georg] Jung's address.

In my treatment I must necessarily discuss the general essence of religion, and thus to some extent come into collision with Feuerbach, a collision which does not involve an attack on his principles but on his style. At any rate, religion will not gain by it.

I have not heard from Koeppen for a long time. Have you ever been in touch with Christiansen in Kiel? I know him only from his history of Roman law, which also contains some things about religion and philosophy in general. He seems to be a man of superior intelligence, although when he comes to philosophy proper he writes with a formalistic style and a frightful lack of understanding. Perhaps by

---

1. The article was never published.
2. Marx gave up his plan to move to Cologne; in April 1842 he returned to Bonn, where he remained, with some interruptions, until the middle of October.

now he writes German. Otherwise he seems to be *à la hauteur des principes* [at the height of principles].

I would be very pleased to see you here on the Rhine.

Your

MARX

P.S. Bauer has just written me that he wants to go north again, in the foolish belief that he could pursue his case against the Prussian Government better there. Berlin is too close to Spandau. In any case, it is a good thing that Bauer does not let the matter go. As I learn here from my future brother-in-law,[3] an aristocrat *comme il faut*, Berlin is angry with Bauer mostly over his *bonne foi* [good faith].

From letter to Arnold Ruge (in Dresden)
TRIER, JULY 9, 1842

Dear Friend:

For the rest, don't you believe that we on the Rhine live in a political Eldorado. It takes the most consistent tenacity for a paper like the *Rheinische Zeitung* to cut its way through. My second article on the Diet, dealing with the church confusions, has been censored out. In it I demonstrated how the defenders of the state took a clerical position and the defenders of the church a political one. This incident is the more unpleasant for the *Rheinische Zeitung* subscribers in that the stupid Cologne Catholics fell into the trap and the subscribers were decoyed into a defense of the Archbishop. Furthermore, you can hardly imagine how vilely and at the same time how stupidly the men of power veered over to the orthodox blockhead. But the work was crowned with success; Prussia has kissed the Pope's slipper before the whole world, and our governmental automata walk the streets without blushing . . . In the Rhineland, the religious party is the most dangerous. The opposition has recently become too accustomed to doing the opposing inside the church.

Yours,

MARX

---

3. Ferdinand Otto Wilhelm von Westphalen, a stepbrother of Jenny Marx, became Prussian Minister of Interior in 1850.

From letter to Dagobert Oppenheim (in Cologne)
BONN, AUGUST 25, 1842

Dear Oppenheim:
    . . . Do send me Mayer's article in the *Rheinische Zeitung* on communalism and, if possible, all the articles by Hermes against Judaism.[1]
I will then send you as soon as possible an article on the latter question, which, if it does not resolve it, will still take it in a different direction.
                                            Yours,
                                                MARX

Postscript to letter to Arnold Ruge (in Dresden)
COLOGNE, MARCH 13, 1843

    Just now the chief or the local Israelites came to see me and asked me to forward a petition for the Jews to the Landtag, and I want to do it. Repulsive [*widerlich*[1]] though the Israelite religion is to me, nevertheless Bauer's opinion[2] seems to me to be too abstract. The point is to puncture as many holes as possible in the Christian state, and to smuggle in, insofar as it is up to us, what is rational. At least one should try it—and the embitterment grows with each petition that is rejected with protest.

*From letter to Arnold Ruge (in Dresden)**
COLOGNE, MAY, 1843

    One will have to reawaken in the breast of these people [Germans] the sense of the self-worth of men—freedom. Only such a sense, which

---

    1. Articles by Carl Heinrich Hermes, in *Kölnische Zeitung*, July 6 and 30, and August 23, 1842.

---

    1. The German word *widerlich* can also be translated as "disgusting," "repulsive," "loathsome," "nauseating."
    2. In *Die Judenfrage* (*The Jewish Question*), 1843.
    * For the complete text, see *Karl Marx on Revolution*, Vol. I of The Karl Marx Library (1971), pp. 511–15.

vanished from the world with the Greeks and evaporated into the blue with Christianity, can transform society again into a community of people for their highest ends—a democratic state.

From letter to Arnold Ruge*
KREUZNACH, SEPTEMBER, 1843

... Just as *religion* is the index to the theoretical struggles of mankind, so the *political state* is the index to its practical ones. ...

The reform of the world's consciousness consists only in making it aware of its perception, in waking it up from its own dream, in explaining to it its own actions. Our whole purpose can consist of nothing else than in bringing out religious and political questions in self-aware human form, as Feuerbach did in his critique of religion.

Our slogan must therefore be: reform of consciousness, not through dogmas but through analysis of the mystic consciousness which is unclear to itself, regardless of whether it is religious or political. It will then be shown that the world has long possessed the dream of a thing, of which it only needs to have awareness in order to possess it in reality.

Letter to Ludwig Feuerbach (in Bruckberg)
PARIS, 38 RUE VANEAU, AUGUST 11, 1844

Esteemed Sir:

Since I have this opportunity, I take the liberty of sending you an article of mine in which certain elements of my critical philosophy of law[1]—which I had finished once but rewrote to make it comprehensible to the general public—are indicated. I do not place any special value on this article, but I am pleased to find a chance to be able to assure you of the distinguished respect and—excuse the word—

---

* For the complete text, see *Karl Marx on Revolution*, Vol. I of The Karl Mark Library (1971).
1. "Toward the Critique of Hegel's Philosophy of Law. Introduction," in *Deutsch-Französische Jahrbücher*, 1844.

love that I have for you. Your *Philosophie der Zukunft*[2] and the *Wesen des Glaubens*,[3] despite their limited scope, are, at any rate, of more weight than all the present-day German literature put together.

In these books—I do not know whether intentionally or not—you have given socialism a philosophical foundation, and the communists too have understood these works in the same way. The unity of man with man, which is also rooted in the actual difference among men, the concept of the human species, pulled down from the heaven of abstraction to the real earth—what else is this than a *societal* concept!

Two translations of your *Wesen des Christentums*,[4] one in English and one in French, are being prepared and are practically ready for the printer. The former will appear in Manchester (Engels has supervised it), the latter in Paris (a Frenchman, Dr. Guerrier, and a German communist, Ewerbeck, have translated it with the help of a French stylist).[5]

At this particular time the French will immediately pounce on the book, for both parties—parsons and Voltaireans and materialists—are looking for outside help. It is a remarkable phenomenon that, in contrast to the eighteenth century, religiosity has descended on the middle and upper classes, while irreligiosity—but an irreligiosity of men sensing their humanness—has reached the French proletariat. You would have to attend one of the meetings of the French *ouvriers* [workers] to be able to realize the virginal freshness and nobility that is generated among these workingmen. The English proletarian also makes giant steps, but he lacks the cultural character of the French. But I must not forget to mention the theoretical services of the German artisans in Switzerland, London, and Paris. The only thing is that the German artisan is still too much an artisan.

At any rate, history is preparing among these "barbarians" of our civilized society the practical element for the emancipation of humanity.

The contrast between the French character and that of us Germans has never struck me so sharply and strikingly as in the Fourierist book,[6]

---

2. Feuerbach, *Grundsätze der Philosophie der Zukunft* (*Principles of the Philosophy of the Future*) (Zurich and Winterthur, 1843).

3. Feuerbach, *Das Wesen des Glaubens im Sinne Luther's. Ein Beitrag zum 'Wesen des Christentums'* (*The Essence of Faith in Luther's Sense. A Contribution to the "Essence of Christianity"*) (Leipzig, 1844).

4. Feuerbach, *The Essence of Christianity* (Leipzig, 1841). It was translated into English by the novelist George Eliot under the title *The Essence of Religion* (London, 1853). The Engels-supervised translation to which Marx refers was never published.

5. August Hermann Ewerbeck, *Qu'est ce que la religion d'après la nouvelle philosophie allemande* (Paris, 1850).

6. E. de Pompery, *Exposition de la science social, constituée par C. Fourier* (*Exposition of Social Science, as Constituted by C. Fourier*) (2d ed., Paris, 1840).

which begins with the following sentences: *"L'homme est tout entier dans ses passions." "Avez-vous jamais rencontré un homme qui pensât pour penser, qui se ressouvint pour se ressouvenir, qui imaginât pour imaginer? qui voulait pour vouloir? cela vous est-il jamais arrivé à vous même? . . . Non, évidemment non!"*[7]

The main motive force of nature, as of society, is therefore the *magical,* the *passionate,* the *nonreflecting attraction,* and *"tout être, homme, plante, animal, ou globe, a reçu une somme des forces en rapport avec sa mission dans l'ordre universel."*[8]

From this it follows: *"Les attractions sont proportionnelles aux destinées."*[9]

Do not all these sentences seem as if the Frenchman had deliberately contrasted his passion for the *actus purus* [pure act] to the German kind of thinking? One does not think in order to think, etc.

How difficult it is for the German to emerge from the one-sidedness contrasted above has been given new evidence by my friend of many years—but now somewhat estranged—Bruno Bauer, in his critical Berlin *Literatur-Zeitung.*[10] I do not know whether you have seen it. There is much unspoken polemic against you in it.

The character of the *Literatur-Zeitung* can be reduced to this: "Criticism" is transformed into a transcendental essence. Those Berliners do not behave like *human beings* who *criticize* but like *critics* who happen to have the misfortune of being human. Thus they recognize only one real need, the need for theoretical criticism. They reproach people like Proudhon, therefore, for taking their point of departure from a "practical need." This kind of criticism devolves into a sad and supercilious spiritualism. Consciousness or self-consciousness is regarded by it as the *sole* human quality. Love, for example, is denied, because in it the beloved is merely an "object." *A bas* [down] with the object! Hence this criticism considers itself as the only *active* element in history. It views all of humanity as a *mass,* a sluggish mass that has value only as a contrast to the spirit. Thus in a critic the highest crime is *mind* or *passion;* he must, instead, be an ironic, ice-cold σοφός [guide].

Thus Bauer states *literally:* "The critic participates neither in the sufferings nor in the joys of society; he knows neither friendship nor

---

7. "Man is revealed in his passions." "Have you ever encountered a man who thought for the sake of thinking, who remembered for the sake of remembering, who imagined for the sake of imagining, who wished for the sake of wishing? Did this ever happen to you personally? . . . No, obviously no!"

8. "Every being, man, plant, animal, or the globe, has received a sum of forces corresponding to its mission in the universal order."

9. "The forces of attraction are proportional to their destinies."

10. *Allgemeine Literatur-Zeitung (General Literary Journal),* a monthly which Bauer published in Charlottenburg from December, 1843, to October, 1844.

love, neither hatred nor envy; he reigns in solitude, where now and again the laughter of the Olympian gods over the perversity of the world rings from his lips."

The tone of Bauer's *Literatur-Zeitung* is therefore a tone of passionless *contempt,* and he makes this the more facile in that he turns upside down your findings and contemporary findings in general. He discovers only contradictions, and, satisfied with this business, he leaves it with a contemptuous "Hm." He states that criticism is not in *vogue,* it is much too spiritual for that. Yes, he expresses the hope that: "the time is not far distant when all of decadent humanity will assemble before the critique"—and "the critique" is Himself and Company—"it will separate this mass into various groups and hand out to all of them the *testimonium paupertatis* [pauper's certificate]."

It seems Bauer fought against Christ out of rivalry. I intend to publish a small brochure against this aberration of criticism.[11] It would be of the *highest* value to me if you would let me know *your* opinion, and in general a prompt sign of life from you would make me happy. This summer, twice weekly, the German artisans here—that is, the communist element among them, several hundred of them—have heard lectures on your *Essence of Christianity* by their secret chiefs,[12] and have shown themselves to be remarkably receptive. The short excerpt from a letter by a German lady in a *feuilleton* in No. 64 of *Vorwärts!*[13] was part of a letter from my wife, who is visiting her mother in Trier, and has been published without the author's knowledge.[14]

With the best wishes for your well-being,

Yours,

KARL MARX

From letter to Frederick Engels (in Manchester)
LONDON, JULY 31, 1851

Dear Engels:
 ... For approximately the past fourteen days I have written nothing, because during the time that I did not spend in the library [British

---

11. *The Holy Family,* a 220-page book (not a "small brochure"), which Marx wrote in collaboration with Engels, and which was published in Frankfurt in 1845.

12. Of the League of the Just, a communist group organized in 1836–38. In 1846 it was succeeded by the Communist League.

13. *Vorwärts!* was a German-language publication that appeared in Paris twice a week. Marx was one of its contributors.

14. On August 10, 1844, *Vorwärts!* published anonymous excerpts from a letter of Jenny Marx to her husband.

Museum] I was hunted like a dog in such a way that, despite the best of intentions, I was distracted from writing.

After the two Bambergers, father and son, procrastinated from week to week—first from month to month—with promises to discount a promissory note for me, and after I went to that Jew den with an appointment for that purpose, bringing with me stamped paper, the young one informed me that the old one, who was also present, could not, etc., etc.

That I did not box the ears of these two Jews for this infamous procrastination, waste of time, and placing me in a false position, was most regrettable. . . .

Yours,

K. M.

From letter to Frederick Engels (in Manchester)
LONDON, OCTOBER 13, 1851

Dear Engels:
. . . A week ago Blind and his wife (Madame Cohen) arrived here . . . Last Monday he and his wife visited me . . . Mrs. Blind is a lively Jewess, and we laughed and chattered quite gaily, when the Father of all Lies introduced the subject of religion. She bragged about atheism, Feuerbach, etc. I attacked Feuerbach, but, of course, in a polite and friendly manner. At first the Jewess seemed to me to be amused by the discussion, and that naturally was the only reason why I entered into this boring theme . . . Suddenly I see the woman dissolved in tears. Blind threw me an expressive, melancholy glance. She stalked out—and was not seen any more, *ni lui non plus* [neither was he]. In my long experience I have never had such an adventure. . . .
Salut!

Yours,

K. MARX

From letter to Frederick Engels (in Manchester)
LONDON, JUNE 2, 1853

Dear Frederick!
. . . In regard to the Hebrews and Arabs, your letter was very

interesting.[1] In other respects: (1) a *general* relationship, since history began, can be proved among all Oriental tribes, between the settlement of one portion of the tribes and the continuation of nomadism among the others. (2) In Mohammed's time the trade routes from Europe and Asia had been considerably modified, and the cities of Arabia, which had participated importantly in the trade with India, etc., were in a state of commercial decline . . . (3) As to religion, the question resolves itself into the general and, therefore, easily answered one: Why does the history of the Orient *appear* to be a history of religions?

On the formation of Oriental cities, one can read nothing more brilliant, perceptive, and striking than old François Bernier's (for nine years physician to Aurangzeb) *Voyages contenant la description des états de grand Mogul, de l'Indoustan, du Royaume de Cachemire,* etc.[2] He also describes very well the military system, the way these great armies were fed, etc.

Bernier rightly considered the basis of all phenomena in the Orient —he speaks of Turkey, Persia, Hindustan—to be the *absence of private property in land.* This is the real key, even to the Oriental heaven. . . .

Vale faveque,[3]

C. M.

From letter to Frederick Engels (in Manchester)
LONDON, DECEMBER 2, 1854

Dear Engels!

I think not, sir,[1] that your letter[2] or even your name can be used in connection with the worthy "Freund."[3] (The Jew is so insistent because, owing to the *genteel* academy which he had his wife establish in St. Johns Wood, he finds himself at the very brink of bankruptcy. I have now heard the details from Cornelius.) Basing myself on your letter, I wrote him the following: (1) Am enclosing a letter from

---

1. Engels to Marx, May 26, 1853: "It is now completely clear to me that the Jewish so-called Holy Writ is nothing more than an account of the Old-Arabic religious and tribal tradition, modified by the early separation of the Jews from their tribal-related but nomadic neighbors. . . ."
2. *Travels Containing a Description of the Dominions of the Great Mogul, of Hindustan, of the Kingdom of Kashmir, etc.* (Paris, 1830).
3. Be well and devoted to me.

---

1. Marx wrote these first four words in English.
2. The letter has not been found.
3. Freund was the Marx family doctor, to whom Marx owed money. Since *Freund* means "friend," Marx put it in quotation marks to indicate satire.

Dana, from which he could see how the commercial crisis in America affected *me*, and through me, *him;* (2) to cover my shortage, I have entered into new literary connections, on account of which I will obligate myself in writing to pay him £4 on the tenth of each month, beginning January, 1855. The sum still amounts to *ca.* £17. If Mr. Freund does not agree to this, he can sue me. Dana's letter covers me in every court, as he will see for himself. If I drag you in directly, I will (1) lose my whole position vis-à-vis Freund, (2) he will tell (and report on the letter) the teacher in his institution, Herr Gottfried Kinkel, the latter will tell Herr Gerstenberg, who in turn will tell every German Jew in the City, until it reaches Blanc, which would be by no means desirable. . . .

Vale [Farewell].

Yours,
K. M.

From letter to Frederick Engels (in Manchester)
LONDON, MARCH 5, 1856

Dear Frederic:

. . . Father Leo delivered a lecture on Münzer before the King[1] (partly printed in the *Neue Preussische Zeitung*). One could say that it is directly aimed against your essay ("The German Peasant War") in the *Neue Rheinische Zeitung. Politisch-ökonomische Revue.*[2] The Reformation must, of course, be rid of the reproach of being the mother of revolution. Münzer [according to this view] was, of course, a "fanatic," who said *"intelligo ut credam."* ["I understand in order to believe"]. Luther said *"credo ut intelligam"* ["I believe in order to understand"]. The "Speners"[3] replied: In his last years Luther regretted the miserable political role he had played, etc. You see how the ferment breaks through even into the official ranks.

Apropos of the Reformation, from the very beginning Austria laid the foundation for the dangerousness of the Slavs, whereby all Slavic tribes, except the Russians, became Reform-minded. The Reformation brought about a translation of the Bible into all the Slavic dialects. This, indeed, stirred up nationalist feeling. On the other side, a firm alliance with the Protestant German North. If Austria had not

---

1. Frederick William IV of Prussia.
2. The *Revue* was published by Marx and Engels in 1850.
3. The *Berlinische Nachrichten,* a Berlin daily, was called *"Spenersche Zeitung,"* after Spener, its publisher.

suppressed the movement, Protestantism would have become the basis for the preponderance of the German spirit as well as a rampart against Greek Catholic Russia. Austria had driven the Germans into all the muck and prepared the way for the Russians in Germany as well as in the East.

Your
K. M.

From postscript to letter to Frederick Engels (in Manchester)
LONDON, MAY 8, 1856

Apropos! Have seen Heine's Testament![1] Return to the "living God," and "apology before God and Man" if he had ever written anything "immoral"!

From letter to Frederick Engels (in Manchester)
LONDON, SEPTEMBER 22, 1856

Dear Engels:
. . . Still another story apropos of Moses Hess. The fame of this young man was due in great part—to Sasonov. At the time when Hess and *Moesin* [she-Moses: Hess's wife Sybille] came to Paris, this Russian was very much down and out, in rags, without money or credit, and hence susceptible to plebeian and revolutionary ideas for overthrowing the world. Sasonov heard that Moses was not without "*Moneten*" [money]. Hence he played up to the *Moesin* behind the back of Moses. He ensnared the former and trumpeted the latter as a great literary light, introducing him to journal and newspaper editors. Vladimir,[1] of course, had a hand in everything and entrée everywhere. So he squeezed out of the stingy Moses enough *Moneten* to "shine" again and to be a decoy to get new credit. And with it, he lured an old Jewess and took her in kosher wedlock. Since then, however, he has become genteel again and turned his back on Moses, declaring him to be a very common and inferior fellow. But he faithlessly deserted

---

1. Heinrich Heine's third will, dictated November 13, 1851.

---

1. Nicolai Sasonov.

the *Moesin*, and now she runs all over Paris cursing and blustering and telling anybody who will listen about the betrayal by the perfidious Muscovite. This is to a certain extent the history of the Grandeur and Decline of the *Maison* Moses. . . .

Yours,

K. M.

From letter to Frederick Engels (in Manchester)
LONDON, FEBRUARY 25, 1859

Dear Engels:

I am writing you again this evening because time presses. I am morally certain that Duncker,[1] after my letter to Lassalle, will accept the brochure.[2] Jew-boy Braun[3] has not, to be sure, written me about my manuscript, although four weeks have already elapsed. For one thing, he has been busy with the publication of his own immortal "flaming" work[4] (even so, the Jew-boy, even his *Heraclitus*, although miserably written, is better than anything the democrats can boast of), and then he will probably want to do the final corrections on my own scrawl. . . .

Naturally, I have not paid the slightest attention to this Talmudic wisdom, but only to the abuse of Ricardo because of his money theory, which, by the way, is not his but derives from Hume and Montesquieu. Lassalle may be personally insulted by this. In itself, there was nothing to it, for in my book against Proudhon,[5] I myself accepted Ricardo's theory. But Jew-boy Braun wrote me a very ridiculous letter in which he stated that he has "interested himself in the forthcoming publication of my book," *although* he himself is "writing a major economic work"[6] to which he is "devoting two years." . . . .

Salut.

Yours,

K. M.

---

1. Franz Gustav Duncker, the Berlin publisher of Marx's *Critique of Political Economy* (1859).
   2. Engels' "Po und Rhein" ("Po and Rhine") (Berlin, 1859).
   3. One of Marx's anti-Semitic nicknames for Ferdinand Lassalle.
   4. Lassalle's drama, *Franz von Sickingen* (Berlin, 1859).
   5. *The Poverty of Philosophy. Reply to the Philosophy of Poverty by M. Proudhon* (Paris and Brussels, 1847).
   6. Lassalle, *Herr Bastiat-Schulze von Delitzsch, der ökonomische Julian, oder: Capital und Arbeit (Mr. Bastiat-Schulze von Delitzsch, the Economic Julian, or: Capital and Labor)* (Berlin, 1864).

From letter to Frederick Engels (in Manchester)
LONDON, FEBRUARY 9, 1860

Dear Engels:
... I have been in secret and confidential correspondence with the
Daily Telegraph ever since the day when the shit appeared.[1] The fellow—to whom I wrote rudely—wants to hear the answer from his
correspondent before he makes *amende honorable.* I, on the other
hand, demanded that he *immediately* publish a notice at least. I will
then, no matter what he does, bring a libel action against him ... For
the rest, on the same Tuesday the thing was published, I wrote to the
editor of Palmerston's mob paper [the *Daily Telegraph*], among
others: "That letter purporting to have been written from Frankfort
am Main, but which was in fact indited at Berlin, is nothing but a
clumsy amplification of two leaders, etc., etc.,"[2] of the Berlin *National-
Zeitung.* The author, that is, the swinish Berlin correspondent of the
Daily Telegraph, is a Jew named Meier,[3] a relative of the City proprietor, who is an English Jew named Levy. Hence both fellows correctly—*juvante* [with the help of] Vogt—reproach Heine with being
a converted Jew. Am enclosing the latest letter from Itzig,[4] which you
must preserve as a rarity. This objective one! One thinks of the
plasticity of this most un-Greek of all water-Polack Jews. ...

Yours,
K. M.

From letter to Frederick Engels (in Manchester)
LONDON, APRIL 12, 1860

Dear Engels:
... You will have seen from the newspapers the joke that Palmerston allowed himself, in presenting Herr Reuter (the Trieste tele-

---

1. On February 6, 1860, the *Daily Telegraph* published an article by Karl Abel
repeating Karl Vogt's charges against Marx which had appeared in the Berlin
National-Zeitung. Marx considered them calumnies.
2. The sentence was written in English.
3. On May 30, 1860, Marx heard from Eduard Fischel in Berlin that the
author of the article was not Meier, but Karl Abel.
4. "Ikey," another nickname for Lassalle.

graph Jew) to the Queen [Victoria]. Reuter's factotum is the Jew Siegmund Engländer, who cannot spell, and who has been expelled from France because, although a paid French spy (600 francs per month), he was revealed to be at the same time a "secret" Russian spy....

Yours,

K. M.

From letter to Frederick Engels (in Manchester)
LONDON, MAY 10, 1861

Dear Frederick:
. . . Apropos. Lassalle-Lazarus. In his great book on Egypt, Lepsius has proved that the exodus of the Jews from Egypt is nothing more than the history that Manetho relates about Egypt's expulsion of "the nation of lepers," headed by an Egyptian priest named Moses. Lazarus, the leper, is thus the prototype of the Jews and of Lazarus-Lassalle. But in our Lazarus the leprosy lies in the brain. His illness was originally a badly cured case of syphilis. This resulted in caries in one of his legs, of which there are still traces....

Totus tuus [All yours],

K. M.

From letter to Ferdinand Lassalle (in Berlin)
LONDON, JULY 22, 1861

In England the will and testament itself is very old and there is not the slightest doubt that the Anglo-Saxons took it over from Roman jurisprudence. That the English quite early considered, not the intestate person, but the right of inheritance based on a testament, appears from the fact that in the High Middle Ages, when the paterfamilias died *ab intestato* [without leaving a will], only the legal portions went to his wife and children, according to circumstances, but from a third to a half fell to the Church. For the parsons assumed that if he had made a will, he would have left a certain quantity to the Church for the salvation of his soul.

Your

K. M.

From letter to Ferdinand Lassalle (*in Berlin*)
LONDON, JUNE 16, 1862

Dear Lassalle:

Bucher did, indeed, send me three copies of *Julian Schmidt*,[1] but none of the other writings you mentioned.[2] The "Herr Schmidt, Herr Schmidt" (I sent Engels and [Wilhelm] Wolff each a copy) was the more welcome as it found me in a by no means happy mood. Moreover, although I have read little of it but only leafed through it, the fellow was repulsive to my soul as the epitome of such disgusting middle-class snobbism even in literature. You rightly make it clear that your attack is indirectly aimed at the middle-class culture mob. In this case it signifies: You beat the donkey, but you mean the purse. Since for the time being we cannot directly "crop" the ears of that purse, it becomes more and more necessary that we knock off the heads of their loudest and most arrogant culture donkeys—with the pen, although poor Meyen in the *Freischütz* found this "literary guillotine game" childish and barbaric.[3] Above all, I was most delighted by the "Schwabenspiegel" and the "seven" wise men—I almost said the "seven Swabians" from Greece.[4] Incidentally, since one will perceive Julian the Grabowite[5] in Julian Schmidt (which is, however, unjust, because it appears to be a sarcastic remark at the Apostate,[6] or at least some ridicule of the other Julian), I can remark that the σοφὸς[7] as the proper character mask (but here the mask in a good sense) of Greek philosophy has occupied me very much earlier. First, the seven Swabians or Wise Men as the forerunners, the mythological heroes, then Socrates in their midst, and finally the σοφὸς as the ideal of the Epicureans, Stoics, and Skeptics. In addition, I was amused to see a comparison between that σοφὸς and the French "sage" of the eighteenth century. Then the σοφιστὴς[8] as a necessary variation of the σοφὸς. For moderns,

---

1. Lassalle's *Herr Julian Schmidt der Literarhistoriker* (*Herr Julian Schmidt, the Literary Historian*) (Berlin, 1862).

2. Lassalle to Marx, June 9, 1862: "In the meantime you will have received through the mediation of Bucher my *Julian*, my *Fichte*, and my speech on the constitution. . . ."

3. Eduard Meyen, "Berliner Briefe," in *Der Freischütz*, April 23, 1861.

4. The "Schwabenspiegel" was an inventory of land and loan laws in Swabia, modeled after the "Sachsenspiegel" of the thirteenth century.

5. An ironic reference to the followers of Wilhelm Grabow (1802–1874), a politician who was vice-president and then president of the Prussian Diet.

6. Julian, the so-called Apostate A.D. 332–363, Roman Emperor from 361 to 363.

7. *Sophos*, "sage."

8. *Sophistas*, "Sophist."

it is characteristic that the Greek connection between character and knowledge, which is contained in the σοφὸς, has been preserved in the national consciousness only in the Sophists.

As regards Julian, not Julian the Grabowite but Julian the Apostate, recently I had an altercation with Engels, who, as soon became apparent at the opening of the row, was essentially correct. But my aversion for Christianity is so pronounced that I have a bias in favor of the Apostate, and I could not identify him with either Frederick Wilhelm IV or any other romantic reactionary, not even *mutatis mutandis*. Do you not feel the same? ...

Your

K. M.

From letter to Frederick Engels (in Manchester)
LONDON, JULY 30, 1862

Dear Engels:

... The Jewish nigger Lassalle, who fortunately departs at the end of this week, has luckily again lost 5,000 Taler in a fraudulent speculation. The fellow would rather throw his money into the muck than lend it to a "friend," even if the interest and capital were guaranteed. In addition, he acts on the notion that he must live like a Jewish baron or baronized (probably by the Countess[1]) Jew. ...

It is now completely clear to me that he, as is shown by his cranial structure and curly hair—descends from Negroes who joined Moses' exodus out of Egypt (assuming that his mother or grandmother on his father's side did not interbreed with a nigger). Now this union of Judaism and Germanism with a basic negroid substance must produce a peculiar product. The impertinence of the fellow is also niggerlike. ...

Salut.

Yours,

K. M.

One of the great discoveries of our nigger—which he confides only to his "most trusted friends"—is that the Pelasgians descend from the Semites. Main proof: In the book of Maccabees the Jews send emis-

---

1. Sophie, Countess von Hatzfeldt (1805-1881), Lassalle's intimate friend.

saries to Greece for help, appealing to the tribal relationship. Furthermore, an Etruscan inscription was found in Perugia, and Privy
Councilor Stuecker in Berlin and an Italian have simultaneously de-
ciphered it and have independently resolved the Etruscan alphabet
into the Hebraic. . . .

From letter to Frederick Engels (in Manchester)
ZALTBOMMEL, HOLLAND, JANUARY 20, 1864

Dear Frederick:
    You see, I am still here, and "I will tell you more," I am in fact
incapable to move about.[1] This is a perfidious Christian illness. When
I received your letter I was congratulating myself on the healing of the
old wounds, but the same evening a big furuncle broke out on my left
chest under the neck, and an antipodal one in the back. Although painful, that at least did not prevent me from walking, which I did, in fact,
across the Rhine (Waal), in company with my uncle and cousin.[2] But a
few days later another carbuncle broke out on my right leg, directly
under the spot to which Goethe refers: And when the nobleman
has no posterior, how can he sit?[3] This is the most painful of the
known abscesses that I have ever had, and I hope it will finally
terminate the series. In the meantime, I can neither walk, nor stand, nor
sit, and even lying down is damned hard. You see, *mon cher*, how
the wisdom of nature has afflicted me. Would it not have been more
sensible if, instead of me, it had been consigned to try the patience
of a good Christian, a person, say, of the stripe of Silvio Pellico?
Besides the carbuncle on the posterior, you should know that a new
furuncle has broken out on the back, and the one on the chest is
only beginning to heal, so that like a true Lazarus (alias Lassalle), I am
scourged on all sides.
    Apropos Lazarus, I like Renan's *Life of Jesus*, which is in some
respects mere romance, full of pantheistic-mystical giddiness. Still,
the book has some advantages over its German predecessors, and
it is not bulky; you must read it. It is, of course, a result of German
research. Highly remarkable: here in Holland the German critical-

---

1. The last four words were written in English.
2. Lion and Antoinette Philips.
3. *"Und wenn er keinen Hintern hat, wie mag der Edle sitzen?* From Goethe's
epigrammatic poem, "Totalitaet."

theological tendency is so very much *à l'ordre de jour* [the order of the day] that the preachers acknowledge it openly from the pulpits. . . .

I am writing only these few lines, and even that is done with great effort, since sitting is painful. But I expect a return answer from you; it cheers me up to see your handwriting.

Don't forget to enclose a photograph. I have promised it to my cousin, and how could she believe in our Orestes-Pylades friendship if I could not *commovere* [move] you even to send a photograph? My address as before: c/o L. Philips. Salut to you and Lupus.[4]

Your
K. M.

From letter to Frederick Engels (in Manchester)
LONDON, JUNE 16, 1864

Dear Frederick:

. . . A Dutch Orientalist, Professor Dozy of Leyden, has published a book to prove that "Abraham, Isaac and Jacob were fantasy mongers; that the Israelites were idolaters; that they dragged with them a 'stone' in the 'Ark of the Covenant'; that the tribe of Simon (exiled under Saul) moved to Mecca, where they built a heathenish temple and worshiped stones; that after the deliverance from Babylon, Ezra invented the legend of the Creation and the history up to Joshua and, in addition, wrote the Law and the Dogma for the propagation of reform and monotheism, etc."[1]

So they write me from Holland, and also that the book has caused a great uproar among theologians there, particularly since Dozy is the most learned Dutch theologian—and a professor in Leyden to boot! At any rate, outside of Germany remarkable movements against religion are afoot (Renan, Colenso, Dozy, etc.). . . .

Your
K. M.

---

4. Wilhelm Wolff.

---

1. Reinhart Dozy, *De Israëliten te Mekka* (Haarlem, 1864).

From letter to Lion Philips (in Zaltbommel)
LONDON, JUNE 25, 1864

Dear Uncle:

My best thanks for your detailed letter. I know how troublesome it is for you to write because of your eyes, and I do not actually expect you to answer every one of my letters. I was pleased to see from your letter that you are physically well and that your spiritual gaiety has remained unshaken even by the discoveries of Professor Dozy.[1] Nevertheless, since Darwin proved our common descent from apes, "our ancestral pride" can hardly be shaken any more by *any shock whatever*.[2] That the Pentateuch was produced only after the return of the Jews from the Babylonian Captivity, Spinoza has already explained in his *Tractatus theologico-politicus*. . . . .

Yours truly,

Ch. Marx

From letter to Lion Philips (in Zaltbommel)
LONDON, NOVEMBER 29, 1864

Dear Uncle:

. . . The *Stammgenosse* [member of our tribe] Benjamin Disraeli has again made a fool of himself this week when at a public meeting[1] he put on airs as the guardian angel of the High Church and of church rates, and as repudiator of critics in religious affairs. He is the best proof of how great talent without conviction produces scoundrels, even though liveried and "right honorable" scoundrels. . . .

Your devoted nephew,

K. M.

---

1. In his letter to Marx, June 12, 1864, Lion Philips discussed Reinhart Dozy's new book (see Marx's letter to Engels, June 16, 1864); Philips observed that the work "makes the whole church fall into ruins," and concluded ironically: "Sorry that *our* [i.e., Jewish] nobility is lost thereby, and in the end we will have only *our Christ*, the plebeian, to boast about. A poor consolation!" (MS., in International Instituut voor Sociale Geschiedenis, Amsterdam.)

2. These three words were written in English.

---

1. On October 25, 1864, at Oxford.

Mrs. Karl Marx, from letter to Johann Philipp Becker
(*in Geneva*)
LONDON, ca. JANUARY 29, 1866*

My Dear Herr Becker:

For a week now my husband has again been stricken with the dangerous and extremely painful illness [carbuncles]. . . .

In religious matters there is now a significant movement in this dank England. The foremost men of science, headed by Huxley (Darwin's follower), with Tyndall, Sir Charles Lyell, Bowring, Carpenter, etc., etc., gave in St. Martins Hall (of the glorious waltz-commemoration[1]) extremely enlightened, truly free-thinking and audacious lectures for the people, and on Sunday evenings at that, precisely at the hour when ordinarily the little sheep used to go to the pasture of the Lord. The Hall was so jammed and the jubilation of the people so great that, on the first Sunday evening when I went there with my girls, 2,000 people could not get into the place, which was already filled to suffocation. Three times the parsons let this [to them] dreadful occurrence [the lectures] happen. But last night [Sunday] the audience was informed that no more lectures would be allowed until the lawsuit of the parsons against the "Sunday evenings for the people" had been settled. The indignation of the assemblage expressed itself decisively, and more than £100 was collected for defense against the lawsuit. How stupid of the little parsons to meddle in this! To the anger of that gang, the evenings ended with music. Choruses sang Handel, Mozart, Beethoven, Mendelssohn, and Gounod, and were received with enthusiasm by the English, who had hitherto only been allowed to bawl "Jesus, Meek and Mild" or to wander into the gin palaces.

Karl, who lies in great pain, and my girls send you their hearty regards; the little one [Eleanor] especially sends much friendliness to the "good Becker." But I, from a distance, extend my hand to you.

Yours,

JENNY MARX

---

* This letter is included here not only for its own intrinsic interest, but also because in intellectual, political, and spiritual matters Mrs. Marx shared her husband's opinions.

1. The ball that commemorated the founding of the First International, September 28, 1865, in St. Martins Hall.

From postscript to letter to Frederick Engels (in Manchester)
LONDON, NOVEMBER 7, 1867

Dear Fred:

   ... The old Urquhart with his Catholicism, etc., grows more and more disgusting.

On lit dans un registre d'une inquisition d'Italie cet aveu d'une religieuse; elle disait innocémment à la Madonne: "De grâce, sainte Vierge, donne-moi quelqu'un avec qui je puisse pécher.[1] In this respect, too, the Russians are stronger. It has been established that a thoroughly healthy chap, who spent only twenty-four hours in a Russian nunnery, came out dead. The nuns rode him to death. Of course, their father confessor does not come every day.

From letter to Ludwig Kugelmann (in Hanover)
LONDON, APRIL 6, 1868

Dear Kugelmann:

   ... The Irish question predominates here just now. It has, of course, been exploited by Gladstone and Co. only so they can come to the helm again, and, above all, have an electoral cry in the next election, which will be based on household suffrage.[1] Chiefly, this turn of events is harmful to the workers' party. Specifically, the intriguers among the workers, such as Odger and Potter, who want to get into the next Parliament, now have a new excuse for attaching themselves to the bourgeois liberals.

Still, this is only a penalty that England—and hence also the English working class—is paying for the great crime it has been committing for many centuries against Ireland. And in the long run it will benefit the English working class itself. Specifically, the English Established Church in Ireland—or what they used to call here the

---

1. One reads in an Italian Inquisition record the following avowal of a nun, who innocently prays to the Madonna: "I beseech you, Holy Virgin, give me somebody with whom I could sin."

---

1. The Parliamentary elections of November, 1868, were based on the Reform Bill of 1867, which extended the suffrage to male householders who paid an annual rent of £10 or more.

Irish Church—is the religious bulwark of English *landlordism* in Ireland and at the same time the outpost of the Established Church in England itself (I speak here of the Established Church as a *landowner*). With the overthrow of the Established Church in Ireland comes its downfall in England, and both will be followed (in ruin) by landlordism in Ireland, then in England. But I have been convinced from the first that the social revolution must begin *seriously* from the ground up, that is, from ground and soil ownership.

In addition, the thing will have the very useful consequence that, as soon as the Irish Church is dead, the Protestant Irish tenants in the province of Ulster will join the Catholic tenants in the three other provinces of Ireland, whereas up to now landlordism has been able to exploit this *religious* antagonism. . . .

Yours,

K. MARX

From letter to Frederick Engels (in Manchester)
HANOVER,[1] SEPTEMBER 25, 1869

Dear Fred:

. . . On this tour through Belgium, my stay in Aachen, and my voyage up the Rhine, I have become convinced that the priests, especially in the Catholic districts, must be energetically attacked. I shall work along these lines through the International. The dogs (for example, Bishop Ketteler in Mainz, the priests at the Düsseldorf Congress, etc.) are flirting, where they find it suitable to do so, with the labor question.[2] Indeed, it was for them we worked in 1848; only they have enjoyed the fruits of victory during the period of Reaction. . . .

Greetings.

Yours,

K. M.

---

1. Marx visited Dr. Ludwig Kugelmann in Hanover between September 18 and October 7, 1869.

2. The General Convention of the Catholic Societies of Germany, meeting in Düsseldorf, September 6, 1869, resolved to appeal to Christians to show concern for the working classes as a cowriter to socialist propaganda.

From letter to Frederick Engels (in Manchester)
LONDON, SEPTEMBER 2, 1870

Dear Fred:

. . . The correspondence between the Swabian ex-seminarian D. Strauss[1] and the French ex-Jesuit pupil Renan[2] is a hilarious episode.[3] Parson remains parson. Herr Strauss's lecture course in history seems to have its roots in intoxication or some similar schoolbook. . . .

Yours,

K. M.

From letter to Frederick Engels (in Ramsgate)
RYDE, ISLE OF WIGHT, JULY 15, 1874

Dear Fred:

. . . Religion flourishes everywhere among the natives here, but in addition, they are practical people. "Vote for Stanley, the rich man," was a poster we found everywhere in the vicinity. The Town Council of Ryde, on which various members of the Ryde Pier and Railroad Company sit, and whose proceedings replace the English House of Commons in the local press, is a veritable model of jobbery.

Our landlord is a Scripture reader for the poor, and his theological library, about two dozen volumes, adorns our sitting room. Although he belongs to the Church of England, I found among his books Spurgeon's Sermons. In Sandown, where I took a warm bath, I found a similar library in the Bath House, and one cannot take a step without seeing announcements of pious meetings. In reality, the plebs here are very poor and seem to find the church their main diversion. It would be interesting to investigate how this original fishermen population was in no time crushed down to this idol-grinding condition. "Overpopulation" certainly did not do it, for altogether there are not even 100,000 permanent inhabitants here. . . .

Yours,

MOHR[1]

---

1. David Friedrich Strauss, a Young Hegelian, was the author of *Das Leben Jesu* (*The Life of Jesus*) (2 vols., 1835–36).

2. Ernest Renan was the author of *The History of the Origins of Christianity* (8 vols., 1863–83, Volume I of which was *The Life of Jesus.*

3. Letter from Strauss to Renan, in *Allgemeine Zeitung*, August 18, 1870.

1. Marx's nickname—"Moor"—used by his family and friends because of his dark complexion.

From letter to Frederick Engels (in Ramsgate)
KARLSBAD, AUGUST 21, 1875

Dear Fred:

I arrived here last Sunday. . . .[1]

In London, a cunning-looking little Jew [*Juedel*] entered our carriage in great haste, carrying a small trunk under his arm. Shortly before Harwich, he searched for his keys to see, as he said, if his clerk had packed his necessary clothing . . . After much searching, he finally located, not the key but a key that opened the trunk, and found that pants and coat did not match, that nightshirts, overcoat, etc., were missing. On the boat, the little Jew opened up his heart to me. "Such cheating," he exclaimed again and again, "has never been seen in the world before." This was the story: A German Yankee named Boern, or Bernstein, recommended to him by his Berlin friend Neumann, swindled him out of £1,700—him, considered to be one of the shrewdest businessmen! That swindler, presumably in the African trade, had shown him bills for goods, worth thousands of pounds sterling, which he had bought from the best firms in Bradford and Manchester; the ship with the goods lies at anchor in Southampton. He gave him [the swindler] the advance payment he had asked for. As he does not hear anything from him, he becomes anxious. He writes to Manchester and Bradford; and he shows me the replies: Bernstein had taken samples and bought goods from them, the price to be paid upon *receipt of the goods;* the bills were therefore merely forms; the goods were never picked up. They were seized in Southampton and it was found that the bales were filled with straw mattresses.

What chagrined our little Jew most, apart from the loss of the £1,700, was that a sharp dealer like himself could be so diddled. He wrote to his friend Neumann and to his brother in Berlin. The latter informed him by telegram that Bernstein had been found in Berlin and denounced to the police, which keeps an eye on him, but was preparing to take to his heels. Do you want, I asked him, to hale him to court? "Not his carcass I want," he replied; " 'tis the money I want back." I: "He will have squandered it by now." He: "Not his carcass I want! He may have tricked those gents in the City" (he mentioned all possible characters there) "out of £12,000, but me he must pay. The others can go and see where they can nab him." The best of it was that upon our arrival in Rotterdam it turned out that he had a ticket only

---

1. August 15. Marx remained in Karlsbad until September 11, 1875.

to Minden and that he had to wait until eleven o'clock next morning before he could take off. The fellow cursed the Railway Administration like mad. Did him no good. . . .

Yours,
MOHR

From letter to Ferdinand Domela Nieuwenhuis (in The Hague)
LONDON, FEBRUARY 22, 1881

Honored Party Comrade:
. . . The doctrinal and necessarily illusory anticipation of the action program of a revolution of the future emerges only from contemporary struggle. The dream of the imminent destruction of the world inspired the early Christians in their struggle with the Roman world empire and gave them a certainty of victory. Scientific insight into the unavoidable and continuing disintegration of the dominant order of society . . . serves as a guarantee that at the moment of outbreak of a real proletarian revolution its very conditions . . . will directly bring forth the next *modus operandi.*

Your most devoted
KARL MARX

From letter written in English to Laura Lafargue (in London)
ALGIERS,[1] APRIL 14, 1882

Dearest Cacadou:[2]
. . . Most striking this spectacle: Some [of] these Maures [Moors] were dressed pretentiously, even richly, others in, for once I dare call it *blouses,* sometimes of white woolen appearance, now in rags and tatters—but in the eyes of a true Mussulman such accidents, good or bad luck, do not distinguish Mahomet's children. *Absolute equality in their social intercourse,* not affected; on the contrary, only when demoralized, they become aware of it; as to the hatred against

---

1. Marx was on a cure in Algiers from February 20 to May 2, 1882.
2. Marx's nickname for his daughter Laura.

Christians and the hope of an ultimate victory over these infidels, their politicians justly consider this same feeling and practice of absolute equality (not of wealth or position but of personality) a guarantee of keeping up the one, of not giving up the latter. (Nevertheless, they will go to the devil without a revolutionary movement). . . .

OLD NICK[3]

---

3. A Marx family nickname.

Bibliography

There is little scholarly work in English on Marx's religious ideas, although there have been some translations of his essay, "On the Jewish Question." A great deal of the scholarly writing on the subject is in French and German, most of it dealing with the question of Marx's anti-Semitism.

GENERAL

Cottier, Georges
    L'Athéisme du jeune Marx: ses Origines Hégeliennes (Paris, 1959)
D'Arcy, Martin
    Communism and Christianity (London, 1956)
MacIntyre, Alexander C.
    Marxism and Christianity (1969)
Miller, Alexander
    The Christian Significance of Karl Marx (n.d.)
Nell-Breuning, Oswald von
    Auseinandersetzung mit Karl Marx (1969)
Niebuhr, Reinhold, ed.
    Karl Marx and Friedrich Engels on Religion (1964)
Röhr, Heinz
    Pseudoreligiöse Motive in den Frühschriften von Karl Marx (Tübingen, 1962)

JEWS AND JUDAISM

Avineri, Shlomo
    "Marx and Jewish Emancipation," in *Journal of the History of Ideas*, XXV, pp. 445–50

Bloom, Solomon F.
"Karl Marx and the Jews," in *Jewish Social Studies*, IV, pp. 3–16
Blumenberg, Werner
"Eduard von Müller-Tellering, Verfasser des ersten Antisemitischen Pamphlets gegen Marx," in *Bulletin of the International Institute of Social History*, VI, pp. 178–97
Bottomore, T. B.
"On the Jewish Question," in *Karl Marx: Early Writings* (1963), pp. 3–40
Davidsohn, Georg
"Die Juden im preussischen Staate von 1837," in *Zeitschrift für die Geschichte der Juden in Deutschland* (1937), pp. 114–16
Glickson, Moses
The Jewish Complex of Karl Marx. Theodore Herzl Institute, Pamphlet No. 20 (New York, 1961)
Haubrich, Don Fritz
Die Juden in Trier (Trier, 1907)
Hirsch, Helmut
"Karl Marx und die Bittschriften für die Gleichberechtigung der Juden," in *Archiv für Sozialgeschichte*, VIII, pp. 229–45
Hirsch, Helmut
"Mariana Judaica," in *Cahiers de l'Institut de Science Économique Appliquée* (1963), pp. 5–52
Kober, Adolf
"Jews in the Revolution of 1848 in Germany," in *Jewish Social Studies* (1948), pp. 135–64
Kober, Adolf
"Karl Marx' Vater und das napoleonische Ausnahmgesetz gegen die Juden 1808," in *Jahrbuch des Kölnischen Geschichtsvereins*, Jahrg. 1932, pp. 111–25
Künzli, Arnold
"Der jüdische Selbsthass," in his *Karl Marx: Eine Psychographie*, Part II (Vienna, 1966), pp. 195–226
Lamm, Hans
Karl Marx und das Judentum (Munich, 1969).
Lesser, E. J.
"Karl Marx als Jude," in *Der Jude*, ed. by Martin Buber, Heft 3, Jahrg. VIII (March, 1924), pp. 173–81
Lessing, Theodor
Der jüdische Selbsthass (Berlin, 1930)
Liber, M.
"Judaisme et Socialisme: Henri Heine, Karl Marx, et le Judaisme," in *La Revue de Paris*, August 1, 1928 (*see also* Salluste)
Mayer, Gustav
"Der Jude in Karl Marx," in *Neue jüdische Monatshefte*, Jahrg. II, 1917–18

Rotenstreich, Nathan
"For or against Emancipation," in *Year Book IV*, Leo Baeck Institute, 1950, pp. 3–36

Salluste
"Henri Heine et Karl Marx," *La Revue de Paris*, July 1, 1928, pp. 153–75; and July 15, 1928, pp. 426–45 (*see also* Liber)

Scholz, Dietmar
"Politische und menschliche Emanzipation—Karl Marx Schrift 'Zur Judenfrage' aus dem Jahre 1844," in *Geschichte und Wissenschaft und Unterricht*, Jahrg. 8, Heft 1 (January, 1967)

Silberner, Edmund
Sozialisten zur Judenfrage (1962)

Silberner, Edmund
"Was Marx an Anti-Semite?" in *Historia Judaica*, XI (1949), pp. 3–52

Stein, Hans
"Der Uebertritt der Familie Heinrich Marx zum evangelischen Christentum," in *Jahrbuch des Kölnischen Geschichtsvereins*, XIV, 1932

Biographical Index

Subject Index*

Absolute Idea, 45
Afghanistan, 113–114
Alexandria, 15
Algiers, 256 & n
Alienation, 40–41, 43–47, 64, 179, 191
Allgemeine Augsburger Zeitung, 21
Allgemeine Literatur-Zeitung, 48n, 201, 237–238 & n
American Revolution (*see* United States of America)
Amsterdam, *see* Bankers, Jewish
Anarchy, 211
Anekdota zur neuesten deutschen Philosophie und Publicistik, 32n, 232
Anglicans (*see* Church of England)
Animals (and religion), 9, 231
  (*See also* Zoology)
Anthropology, 9
Antichrist, 33
  (*See also* Christ)
Anticlericalism, 109–111
  (*See also* Clergy)
Antiquity, 100–104, 137, 146
  (*See also* Greece; Rome)
Anti-Rent movement, 89
  (*See also* United States of America)
Antisemitism, xii–xiii, xxii–xxv, 170, 214, 259
  (*See also* Jews; Judaism)
Apostles, 145
  (*See also* Bible)
Arabs, 218, 239–240
  (*See also* Moslems)
Aristocracy, 125
Art, 41, 44, 45, 146, 190, 232
Asia, 137, 240
Atheism, atheists, 31, 38, 41–42, 46, 51, 69–70, 143, 204, 251
  (*See also* God)

Augsburg, Peace of, 162, 165
Augsburger Allgemeine Zeitung, 101
Austria, 37, 116, 219–221, 241–242
Authority, 24, 36, 72
  (*See also* State)

Babylon, 249
Bamberger Zeitung, 101
Bankers, Jewish, 215–217, 219–225
  (*See also* Jews; Judaism)
Bavaria, xxv, 104
Beer Bill, 125
  (*See also* Sunday closing)
Belgium, 95–96, 195, 220, 253
Berlin University, ix, xvii
Berliner Politisches Wochenblatt, 21
Berlinische Nachrichten, 241 & n
Bible, xiii, xvii–xviii, 9, 23, 26, 28–29, 31, 34, 58, 69 & n, 72–74, 80, 150, 158, 178–179, 188, 240n, 241
Blätter für literarische Unterhaltung, 101
Bonn University, xvii, xviii, 206, 232
Bourgeois, bourgeoisie, 38, 65, 97, 104, 105, 112, 135, 148, 175, 183, 213
Brahmins (*see* Hinduism)
Breslau, xxv
Brunswick, 160–161
Buddhism, 114
Byzantium, 24, 114–115, 121
  (*See also* Greek Orthodox Church)

Cambridge University, 141
Capital, 136, 143–144
  (*See also* Bankers, Jewish; Money)
Capital (by Marx), xxvi, 92n, 135n, 136–144
Carbuncles, 248, 251
Cartesianism (*see* Descartes)
Catalonia, 75

---

* Page references for the names of individuals in cross-references are given in the preceding Biographical Index.

[271]